WHITEWASH

WHITEWASH

What the Media Won't Tell You About Hillary Clinton, but Conservatives Will

L. BRENT BOZELL III

with Tim Graham

CROWN
FORUM
New York

Published in the United States by Crown Forum, an imprint of the
Crown Publishing Group, a division of Random House, Inc., New York.
www.crownpublishing.com

Crown Forum and the Crown Forum colophon are trademarks of
Random House, Inc.

Library of Congress Cataloging-in-Publication Data
Bozell, L. Brent.
  Whitewash : what the media won't tell you about Hillary Clinton, but conservatives
will / L. Brent Bozell III with Tim Graham. — 1st ed.
    p. cm.
  Includes index.
  1. Clinton, Hillary Rodham—Relations with journalists.   2. Press and
politics—United States.   I. Graham, Tim.   II. Title.

  E887.C55B69 2007
  973.929092—dc22

                                                                2007031640
978-0-307-34020-7

Printed in the United States of America

Design by Lauren Dong

10 9 8 7 6 5 4 3 2 1

First Edition

Dedicated in memory of

David Thibault,

1958–2007

Contents

Introduction
"Why Hillary?"

Friends of Hillary Clinton would have you believe she's an amalgam of Betty Crocker, Mother Teresa, and Oliver Wendell Holmes. . . . Fortunately, Hillary Clinton, the latest wife to be challenged to fit perfectly into the ill-defined role of political spouse, is more interesting than that. . . . Clinton is now a top-dollar litigator at the old-line Rose Law Firm in Little Rock. . . . She serves on 17 civic and corporate boards, hardly ever missing a softball game or school play.

—MARGARET CARLSON, *Time*, January 27, 1992

The overriding question is: Why Hillary? She is the de facto *nominee, the presumptive nominee. But what has she done?*

—RUSH LIMBAUGH, in an interview with the authors

What makes Rush Limbaugh America's number-one talk-radio host is his extraordinary ability to slice through analytical fog. When we interviewed Limbaugh for this book, we asked him a number of questions about Hillary Rodham Clinton and her years on the national scene. As usual, Rush got to the nub of the issue.

For all the focus on Hillary's presidential prospects, the most intriguing question of all is usually ignored: *Why* Hillary? How did she arrive at her position as a leading presidential contender—a sure bet, in the eyes of many political observers, to become the next president of the United

States? She has been in the national spotlight for a decade and a half but had never been elected to political office prior to running for the U.S. Senate from a state in which she'd never lived. And yet, before she'd even set foot in the U.S. Capitol—indeed, before she even announced her Senate candidacy—political analysts were already telling us that this scandal-plagued wife of an impeached president was presidential timber, and that, in fact, she'd vault to the top of the Democratic field the moment she chose to run for the White House.

This is, to say the least, not the typical path to the Oval Office.

Which brings us to Limbaugh's question. *What has she done?* How is it that Hillary is positioned to become the forty-fourth president of the United States? How did this woman come so far, so fast, having accomplished so little?

So how *did* Hillary get here?

The answer is that she had at her disposal what is arguably the most powerful weapon in politics. For all the books that have explored her life and times, none has exposed this secret weapon, the real key to her political success, which allowed her to build a political career of her own and is now proving crucial to her presidential campaign.

The weapon? The news media.

The national media have flagrantly abandoned their duty as a supposedly independent, dispassionate press when it comes to coverage of Hillary Clinton. They have shamelessly served as cheerleaders for Mrs. Clinton from the moment she emerged on the national scene in 1992 (note the gushing *Time* magazine "news" story quoted at the top of this chapter). Liberal reporters—and, truth be told, female liberal reporters especially—have consistently hailed her as a trailblazing pioneer, a feminist role model, a brilliant intellect, a politician of striking compassion, an inspiring leader, and more. What makes the media's coverage of Hillary Clinton even more deplorable are the recurring examples of *non*-coverage. Time and again they have refused to cover Mrs. Clinton's staggering number of personal, political, and financial scandals. They have downplayed or simply ignored her leftist political agenda, which stands at the fringes of American political thought. And they dramatically downplayed her significant political failures. Plain and simple, they have whitewashed her record to turn her into the formidable presidential candidate she has become.

You can hear the response already. Hillary's supporters, in and out of the media, have consistently stated and will continue to trumpet the line that *no one has been more investigated or scrutinized than Hillary Clinton.* But as this book will reveal, that claim is not just incorrect, it is utterly absurd.

We need to take a step back to discuss what constitutes an investigative news story in the first place. An investigative news story on a political scandal involves several stages. First there is the allegation, which will (and should) die an immediate death if it is neither corroborated nor believable. But if it carries the scent of credibility, it leads to the second step—investigation. A thorough investigation, examining all the angles while seeking independent confirmation of charges, is complete when, *and only when,* it has reached the third stage of the process—resolution, where the theoretical, the hypothesis, is proven or disproven and there is now fact, truth.

That is how the investigative process *should* work. But as this book will prove, in the case of Hillary Rodham Clinton, the so-called (and misnamed) "mainstream news media" have consistently refused to investigate—thoroughly investigate—credible allegations, even when other media sources were uncovering one scandalous action after another. In fact, *not one* scandal involving Hillary Clinton has ever reached the final step of resolution, with every question answered, the complete story told.

Instead, the national "news" media have ignored charges against Mrs. Clinton, and reported credible allegations only when they could no longer be ignored—say, when an indictment was handed down. Even when the media have reported on certain allegations that begged investigation, they've stopped well short of resolution, bailing out of an investigation before the answers might damage Hillary's reputation.

Making matters even more outrageous, in most cases the only serious investigation following an allegation has focused not on Hillary but, amazingly, on her critics, constantly calling into question her accusers' integrity and honesty. Every disagreement with her ideological agenda is presented as an episode in discrimination, carried out by those who are made uncomfortable by strong women. Every attempt to address her scandalous behavior is presented as an exercise in the politics of character assassination. In the court of Hillary media coverage, the plaintiff always becomes the accused.

When Hillary's defenders—often led by Senator Clinton herself—become outraged at her "attackers," they are expressing an anger common on the left these days: anger at the fact that they no longer have a monopoly on the news in this country. To be sure, the liberal media still dominate the airwaves and the presses, meaning that they retain extraordinary influence over the national conversation. But the "alternative media"—cable television, talk radio, news websites, and blogs—have grown by leaps and bounds in recent years, precisely at the time that Hillary Clinton emerged as a national figure. Many of these outlets have stepped in where the traditional media have abandoned their duty to explore serious questions about our political leaders. For having the temerity to seek the truth, they are blasted as "Clinton-haters" and "angry conservatives," "persecutors" straight out of the "vast right-wing conspiracy."

Even in the face of these relentless attacks, the upstart alternative media and some intrepid government investigators have done important work trying to get at the truth. It also needs to be recognized that several times some in the establishment media have dipped their toes in the investigative waters and reported their initial findings before abandoning the search. Were it not for their efforts, the American people never would have learned of virtually any of the scandals surrounding and involving Hillary Clinton.

Yet despite those efforts, the truth about Mrs. Clinton remains hidden from most Americans because the still-powerful liberal media have buried these scandals or exercised damage control on behalf of Hillary when they could no longer dismiss a topic altogether.

We need the truth. For years we've been told that the presidency is Hillary's for the taking. Even when she began to face some unexpected challenges from Democratic rivals for her party's nomination in 2007, many members of the media were quick to remind us that she was "inevitable" and "unbeatable." This is in keeping with the fawning treatment the elite media gave Hillary in the early years, when they portrayed her as the most qualified First Lady in American history, and in recent years, when they packaged her as an extraordinarily accomplished congressional legislator. How in the world did she become an obvious choice to be president of the United States? As Landmark Legal Foundation president and popular talk-radio host Mark Levin wryly observed when we interviewed him, "She's managed to move from being the poor victim, wife, and mother to one of the greatest lawyers to ever not litigate a case, to a great leader."

This book shows how it happened, and not only reveals the ugly truths that the media have labored to hide from the American people, but also documents how they have kept them from the public. To write this book, we have drawn on a wealth of studies and data compiled exclusively by our organization, the Media Research Center, which for two decades has been carefully and systematically documenting the news media's left-wing bias. As we discovered in the course of researching this book, it is truly shocking to see how blatantly the media have shilled for Hillary at every step along her path to power. The extent and sheer audacity of the media's Hillary cheerleading startled even us, who have spent our careers closely analyzing the media.

Team Hillary are always quick to dismiss any mention of the candidate's ugly record as "old news." The "objective" news media, still obsessed with George W. Bush's 1971 National Guard record, will agree, simply yawn—*oh, we've heard it all before.* But in fact we *haven't* heard it before, because the liberal media have made sure the real story was never reported.

That is why it is so essential to chronicle Mrs. Clinton's years on the national scene—not to rehash "old news," but to *expose* the flaws, failures, and scandals for which the press corps have never held Hillary accountable. As you'll see, even on the campaign trail for Bill Clinton in 1992, she was the same scandal-plagued, domineering, and, yes, deceitful figure we recognize today. The ugly character traits, as well as the radical ideology and poor political judgment, have been there from the beginning. But a servile press corps will never tell you that. We wrote this book to document that reality as well. We will name names, telling you who in the national "news" media are advancing Hillary Clinton's candidacy, how they are whitewashing her record, and why.

In writing this book we interviewed dozens of conservative political and opinion leaders who have carefully studied Mrs. Clinton and the national media over the years, including Rush Limbaugh, Newt Gingrich, Sean Hannity, Ann Coulter, Mark Levin, Mary Matalin, Cal

Thomas, Laura Ingraham, Tony Blankley, Kate O'Beirne, Phyllis Schlafly, Ed Gillespie, and Congressmen Dan Burton and Jack Kingston. These are just some of the many people who have worked to let Americans hear the full story on Hillary Clinton.

Without question, no political figure in America today has benefited more from a water-carrying media than Hillary Rodham Clinton. The flattery and damage control only continue as Hillary ramps up her presidential campaign. If the media refuse to seek out the truth, we must step in to fill the role they have abandoned. It's not about "attacking," it's about letting the American people have the full story so they can judge for themselves whether this media phenomenon is fit to be president.

Chapter 1
Definitely Not Tammy Wynette

I just don't believe any of that.

—HILLARY CLINTON on Gennifer Flowers's allegations of an affair
with Bill Clinton, January 1992

*I thought the whole thing was disingenuous, because at the time I
found it impossible to believe that Hillary didn't know anything
about it. Just like I don't believe for a moment she didn't know about
Monica Lewinsky.*

—RUSH LIMBAUGH on the Clintons' handling of the 1992 Gennifer
Flowers scandal, in an interview with the authors

For years, the worst-kept secret in Washington was that Hillary Rodham Clinton would run for president. Her candidacy was such a foregone conclusion for so long that it's hard to remember a time when her designs on the Oval Office weren't being closely analyzed. But it's worth recalling the unlikely path Mrs. Clinton has taken to becoming a presidential front-runner. Before she ran for the Senate in 2000, for example, she had never even held elective office. And when did the buzz about her possible Senate run begin? Right in the midst of her husband's impeachment trial—only the second presidential impeachment in U.S. history.

Just how did this happen?

To answer that question requires going back to the time when Hillary Clinton emerged upon the national scene, in January 1992. As a close examination of the record reveals, Mrs. Clinton had a vast army of supporters building up her credentials from the very beginning. Those supporters were found in the media.

Indeed, from the moment Hillary walked onto the national stage, the media hailed her as a woman on the verge of history, a feminist trailblazer, a pioneer of women's liberation, like a female Neil Armstrong landing on the moon in Guccis. If her husband was elected president, she would be the first First Lady to have an "independent" career of her own. The many liberals and feminists now in the press corps could visualize one of their own as a White House spouse, chafing at the demand to glue on a plastic smile and pretend she lived for the annual Easter Egg Roll, choosing instead to use her honorary office to strike blows for "social justice." Empathy for Hillary's pioneer plight oozed between every sentence of many Woodstock generation media accounts.

It's a pattern we have seen repeated again and again in the fifteen-plus years since.

"I Don't Think It's Worthy of Comment"

Hillary Clinton entered the national picture in a less-than-traditional way, in the middle of a political crisis for her husband. A scandal threatened to bury her husband's campaign for the Democratic presidential nomination just as he had pulled ahead in polls. A tabloid newspaper had paid a six-figure sum to Gennifer Flowers, a blond former TV reporter from Little Rock who claimed that Bill Clinton had cheated with her for twelve years behind Hillary's back, and had rewarded her services with a state job while he served as governor of Arkansas. Most people were introduced to Hillary on *60 Minutes* as she sat in a turquoise turtleneck and jacket and a girlish black headband, her husband's political career teetering on a precipice, and defended him with a clenched fist as he mumbled vague admissions about inflicting "pain" in their marriage.

The world would one day recognize the Gennifer Flowers incident as not a marital slip but just another episode in Bill's serial adultery. Ultimately we would also learn that her husband's constant philandering was well known to Hillary. The marriage as a loving relationship was a farce. So why did Hillary so stoutly stand by her man? Why endure the tortured embarrassment of a national spectacle?

From a political standpoint, the answer seems obvious: A public termination of the marriage would destroy Bill Clinton's national political aspirations—and hers.

But beyond that long-term benefit, Hillary also reaped an immediate public relations bonanza. She evoked an outpouring of sympathy, a feeling so strong that even Flowers wrote in her book *Passion and Betrayal* about how Hillary passed right in front of her face without looking at her at the Governor's Mansion. "She could have slapped me right off the sidewalk and I would have deserved it. I actually sympathized with her."

Rumors about Bill Clinton's infidelities had been circulating for months, but there were no specifics. On September 17, 1991, about two weeks before the Clinton campaign officially took off in Little Rock, the Clintons went to Washington, D.C., for the Godfrey Sperling press breakfast. There they employed what would be their strategy on adultery allegations: to muddle through them with vague spin in order to convince the news media to take Bill's past sins off the table. Robert Novak was at the press breakfast that morning, and he remembered that the Clintons "seemed uneasy waiting" to get to their marital message. When finally a question was raised, Bill Clinton's answer, as reported by Novak, was typically Clintonian, a clever parsing of words ultimately signifying nothing: "Like nearly anybody that's been together twenty years, our relationship has not been perfect or free of difficulties. But we feel good about where we are. We believe in our obligations. And we intend to be together thirty or forty years from now, regardless of whether I run for president or not." For his part, Sperling, of *The Christian Science Monitor*, remembered Hillary "nodding emphatically."

This breakfast was a smashing success. The nonanswer was good enough for reporters, perhaps because the Clintons already had them at "Hello." *Time* political writer Michael Kramer ratified the vague-answers-are-enough consensus of the press, writing that the amorphous admission of "pain" was "received as a welcome exercise in truth telling." Sperling expressed the media's conventional wisdom when he wrote that if the two of them had reconciled, there was no political problem. In short, only Hillary would have the moral authority to decide if adultery mattered—a victim's veto. If she'd decided his straying was okay, then the matter was settled.

On January 16, 1992, the national tabloid *The Star* printed recycled allegations of adultery from a 1990 lawsuit by Clinton adversary Larry Nichols, but even then the Clinton campaign barely broke a sweat. Reporters viewed this story as little more than shaky gossip coming from embittered Clinton foes. At this point Hillary was still telling *Time's* Margaret Carlson, "My marriage is solid, full of love and friendship, but it's too profound to talk about glibly."

But a week later *The Star* was back, and this time promised evidence. Gennifer Flowers stepped forward to say that she'd enjoyed a long-standing affair with Clinton and had tapes of phone conversations with him to prove it. Samples of the taped conversations were released, and now the Clinton machine knew it had a potential disaster on its hands. Former Clinton aide George Stephanopoulos recalled in his memoir *All Too Human,* "I couldn't bear the thought that an old dalliance dredged up by a tabloid would curtail the professional experience of my life." If that "experience of my life" was in month number three of his professional affiliation with Clinton, one can just imagine how Mrs. Clinton felt after more than two decades molding her husband's chance at national office.

To put out the fire, the Clintons sent trusted adviser Mandy Grunwald to do their bidding on ABC's *Nightline.* Bill and Hillary must have enjoyed watching her beat Ted Koppel senseless even though he was taking a relatively soft approach to the adultery issue. "You haven't been talking about the middle class!" Grunwald charged. "You haven't talked about why Bill Clinton has captured people's imagination." Koppel was left to applaud her aggression: "So far you've done a very effective job of putting me on the defensive and asking me questions, which is perfectly appropriate."

Nightline reporter Jeff Greenfield, who delivered the setup piece for the interview, had no aggressive journalism to offer, either. His report featured a sound bite of Bill Clinton saying, "I read the story. It isn't true. And I told her [Flowers] over and over, I said, 'Just tell the truth. Tell the truth.'" Then Greenfield added this Hillary quote: "I just don't believe any of that and I don't think it's worthy of comment."

The media were focusing on Hillary's final point—the story wasn't worthy of comment—but ignoring the factual particulars. Greenfield ran a portion of the transcript discussing the affair. Judge for yourself whether Clinton and Flowers had an affair and were discussing a cover-up:

> CLINTON: I thought they'd look into it. But, you know, I just think a crazy person like Larry Nichols is not enough to get a story on the television with names in it.

> FLOWERS: Right. Well, he better not get on there and start naming names.

> CLINTON: Well, that's what I mean. You know, if all the people who are named . . . deny it . . . That's all, I mean, I expected them to come look into it and interview you and everything, uh, but I just think that if everybody's on record denying it, you've got no problem.

> FLOWERS: Well, I don't think . . . I don't think . . . I don't . . . Well, why would they waste their money and time coming down here unless someone showed 'em some interest? See, they weren't here tonight and they're not going to be there.

> CLINTON: No, no. See, that's it. I mean, they're gonna run this Larry Nichols thing down, they're gonna try to goad people up, you know, but if everybody kinda hangs tough, they're just not going to do anything. They can't.

> FLOWERS: No, they can't.

> CLINTON: They can't run a story like this unless somebody said, "Yeah, I did it with him."

What about the charge that Clinton used his power to award Flowers a job on the state payroll?

> FLOWERS: The only thing that concerns me, where I'm, I'm concerned at this point, is the state job.

> CLINTON: Yeah, I never thought about that. But as long as you say you've just been looking for one, you'da check on it. If they ever ask you if you've talked to me about it, you can say no.

The transcript contradicted the Clinton campaign's explanation that he had simply advised Flowers to tell the truth, a sound bite of which had aired just seconds earlier. Nevertheless, Greenfield dismissed Clinton's obvious attempt at obfuscation: "But that conversation by itself establishes nothing."

Oh really? The Flowers tapes clearly implicated Clinton in a relationship with Flowers, and they revealed Clinton advising Flowers to stick with the untrue Clinton cover story that there was no affair and that nothing was fishy in a new state job she had been given.

Koppel, supposedly that roaring lion of journalistic skepticism, was meowing, asking only about whether the voters had a right to know answers from the Clintons, and not demanding answers himself. This was not the approach Koppel took to conservative national candidates like Dan Quayle and Pat Robertson. In 1988 he picked Robertson apart on his military record, forcing the evangelist to admit that he was in a support unit in the Korean War, not on the front lines. Later that year, Koppel lectured Quayle aides that Quayle's joining the Indiana National Guard was an act of hypocrisy: "He was very much in favor of the war in Vietnam and yet . . . leaves this image now of having said, 'Here, I'll hold your coat, you go and fight in Vietnam.'" (But Bill Clinton's draft record, Koppel claimed, was not "germane" to the 1992 campaign.) He didn't let conservatives claim that their biographies were none of the people's business. He didn't let them change the subject to their 37-point plans for economic recovery. They were there to be exposed.

Grunwald was effective only because reporters had surrendered. They would not press the Clintons or their advisers on the investigative facts at hand. The media would declare that the charges were unsubstantiated, and make no attempt to substantiate them. The press's acquiescence would benefit not just Bill, but Hillary as well.

"Hit by a Meteor"

Though the media were obviously uncomfortable with the Flowers scandal, the Clintons had no choice but to step out when, on Thursday, January 23, Gennifer Flowers announced that the following Monday she would hold a press conference to play the incriminating tapes. It was time for Bill and Hillary to employ the tactic that would become a trademark of their damage-control efforts for years to come: the preemptive strike.

The Clintons agreed to be interviewed by CBS *60 Minutes* correspondent Steve Kroft for airing right after the Super Bowl, a gift of remarkable national visibility for a presidential candidate—and one day before Flowers's anticipated attack. Hillary was not only the costar but the crucial behind-the-scenes stage manager as well. "Both Clinton and Hillary were adamant about the A word [*adultery*], arguing that it was too grating, too harsh, too in-your-face to the viewers at home," said Stephanopoulos. The night before the *60 Minutes* interview the Clintons held a meeting with their closest aides; showing Mrs. Clinton's leadership role, Stephanopoulos wrote, "Hillary adjourned the meeting around one A.M." And then after Flowers played her tapes, Hillary took command again: "Hillary rallied all of us that night with a conference call from Minneapolis, foreshadowing another pattern that would be repeated again on a larger stage. If she was standing by her man, then so were we."

Steve Kroft's interview had the same weakness as Ted Koppel's: it allowed the Clintons to set the terms of discussion, and to argue that only a crotch-obsessed press wanted to discuss hanky-panky at the Quapaw Towers apartments when people were out of work in New Hampshire. Kroft established the tone from the beginning, when he underlined for viewers that the "tabloid" charges were unsubstantiated.

Kroft did ask about adultery multiple times ("You've been saying all week that you've got to put this issue behind you. Are you prepared tonight to say that you've never had an extramarital affair?" "You keep saying that you've made mistakes. What kind of mistakes? What mistakes—mistakes with women?"). He also wanted Clinton to address questions about his veracity ("A good friend of yours, one of your campaign advisers, told us the other day, 'Bill Clinton has got to level with the American people tonight, otherwise his candidacy is dead.' Do you feel like you've leveled with the American people?"). And he wanted to know whether Clinton was feeling good about it all ("You came here tonight to try and put it behind you. Are you going to get on the plane when you walk out of this room and go back to New Hampshire? You think you've succeeded?").

But if Kroft's questions were persistent, they were not at all specific. He didn't ask a single question about the Flowers tapes. He didn't ask about Flowers's state job. And he didn't ask whether Clinton had suggested she lie about the job if pressed on the subject.

Viewing the 1992 interview today is fascinating not simply because the edited eleven-minute piece looks like CBS's attempt to get Bill Clinton past the charges—it allowed him to plead that no one in history had been so maligned, to claim that admitting to an affair would never end the questions, and to insist that the scandal was a test not so much for Bill Clinton but for "the character of the press." Watching the interview now is especially interesting for Hillary's performance. Putting on the hillbilly accent like an ill-fitting straw hat, she delivered statements— unchallenged by her interviewer—that were truly preposterous. In her first answer, she claimed to have met with women implicated in affairs with her husband. (Note how she used "this woman" to describe Flowers, the same way her husband would later distance himself from Monica Lewinsky.)

> When this woman first got caught up in these charges, I felt like I've felt about all of these women. They've just been mindin' their own business and they got hit by a meteor [pronounced: mee-tee-oar] and it was no fault of their own. We reached out to them. I met with two of them to reassure them they knew they were friends of ours. I felt terrible about what was happening to them. You know, Bill talked to this woman every time she called, distraught, saying her life was going to be ruined [pronounced: rooned]. You know, he'd get off the phone and tell me she said sort of wacky things, which we thought were attributable to the fact that she was terrified.

Phony accents aside, imagine the spectacle of Mrs. Clinton meeting the "bimbos" in question and "reassuring" them that they were her "friends"! Creepy as it sounds, it has been at least partially confirmed. Juanita Broaddrick has asserted publicly that after Clinton sexually assaulted her, Hillary approached her at a reception, gripped her hand, and thanked her for "all her help." *Reassuring* is probably the last word Mrs. Broaddrick would employ to describe that meeting.

The quotes CBS put in heavy rotation on the next day's newscasts featured Hillary insisting on a "zone of privacy" and what would become the infamous Tammy Wynette quote, complete with the *g*'s dropped and her fist pumping: "I'm not sittin' here like some little woman standing by my man, like Tammy Wynette. I'm sittin' here 'cause I love him, I respect him, and I honor what he's been through, and what we've been through together, and you know, if that's not enough for people, then heck, don't vote for him."

And yet Hillary was never the "little woman," never a sappy doormat who would offer, as the song says, "two arms to cling to" when her husband was embattled by what the Clinton campaign called "bimbo eruptions." She was the leader of the antibimbo shock troops, ruthlessly organizing the she's-nutty-and-slutty talking points. She was the most enthusiastic destroyer of Clinton accusers.

In *All Too Human*, Stephanopoulos remembered his first bimbo eruption, in November 1991. Rock groupie Connie Hamzy charged in *Penthouse* that Clinton had propositioned her at a hotel. Stephanopoulos recalled that while Clinton seemed amused in recounting his version of the Hamzy story, Hillary was blunt: *"We have to destroy her story."* (Italics his.) When he succeeded in getting the story killed in the press, he received "an appreciative phone call from Hillary and the governor."

On the Sunday after Steve Kroft's Super Bowl special with Hillary and Bill, *60 Minutes* turned to another feminist hero, Anita Hill, and during that mostly sappy interview, Ed Bradley asked Hill, "People say, 'Well, I sat there, and I watched her, and I wanted to believe her, but I don't understand how she could say nothing for ten years. I don't understand how she could stay with him. I don't understand how she could follow him to another job.' How do you make those people understand?" This would have been a great line of questioning to apply to Mrs. Clinton. America still hasn't received her answer to that question. Why did she stay in that train wreck of a marriage?

HILLARY TOUTS THE TEN COMMANDMENTS

Having put the media on trial in the *60 Minutes* interview, the Clintons watched as the press dropped the Flowers scandal. After Kroft's 1992 report, ABC, CBS, NBC, and CNN aired a grand total of fourteen stories on the evening news, and eight of those were brief anchor-read blurbs, which typically highlighted the money Flowers received from *The Star*. The weekly news magazines touched on the allegations in only one issue, with hectoring headlines in the February 3 editions betraying their biases. There was "Money for Mischief" *(U.S. News & World Report)*, "We're Voting for President, Not Pope" *(Newsweek)*, and "Who Cares, Anyway?" *(Time)*. As for the Flowers tapes—the real story—only *Nightline* and the *CBS Evening News* aired snippets . . . and they were small snippets.

Nonetheless, five months later, at a luncheon held for top Democratic donors soon before the Democratic National Convention, the top media stars beat their breasts over their coverage of the Gennifer Flowers story. NBC anchor Tom Brokaw complained, "I think we've made it almost unbearable [for candidates] to enter the public arena." ABC anchor Peter Jennings called coverage of Flowers a mistake: "I realized that the press only cared about Gennifer Flowers and the people only cared about the economy."

That might have been the end of the Flowers story, but six years later, news of the Monica Lewinsky affair broke. In early 1998, twelve days after the Lewinsky story appeared, *60 Minutes* brought the 1992 Kroft interview out of the archives, running never-before-seen excerpts to shed new light on the Clinton spin. This time Kroft reviewed facts kept from CBS's viewers the first time around. Now he noted the Flowers tapes, saying that on them "the governor was heard coaching her on what to say if any reporters started asking questions." If this was important enough to report six years after the fact, why hadn't he raised it in his initial story? Kroft was seemingly defending himself for history when he added, "But the tapes had been edited, and most people chose to ignore them."

Interestingly, the fact that the tapes had been edited had been a key talking point for Stephanopoulos, James Carville, & Co. back in 1992, and apparently they had convinced the media that the tapes were therefore not believable. Of course, that claim looked a little silly when Bill Clinton personally apologized to Mario Cuomo for saying on those supposedly unbelievable tapes that the New York governor was a "mean son of a bitch" who, he agreed, "acts like a Mafioso" (the Cuomo segment was one of the snippets CBS aired).

In any case, it's always comical to hear TV journalists claim that you can't trust edited conversations. If that's true, why should anyone be asked to trust the edited seven-second snippets on TV news—or the edited eleven-minute *60 Minutes* interview—as reliable, either?

The new material *60 Minutes* released in 1998 showed that Slippery Hillary had been sitting next to Slick Willie that day back in 1992. In a pickle, not only could Hillary lie, but she could also share her husband's chutzpah in supposedly standing up for the truth against all those *other* liars out there.

In the new excerpts, Kroft directly asked Hillary about how they defined "problems" in their marriage: "What does it mean in America in 1992, that you had 'difficulties'?" Hillary struggled to stay vague: "We've had problems. We've had difficulties, in, in the past. And I agree with Bill that we—we think that's between us." Fair enough, but then she went for the zinger: "We don't owe anyone else besides each other the honesty that we've tried to bring as we've worked these problems out." She also said, "Part of what I believe with all my heart is that the voters are tired of people that lie to them. They're tired of people who act like something they're not." Like acting like you have an Arkansas accent?

In another snippet out of the archives, Kroft suggested that Bill's attractiveness to women was a political problem, and Hillary grew snippy: "You know, you are very good, Steve. You ask the same question nine or ten or twelve different ways and it—and—and I don't mean to be avoiding the question," which is precisely what she was trying to do. She chose instead to moralize: "If character only revolves around one question—which is what you're asking in the press—that's a shame, you know, because there are a lot of other questions that are, if not more important, certainly equally important. You know, there are ten commandments, not one. And one of them is, 'Thou shalt not bear false witness against thy neighbor.'"

It was the quintessential Hillary Rodham Clinton moment. Asked about her husband's violations of the Sixth Commandment, Hillary had responded by accusing their critics of violating the Eighth Commandment. It was "creepy and arrogant intimidation," *National Review*'s Kate O'Beirne commented when we interviewed her for this book. "'*Don't dare believe these irresponsible charges.*' It was intimidation."

Kroft betrayed CBS's original point of view at the end of the 1998 segment, claiming, "Tonight, only the president knows whether he is disappointed with himself in his dealings with Monica Lewinsky, the young

White House intern. But this time, his wife is not the only person who has the right to know." Kroft had inadvertently acknowledged that conventional media wisdom had deemed previous Clinton affairs, the Flowers one being the most notable, as none of the public's business—never mind that in 1992 America was being asked to decide if the man was fit to serve as president of the United States.

In the March 9, 1992, issue of *The New Republic*, senior editor Hendrik Hertzberg gave a refreshingly candid assessment of the elite media's take on Bill Clinton. Hertzberg described how he'd asked his political-reporter colleagues covering the New Hampshire primary for whom they would vote were they Democrats registered in that state. The "answer was always Clinton. Almost none is due to calculations about Clinton being 'electable' . . . and none at all is due to belief in Clinton's denials in the Flowers business, because no one believes these denials. No, the real reason members of The Press like Clinton is simple, and surprisingly uncynical: they think he would make a very good, perhaps a great, President."

No one believes these denials. Longtime political consultant and Reagan biographer Craig Shirley agreed with Hertzberg's assessment. When we interviewed Shirley, he illustrated the point with a story: "I can remember playing poker many, many times with national political reporters in the nineties. I'd be the token Republican and I'd talk about the wanton corruption of the Clinton administration, and they'd chuckle. To them it was to be expected. You expect Democrats to be slightly unsavory when it comes to morals, malfeasance, and the like." Likewise, *Washington Times* editorial page editor Tony Blankley, who spoke with scores of mainstream journalists during the 1990s, told us, "It was a matter of joking. They took for granted that he cheated."

Reporters knew all along that Bill Clinton was a serial adulterer, and therefore also a serial liar about his sham of a marriage. That made Hillary a serial liar, of course, as she repeatedly aided and abetted that myth with statements of her own. This, too, the media accepted, as Blankley pointed out: "They took for granted that Hillary knew, and that she was lying, and they chose not to report it. They subordinated their journalism for their support for Hillary."

It wouldn't be the last time.

Chapter 2
Tossing Cookies . . . and Softballs

The political wife that scares people most is usually a super success like Hillary Clinton, who ranks among the nation's most powerful lawyers and got better law-school grades than her husband. Perhaps she would be better off just trailing behind her husband, holding the Nancy Reagan gaze.

—*TIME*'s MARGARET CARLSON, March 30, 1992

Hillary was frequently in the hands of women in the media whose self-conceit was that they, too, were trailblazers against the odds in a hostile patriarchy.

—*NATIONAL REVIEW*'s KATE O'BEIRNE,
in an interview with the authors

If we first got to know Hillary Clinton as the poor wounded wife—thanks, of course, to the media's soft-pedal approach to the Gennifer Flowers story—she would soon step into the spotlight in her own right. Even in those early days the Hillary that emerged was the duplicitous, scandal-plagued, controlling figure we recognize today, except that the media, then as now, worked overtime to obscure these realities and keep them from the American people.

On March 16, 1992, only a few weeks after Hillary uttered the infamous Tammy Wynette line, she made unwanted headlines again. Prodded by NBC's Andrea Mitchell at the Busy Bee coffee shop in Chicago on a Monday morning about possible conflicts of interest between her lawyer's job and her husband's job, Hillary snapped, "I suppose I could have baked cookies and had teas. But what I decided to do was fulfill my profession, which I entered before my husband was in public life." As *National Review*'s Kate O'Beirne put it, this foot-in-mouth moment revealed Hillary's "contempt for the traditional role of women." O'Beirne told us in an interview, "She always saw herself as a brave pathfinder. She always thought of herself as superior. You could always detect that in Hillary." Once again, the real Hillary was there from the beginning, for anyone who bothered to look.

Let's be clear: The issue at hand was not Hillary's well-paying job as a senior partner at the Rose Law Firm in Little Rock. It was that Hillary's practice represented clients doing business before state agencies in Arkansas as well as representing the state government itself, at a time when the state government was headed by none other than her husband. Hillary typically dismissed questions about conflicts of interest by saying she took no share of income from the Rose Law Firm's state business. But that story of respectable distance soon collapsed. Well, her cover story *should* have collapsed, anyway.

HILLARY'S FIRST SCANDAL

On Sunday, March 8, 1992, the *New York Times* carried a story on the bottom of the front page by reporter Jeff Gerth disclosing the Clintons' peculiar partnership with S&L tycoon Jim McDougal and his wife, Susan. In 1978, they had formed Whitewater Development, which planned to sell vacation properties perched in the hills above northern Arkansas's White River. Gerth reported some fishy details suggesting that the McDougals were helping the Clintons out in a quid pro quo— the Clintons had invested less money in the 50-50 Whitewater partnership than the McDougals. It's not irregular for a 50-50 partner to provide less than 50 percent of the investment when one partner has other intangible benefits to offer. What nonmonetary contribution did an up-and-coming governor bring to the table?

In 1985 state banking regulators began questioning whether McDougal's Madison Guaranty Savings & Loan had enough assets on hand, and lawyers came up with a plan to issue preferred stock to keep the bank afloat. Listed as a lawyer to contact on that plan was one Hillary Rodham Clinton. Beverly Bassett Schaffer, the banking regulator just appointed by Governor Bill Clinton, rubber-stamped that request from Hillary to keep the failing S&L in business. (The letter began with a "Dear Hillary.") Eighteen months later, after more financial erosion, the federal government finally shut Madison down. The final report by Whitewater independent counsel Robert Ray said the failed enterprise cost taxpayers a whopping $73 million.

This was the first Clinton scandal that directly challenged Hillary's professional ethics. Hillary did not, however, wage public war on the *New York Times*, charging that Washington Bureau Chief Howell Raines hated Clinton, or was jealous of him. She and her staff must have realized that an attack on the *Times* would only keep the story alive. As it was, the rest of the media's reaction was downright comatose.

The day the *New York Times* story broke, ABC ran a short story, CBS aired only a brief anchor mention, and NBC reported nothing. Two days after the *Times* scoop, Bill Clinton easily swept eight states on "Super Tuesday." In his victory speech, a confident and shameless Clinton declared that he was running for president "because I thought most people in America were just like me and Hillary and our friends at home, that they were tired of a politics that puts money first and people last." The media not only ignored the story, they allowed the Clintons to play the idealistic anti-greed game all year long.

One week after Gerth's explosive-scoop-turned-hiccup on the McDougal-Clinton financial partnership, Michael Weisskopf and David Maraniss of the *Washington Post* filed their own exposé on Hillary's work at the Rose Law Firm, again raising questions about Hillary's firm handling cases before state agencies run by her husband's appointees. At a televised debate that night in Detroit, candidate Jerry Brown charged that Clinton was "funneling money to his wife's law firm" and called it not just "corruption" but "the kind of conflict of interest that is incompatible with the kind of public servant that we expect as president."

Clinton was ready for that one. In his memoir, George Stephanopoulos said he had coached Clinton that the minute he heard Jerry Brown utter the word *Hillary*, he should "rip his head off." On cue, Clinton reacted to Brown with a squint and a bout of scripted anger: "I don't care what you say about me, but you ought to be ashamed of yourself for jumping on my wife. You're not worth being on the same platform as my wife. I never funneled any money to my wife's law firm. Never!"

Maybe it depends on the meaning of the word *funnel*. Rose *was* making big money off Clinton's state government, coming and going. In the *Post* story Brown was referring to, Weisskopf and Maraniss reported that Rose "offers the full range of representation before the government, from getting environmental approvals from the state Pollution Control and Ecology Commission, to lobbying to protect the poultry industry from strict regulations on animal waste, to writing the rules by which corporations treat their shareholders." Also: "One of Rose's most lucrative clients is the state government, which has issued a number of nonbid contracts to Rose, as well as to other leading firms here, during Clinton's years as governor." (In the current liberal media lingo, cozy "nonbid contracts" sounds a little Halliburtonish, doesn't it?)

That was not all. "The Public Service Commission, appointed by Clinton, paid $115,000 to Rose to represent it in a nuclear power plant dispute with Mississippi. Rose has earned up to $175,000 for bond counsel work for the Arkansas Development Finance Authority since 1985. Although the firm is not the leading earner of bond counsel fees, it did not have any of the state business in most early years of the decade, according to state records." With Hillary on the payroll, the Rose Law Firm was thriving off the state of Arkansas, with nonbid contracts and new bond-counsel business under the Clinton administration.

Surely this would rise to the level of a national issue for the political press corps. After all, during the Reagan-Bush years, liberal Washington reporters were heavy-breathing sticklers about conflicts of interest in government, and even the *appearance* of a conflict of interest. This was what Walter Mondale was referring to when he said Ronald Reagan's regime carried a "sleaze factor." And now the TV networks had strong evidence—provided by two of their own, the *New York Times* and the *Washington Post*—that the country was being asked to elect the personification of corruption as its president, and this man's equally corrupt wife would be its next First Lady.

But these were the Clintons.

In what was becoming a pattern, the *Post*'s version of the Little Rock financial-scandal story could barely be found on TV. As a congressman, Bob Livingston of Louisiana spent many years trying to uncover the web of corruption in Little Rock. "I put my career on the line to prove it, [but] the press never wanted to look at Whitewater," the former congressman told us in an interview. To the degree they did cover the issue, "they were dragged kicking and screaming by Republicans and talk radio," Livingston said. From March 8 to 31, the four networks combined produced only five full stories on Whitewater and mentioned the financial questions in only nine stories in total; they did nothing to investigate the claims independently.

The news magazines were even less interested. In their March 23 editions, *Newsweek* devoted one clause and *Time* reported nothing. Neither did *U.S. News & World Report*—even though, in the previous issue, the magazine had devoted three pages to chronicling the family connections of one George W. Bush, headlined "The Color of Money: The President's Eldest Son and His Ties to a Troubled Texas Firm." Scandal stories about the finances of the Republican president's sons were still newsworthy, but scandals about the finances of the presumptive Democratic nominee and his wife were not.

Two days after the *Post* scoop and the Jerry Brown scrap, Clinton again won the big primaries, this time in Michigan and Illinois, and in their Primary Day reports, the networks were still defending the Clintons. NBC news commentator John Chancellor crowed after the Clinton victory that "Jerry Brown's inaccurate attack on Hillary Clinton's legal fees did not work. The Democrats in these two states today told us that honesty was important, and Clinton got the highest mark in both states."

That line should have collapsed on March 20, when the *Washington Times* reported that contrary to Hillary Clinton's claim that she did not "intervene or attempt to influence" the state concerning the Madison inquiry, she and the Rose Law Firm received a $2,000-a-month retainer for at least fifteen months for Hillary's defending McDougal's Madison S&L before the state's banking regulators. In his 1996 book *Blood Sport*, Pulitzer Prize–winning author James Stewart described how Bill Clinton stopped by Jim McDougal's office during a jog in August 1984 and urged McDougal to throw business Hillary's way. When *New York Times* reporter Jeff Gerth started asking questions about this story during the campaign, the Clinton campaign denied the totality of the jogging story, and that was good enough for the editors at the *Times*. According to Stewart, after Gerth had filed a story regardless, Executive Editor Joe Lelyveld killed it because he said he "didn't want it to look like the *Times* was 'piling on' Clinton."

Now Clinton was winning critical primaries willy-nilly, but liberals still worried about scandal hurting his general-election chances against President Bush. Reporters continued to protect the Clintons, still proclaiming that there was nothing factual in the anti-Hillary complaint and still flat-out ignoring her McDougal retainers. On March 23, after the *Washington Times* report appeared, ABC's Chris Bury sounded like a Team Clinton defense lawyer: "Brown repeated claims that Clinton made money by directing state business to his wife's law firm. Those claims have never been proven." Richard Threlkeld of CBS portrayed it all as an invasion of privacy: "Now Hillary Clinton is asking: Must a wife sacrifice her career if it might interfere with her husband's? Not the sort of campaign issue the voters were expecting."

Echoing Threlkeld's tsk-tsking, *Time* and *Newsweek* ran apologetic articles about unfair scrutiny of working political wives. *Newsweek's* acerbic Ginny Carroll argued that the real issue wasn't Hillary's potentially corrupt practices, but America's outdated sexism. "The core issue, arguably, is whether America is really ready for a self-confident, politically active woman like Hillary Clinton as First Lady." In fact, there wasn't anything debatable about this delicious piece of factual distortion. No Republicans were denouncing Hillary for being a working woman. They were suggesting that she was a *corrupt* working woman.

In an intriguing passage underlining the liberal media's lack of interest in probing the Clintons, Carroll wrote, "[T]here is no convincing evidence that either did anything improper as governor or Little Rock lawyer. But the opposition will undoubtedly comb the fine print of each and every legal transaction she handled, looking for irregularities." Carroll's unintended confession was enlightening: Combing the fine print of Bill and Hillary's cronyism was not to be the job for the press corps. It was a distasteful assignment suited only for Clinton-haters—knuckle-dragging opposition researchers who hated women coming out of the kitchen.

Later that year, Carroll sneered on C-SPAN about her reaction to a

"Rather Biased" button: "My reaction to that button and others, in part, is a button I bought yesterday that says, 'Yeah, I'm in The Media, Screw You!'" Like so many other reporters, Carroll carried the arrogant notion that only the press, and not the public, would determine when a scandal was a scandal.

Time's Margaret Carlson, then the magazine's deputy Washington bureau chief, similarly ascribed evil intentions to those with the audacity to raise questions about Whitewater improprieties. "They are easy to make and hard to refute," she warned, "and can obscure a hidden intent to put an uppity woman in her place."

Newsweek's alleged media critic, Jonathan Alter, was still fussing at Clinton opponents two weeks later, in the April 6 issue. "Jerry Brown was grossly wrong about Clinton 'funneling money' into his wife's law practice," he wrote. "Hillary Clinton takes no share of state fees, but if she did, it would be peanuts." Alter chose to ignore the $2,000-a-month retainer from McDougal, complaining instead that George Bush's sons "make Hillary Clinton's activity look like one of those tea-and-cookies parties she disparages." A week later, Alter's *Newsweek* compadre Eleanor Clift, as eager as Alter to advance the Clintons' fortunes, added for emphasis, "Little Rock is a corporate plantation, but there is no evidence that the Clintons profited personally from hobnobbing with business people or political backers."

These claims could have been rebutted by fellow *Newsweek* reporter Mark Miller, except much of what he learned as a journalist inside the Clinton campaign—a position of access that many reporters would be eager to protect—was not published until *1994*. When *Newsweek* finally published what Miller knew about Whitewater, his reporting thoroughly contradicted what his colleagues Alter and Clift had stated during the 1992 campaign. Indeed, Miller's report disclosed that Hillary possessed her husband's truth problem.

After the 1992 Illinois primary, Mrs. Clinton said in response to a reporter's question that she had "never, ever" profited from state business. But Miller revealed that the Clinton campaign staff "was horrified to discover that this was not entirely true, when it turned up a 1986 memo detailing her decision to give up the bond profits [she had joined Rose in 1977]. The staff ended up sitting on the memo—which fortunately for Clinton, never leaked."

The lack of leaks could have been a function of a press corps that was uninterested in investigating Hillary and Bill.

Toward the end of March 1992, Denver accountant James Lyons released a report produced for the Clinton campaign claiming that the Clintons actually lost money on the Whitewater investments. Even if true, Lyons's report did not address the key issues: the Clintons clearly had received money on a deal they expected to ultimately provide a financial bonanza; Hillary clearly had used her husband's position as governor to keep a corrupt deal afloat; the American taxpayer clearly had been handed the bill for the failed scheme; and clearly, the Clintons—both together and separately—had lied about it. Yet none of this mattered. The scandal all but evaporated not only on television but in the national print press as well. Looking back at campaign coverage, Gannett reporter John Hanchette told the *American Journalism Review* in May 1994, "All of these spreadsheets came out with all this little tiny print on it that looked like a bank statement for a complicated business. People sort of looked at it and said 'What the heck is that?'" *U.S. News* assistant managing editor Harrison Rainie explained in the same *AJR* story, "For better or worse, [the Lyons report] stopped the story." *Stopped* the story? The story never left first gear.

Ann Coulter nailed it when she wrote in *High Crimes and Misdemeanors*, "Whitewater gets interesting only when you understand why it is boring. It is boring by design, like a *New York Times* editorial. Don't skip [Whitewater]! That's just what the Clintons want you to do."

"DOES IT MAKE YOU HURT OR MAKE YOU MAD?"

Why would the media be so quick to drop the Whitewater story? Credit the Times Mirror Center for exploring the question. Its postprimary poll of journalists in June 1992 suggested that a majority of national reporters had a viscerally hostile reaction to news of Bill and Hillary's S&L scandal.

Reporters were asked their initial impressions about certain stories on the presidential candidates. First, the pollsters explored Andrew Rosenthal's infamous *New York Times* story about President Bush's encounter with an automated checkout scanner at a grocery store. Rosenthal had portrayed Bush as out of touch with everyday life by reporting that the president was amazed by a common supermarket scanner, when in fact it was a newly developed high-tech scanner. Forty percent of national reporters said they had a positive journalistic reaction to this silly, misre-ported story—meaning they felt it was well reported and newsworthy—while 34 percent did not.

The pollsters then asked about the first *New York Times* reports on the Clintons' dealings with McDougal. This time, only 17 percent of national reporters had a positive journalistic impression of the story, while a surprising majority—53 percent—had a negative reaction.

The reasons for their disapproval were also fascinating: 16 percent felt the issue was "exaggerated" or "no big deal." Another 10 percent called it "irrelevant." Keep in mind that this story dealt directly with possible financial conflicts of interest in a savings and loan that cost taxpayers a cool $73 million to bail out—and that involved a candidate who had proclaimed in his 1991 announcement speech, "When the rip-off artists looted our S&Ls, the president was silent. In a Clinton administration, when people sell their companies and their workers and their country down the river, they'll get called on the carpet." By contrast, only 5 per-cent thought the Great Bush Grocery Store Scandal was overblown, and only 1 percent considered *that* irrelevant. In one story, millions of tax-payer dollars were lost. In the other one, nothing happened except that the president was caricatured as the dad of Richie Rich.

It wasn't that the press just wasn't interested in the investigation of failed and potentially corrupt S&Ls. In fact, they were zealous in their efforts—if the S&Ls were connected to Republicans. On September 15, 1992, *Dateline NBC* aired a hard-hitting investigative segment on the financial dealings of President Bush's son Neil. NBC reporter Brian Ross aggressively interviewed the younger Bush, and later tried a dramatic "ambush" on the floor of the Republican convention. After airing Neil Bush's claim that it was hard to explain complicated transactions, Ross went on the attack: "It's really not that complicated: quite simply, while his father has been in the White House, American taxpayers have been stuck with millions of dollars in bills from failed business ventures involving Neil Bush, including one deal that only now is fully coming to light, and all the while, the president's son has been living a life that some people say is like that of an American prince." Ross pointed out that Neil Bush had paid himself salaries of $120,000 and $160,000 as his ventures failed.

So why didn't the Neil Bush standard apply to Hillary? In the years before Bill Clinton ascended to the White House, Hillary Clinton made more than Neil Bush's self-declared salaries, more than $200,000 a year, as a lawyer and corporate board member. She not only served as a co-owner of Whitewater Development, but also represented Madison Guaranty Savings & Loan before state agency heads appointed by her husband. That legal work led to a deeper bailout cost to the American taxpayer.

But the week before the Neil Bush report, *Dateline* anchor Jane Pauley interviewed Hillary Clinton—and didn't ask her a single question about her role in representing Madison. This time there were no ambushing camera crews springing out of bushes. Pauley's interview with Mrs. Clinton was very politely taped at the Governor's Mansion in Little Rock and carefully edited, and she very politely asked Mrs. Clinton about her nasty Republican opponents. When Pauley asked why she pushed opponents' hot buttons, Hillary said, "I do have opinions, and I state my opinions," which can be "troubling to people." The question distorted the issue: conservatives were raising questions about the *content* of her opinions and her work; no one was shocked and outraged that she had opinions. Pauley followed with these probing questions: "When you hear yourself held up, as you were at the Republican convention, some people have used the word 'demonized,' does it make you hurt or make you mad?" "What was the worst things you've heard said about you?," and "What was the grossest distortion of your record?"

And then there was the softball that deserves its own plaque in Cooperstown: "Before Governor Clinton declared for the presidency, you prepared Chelsea. Bad things may be said about Daddy. Was Chelsea at all prepared for bad things being said about Mommy?" Hillary smacked the softball over the fence, replying that she told Chelsea their opponents were so desperate that they might start attacking Chelsea, or "maybe go after our cat."

Pauley seemed so impressed by how courageously Hillary was representing her, and all women of the baby-boom generation, that she had no time to ask a specific question about anything Hillary had done in representing S&L thieves. The closest she came to the Whitewater issues was asking whether Hillary would "cede the moral high ground" to Marilyn Quayle, since Mrs. Quayle had set her legal career aside for her husband. Hillary gave the rote answer that all women should be honored for their choices, and that in her own life, she'd tried to avoid the tendency for women to think "we've got to do everything absolutely perfectly." Pauley melted. "What do you not do perfectly?" she cooed, to which Hillary joked, "Oh! I could give you a long list, but I won't. Why would I disillusion you like that?"

This was just too much for Kate O'Beirne, whose years fighting the entrenched liberal media, most prominently on CNN's *Capital Gang,* has earned her folklore status within the conservative movement. When we interviewed her, she blasted women in the media for failing to honestly report on Hillary. According to O'Beirne, feminists in the media see *any* criticism of Hillary as coming from those "threatened by a powerful woman because that's their self-conceit about themselves." These women in the media "have this huge chip on their shoulders. They are the aggrieved sisterhood."

Chapter 3
Circling the Wagons

I think that strong, intelligent women are still threatening to some people. . . . And this country would be, I think, only better to have her in the White House.

—ACTRESS AND HILLARY BUDDY MARY STEENBURGEN
on *Today*, responding to voters with
a negative image of Hillary, July 14, 1992

As far as going after Hillary now is concerned, [many conservatives] are afraid to take on a "strong woman" because they're going to be called sexists or misogynists.

—CAL THOMAS, syndicated columnist,
in an interview with the authors

After the media twisted themselves into pretzels trying to claim that Hillary was a wife who suffered "pain in her marriage" but was never a doormat, and that Hillary was a top-notch lawyer but never a huckster for S&L looters, they turned to what was potentially a far greater political problem: Hillary the brilliant, driven, passionate advocate was also an ideological ultraliberal on the fringes of American political discourse.

One particularly frightening article for Hillary's supportive media circle emerged just before the Democratic convention, when Daniel Wattenberg's August 1992 cover story for *The American Spectator*, "Boy Clinton's Big Mama," hit the stands. Near the article's end, Wattenberg reported that in 1987 and 1988, Hillary served as chair of the board of directors of the New World Foundation, identified by the Capital Research Center as one of the country's ten most liberal foundations. In addition to funding traditional liberal groups (NAACP, People for the American Way), New World under Hillary's leadership was also a major benefactor of the radical left.

New World showed a special devotion to fighting Ronald Reagan's attempt to hold the line against Communism in Central America. It gave $20,000 to the Christic Institute, a far-left anti-American outfit so nutty that it was attacked by the hard-left magazine *Mother Jones* as irresponsible; Christic, for example, claimed that a "secret team" of generals and CIA agents was running a covert and illegal anti-Communist foreign policy. New World also gave $5,000 to CISPES (the Committee in Solidarity with the People of El Salvador), a group organized to offer American support to the Communist guerrillas of El Salvador.

In addition, Hillary's board oversaw grants to the Center for Constitutional Rights, founded by radical lawyer William Kunstler, who told left-wing students in the Vietnam era to learn how to shoot guns because in a revolution, "you may ultimately be bathed in blood." He told the *Village Voice* in 1979 that Joan Baez should not have criticized the Communist government of Vietnam, adding that he "would never join in a public denunciation of a socialist country."

How would the media square this radical philanthropy with the Clintons' supposed home-fried triangulated Southern centrism? Simple. Ignore it, and if some uncooperative conservative insists on bringing it up—rip his head off.

That was certainly the theme on CNN's *Capital Gang* on July 13, 1992, when columnist Mona Charen made—or better stated, tried to make—the point that no matter the spin from the Clinton camp, Hillary still represented the left wing of the Democratic Party. *Wall Street Journal* Washington bureau chief Al Hunt would have none of it. "Well, Mona, I would point out that that is based on law review pieces she wrote twenty years ago. It's utter, complete nonsense. You don't have anything factual." When Charen shifted it to New World grants, awarded just four years earlier—"Her foundation grants to CISPES, and William Kunstler"—Hunt yelled in reply, "No! That is the far-right *American Spectator* kind of neofascist hit nonsense!"

Most of Wattenberg's article was devoted to Hillary's legal writings, the most florid passage coming from a 1974 essay titled "Children Under the Law," which was reprinted in the *Harvard Educational Review* in 1982, after Mrs. Clinton had been the First Lady of Arkansas four years. The "money paragraph" Wattenberg plucked out was this:

> The basic rationale for depriving people of rights in a dependency relationship is that certain individuals are incapable or undeserving of the right to take care of themselves and therefore need social institutions specifically designed to safeguard their position. Along with the family, past and present examples of such arrangements include marriage, slavery, and the Indian reservation system.

She had compared marriage to slavery, a campaign manager's nightmare. A spin-control artist might try to suggest she meant marriage a century or two back, but she'd handcuffed the spinners by writing "past and present examples." For social conservatives who had battled with feminists (primarily) over the sanctity of the nuclear family, this had a routine echo: traditional marriage had placed women in a subservient, dependent relationship with men. As the longtime antifeminist warrior Phyllis Schlafly told us, "Feminists are antimarriage and they look upon marriage as putting women in a lower class, from which they need to be liberated." Recalling her campaign against the Equal Rights Amendment, she said, "In the early days I would be picketed by women with placards reading, 'I'm a second-class citizen.'"

But the exotic references to slavery and Indian reservations obscured Hillary's larger point: that the legal status of minors should be abolished and the legal presumption of incompetence for minors should be reversed. Even liberal admirer Garry Wills understood that Hillary meant something radical, writing in the *New York Review of Books*, "In the past, the child's rights were asserted vicariously through the parent. Ms. Clinton sees those rights as, at times, to be asserted against the parent. This has always been recognized in abuse cases, but she would extend it much farther."

In another article Wattenberg cited from 1979, Hillary extended her revolutionary vision, calling for the "liberation" of teenagers, especially on sexual and lifestyle issues. "I prefer that intervention into an ongoing family be limited to decisions that could have long-term and irreparable effects if they were not resolved. Decisions about motherhood and abortion, schooling, cosmetic surgery, treatment of venereal disease or employment, and others where the decision or lack of one will significantly affect the child's future should not be made unilaterally by parents."

This amounted to a declaration of war against the nuclear family and a direct challenge to the authority of parenthood. Large majorities of Americans have long favored parental notification for abortions, as well as parental consent. Common sense tells us that most parents would also not be wild about their teenagers submitting themselves to cosmetic surgery or venereal-disease treatments without their knowledge and approval. Hillary's thinking, in sum, made her not simply a liberal but someone far outside the mainstream.

That being so, an impartial media should have felt obligated to question the woman who would certainly play a major role on social issues in a proposed Clinton administration. But when it came time to ask Hillary to defend these extreme antiparent positions and grant-making decisions, the press confronted . . . her critics. It was the same pattern we'd seen with Whitewater, and before that, with Gennifer Flowers.

A day after Judy Woodruff's husband, Al Hunt, attacked the "neofascist" *Spectator* exposé, she interviewed Hillary on PBS's *MacNeil/Lehrer NewsHour*. Woodruff suggested that questioning her liberalism should not be part of the campaign: "How important do you think it is that Hillary Clinton not become an issue in this campaign, and I ask that because Republicans, conservatives are already saying, you know about the articles that have been written—'She's very liberal, she came into this campaign being the wife of a governor with a strong set of opinions about everything [from] children's rights to aid to the El Salvador rebels,' and so on, and so on. How important is it that that not enter in, and should it in any way enter in?"

Set aside the fact that the Clintons were the ones who had made Hillary an issue in the campaign, with the promise that they were a bargain deal—"Buy One/Get One Free," said the buttons the campaign handed out. Examine instead how Hillary responded. She couldn't deny what she'd written, so instead she played the victim again, claiming that this was all a "calculated political decision" by the GOP to "go after me." Then she shamelessly twisted reality to suggest that she actually *supported* parental notification before abortions: "Why are they doing that? Particularly, why are they distorting who I am, and taking me out of context, and forgetting that in many areas, be it the death penalty, or parental notice, I would be considered conservative, not liberal?" She answered herself: "It's because they worry I do have more in common with most American women."

Woodruff pitched a bunch of fluff questions to Hillary, including this bit of pandering: "Many people out there, of course, are still trying to figure out who Hillary Clinton is, and one of the images that's been batted around, I guess you would say this year, is 'Well, she's this hard-driving, not only smart, but really pushing [*sic*] mastermind behind her husband, who's even more ambitious than he is.' What do you—you've obviously had to address that—what do you say?" Hillary modestly downplayed the "mastermind" issue by saying, shucks, she was just a mother who served on the board of the local children's hospital and practiced law, but "they may still decide they don't like me because I wear a headband on occasion."

"They" were on trial again.

The *Today* show went even easier on Hillary on July 20. Interviewing Mrs. Clinton and her new running-mate spousal partner, Tipper Gore, Bryant Gumbel tossed up light questions and then, uncharacteristically, let his subjects carry on (and on, and on) uninterrupted for sixty to ninety seconds. Gumbel asked, "You two—this comes as no bulletin—you two have surely seen the widespread speculation that one campaign isn't big enough for two women as strong-willed, independent-minded, outspoken as each of you are. You're laughing. How's that speculation strike you?" Then he took the obligatory swipe at Republicans: "Mrs. Clinton, in an interview with PBS, you said you thought that the Republicans had made a calculated political decision to, in your words, go after you. How big an issue do you think you're yet going to be in this campaign?" For her response, he allowed Hillary seventy-three seconds to make the point that Republicans were "desperate" because they didn't have any new ideas.

No Time for Hillary-Grillers

Controversy over Hillary's ultraliberalism resurfaced on August 17, the first day of the Republican convention in Houston, when Pat Buchanan explicitly attacked Hillary's radicalism in prime time. "Elect me, and you get two for the price of one, Mr. Clinton says of his lawyer spouse. And what does Hillary believe? Well, Hillary believes that twelve-year-olds should have a right to sue their parents, and she has compared marriage as an institution to slavery—and life on an Indian reservation. Well, speak for yourself, Hillary." Buchanan called her beliefs "radical feminism" and decried the left-wing social agenda "Clinton and Clinton" would impose: abortion on demand, gay rights, women in combat, discrimination against religious schools.

This was the speech the Bush campaign wanted delivered, *needed* delivered to bring conservatives home. "The President Bush reelect campaign wanted Pat to speak his mind, but also to expose the [Clintons'] very left-wing agenda that the media in many ways had been hiding from the American public," PR expert Greg Mueller, who served as a senior political adviser to the Buchanan campaign, told us in an interview. They wanted it known that with a Clinton administration America would get "liberalism through and through, including policy initiatives from the radical left that were developed and would be implemented by Mrs. Clinton herself."

The conventional wisdom holds that Buchanan's firebrand speech dramatically hurt President Bush's reelection efforts. This is the stuff of media mythology. The facts speak for themselves. Entering convention week, the Bush campaign trailed Clinton by 17 (CBS News) or 18 (CNN–*USA Today*) points. But in tracking surveys conducted by the *Houston Chronicle* and the Hotline on the night of Buchanan's speech (as well as Ronald Reagan's extraordinary farewell address), the lead had shriveled to 5 points, the closest George Bush would ever come to Bill Clinton in the race.

The media, however, ensured that the Republicans' momentum quickly halted. All pretense of objectivity went out the window in favor of loaded editorials masquerading as "news."

ABC anchorman Peter Jennings rebuked Buchanan in prime time: "Took a number of shots at Hillary Clinton. Didn't get that altogether accurate, but that'll come out in the debate as time goes on."

The same charges of inaccuracy came up on the evening news. Days before the convention, on the August 12 *World News Tonight*, ABC's Cokie Roberts had pilloried hapless Republican National Committee chairman Rich Bond for using the *Harvard Educational Review* article. Without spending more than 15 seconds on the essay, Roberts simply declared the opposite of reality: "She did not equate marriage with slavery," she harrumphed unequivocally as the TV screen read *DID NOT EQUATE MARRIAGE WITH SLAVERY*. "Still, Republicans have seized on the article as evidence that Bill Clinton cannot be a moderate, not if he listens to his liberal wife. There's a concerted Republican effort to portray Hillary Clinton as an out-of-the-mainstream radical." Roberts might have claimed that Hillary's sentence was sloppily constructed, but it was simply inaccurate to claim that she did not equate marriage with slavery. She clearly did, in black and white.

ABC News was at it again the night after the Buchanan speech. Reporter Jim Wooten claimed that what "Mrs. Clinton, an attorney, argued in 1974 was that children have a right to protection from parental abuse, including legal separation from the parent." After airing a clip of Buchanan saying that this was "radical feminism," Wooten rebutted: "In fact, that is now the law." But the ABC reporter had watered down Hillary's claims, failing to mention that she favored completely overturning the presumption of incompetence for children in favor of a general presumption of competence. Reporters like Wooten and Roberts had taken a shrink ray to the issue and reduced it to a completely defensible wall of protection against abusive parents.

Impassioned ABC next took its poor-Hillary crusade to *Nightline*. Both strands of the protect-Hillary message emerged. First, *They're picking on the poor girl.* In his intro Koppel showed a clip of Buchanan and then retorted, "It's a political convention, so they come out swinging. But should the candidate's wife be dragged into it?" (Again, wasn't it Bill Clinton who dragged his wife into the campaign in the first place?) Then it was the other punch: *They hate strong women.* Koppel began the program on a snide note. "Let us not for a moment be confused into believing that this is only a conservative Republican thing, this business of some people feeling threatened by smart, assertive, professional women," he preached. "Women who speak their minds in public are still swimming upstream in this country." Did Koppel ever wonder just how it was that conservatives could admire Golda Meir, revere Margaret Thatcher, cheer Jeane Kirkpatrick, and also somehow hate strong women?

Koppel took off the gloves when he interviewed Phyllis Schlafly, that object of ocean-deep feminist hatred. Abandoning any sense of impartiality, he insisted that the anti-Hillary side was full of knowing lies: "Is truth necessary or even desirable here?" Schlafly replied that Hillary's "views on children are very closely tied to the Children's Defense Fund, on which she served as a director [Hillary was the CDF's chairperson from 1986 to 1992]. That is the principal lobbying agent working for federally funded, federally regulated babysitting of preschool children, and their proposal was so extreme that they couldn't even get this present liberal Congress to pass it. So I think her views are very much an appropriate topic of discussion and the American people should know about them." Koppel's answer was eye-popping: "All right, let us agree just for a moment to disagree on that." Disagree with what? With the fact that Congress failed to pass the CDF proposal? With the idea of even a *discussion* of Hillary's views? Koppel represented the arrogant media viewpoint: the American people don't need to know about Hillary's exotic academic articles. Let's just bury them in the backyard.

In fact, the American people didn't need to know anything about Hillary's background, it seemed Koppel was saying. At one point he cut Schlafly off, saying that she justified her "attacks" on Mrs. Clinton "by saying that she is now presenting herself and that Governor Clinton is presenting his wife as sort of a package deal, you know, you get one, you get both, and you elect one, you elect both. Would it be equally justifiable for Democratic hitmen and -women to go after the president's son, Neil Bush, for his activities in the Silverado [S&L], or something like that?" But of course it wasn't just Democratic hitmen who had done that; it was the media as well. Ted Koppel and *Nightline* had done that, on July 17, 1990! That despite the fact that Neil Bush had never presented himself as part of a "package deal" with his father.

In his memoir, George Stephanopoulos, who appeared opposite

Schlafly that night, offered nothing but praise and gratitude for his future ABC colleague: "What turned the debate was Ted Koppel's using his anchorman authority to subtly suggest the attacks on Hillary were misleading. All I had to do was fall in behind and remind viewers that the Republicans were up to their old tricks." Stephanopoulos was wrong about one thing: Koppel was as subtle as a nuclear bomb.

Indeed, the only time Koppel even veered toward a real and substantive challenge to Mrs. Clinton's side occurred when he said that "folks are worried about . . . the degree to which [Hillary] may have been instrumental in Arkansas in making judicial appointments, and the concern that people who elect Bill Clinton don't necessarily want Hillary Clinton making similar decisions on a national basis." But Stephanopoulos merely batted away the suggestion, twice insisting, "She will not play a formal role in the White House"—a claim that would soon look ridiculous, of course.

On August 18, Judy Woodruff returned to the theme of negative Republican attacks while interviewing First Lady Barbara Bush on PBS. Woodruff pressed Mrs. Bush to distance herself from every Republican attack during the Houston convention that had so ruffled liberal media feathers. The first question was about GOP chairman Rich Bond's questioning the patriotism of Democrats. The second question was about Pat Buchanan's opposing gay GOP activists. The third question was about those outrageous Republican suggestions that Bill Clinton was a "skirt chaser."

Mrs. Bush pushed right back: "Look, you're saying nothing nice. . . . Where were you during the Democrat convention defending us?" Woodruff tried to ignore that, returning to her line of inquiry: "But [Commerce Secretary Robert] Mosbacher said in the last day or so that Governor Clinton's alleged marital infidelity is a legitimate campaign issue!"

Two days later on the *NewsHour*, Woodruff marched Marilyn Quayle through the same gauntlet about *her* convention speech. Mrs. Quayle had said that not every member of the baby-boom generation joined the counterculture, did drugs, had wild sex, and dodged the draft. Woodruff protested this simple point. "I still don't understand what bringing up draft dodging and some of the other points you made has to do with this election," she huffed. She concluded by again taking issue with Republican portrayals of Mrs. Clinton as liberal: "Mrs. Clinton, you have said, at least I saw in an interview that I think ran in the *New York Times* this week, 'Mrs. Clinton's ideas, some of them, are radical.' You used the word *liberal,* I think you used the word *radical* a couple of times. What were you referring to? . . . I'm sure, as you know, they say these words, these terms, expressions that have been brought out, are taking them out of context, or a distortion of what she was trying to write twenty years ago, or fifteen years ago or something like that."

In between Woodruff's interruptions, Mrs. Quayle tried to say of Hillary, "She's a professional woman, she's being treated in a professional manner by looking at what she's done as a professional, and that's good." But reporters weren't at all interested in treating Hillary in a professional manner, refusing as they were to look seriously at what she'd done professionally. To do that apparently made you a Republican.

By week's end the media counterattack had worked. The 5-point spread had disappeared, and Bill Clinton had regained his lead. Even worse, the Bush campaign was in full retreat mode, zigzagging to avoid media artillery rounds, with nervous-Nellie spokesmen like Rich Bond now disavowing any support for the Buchanan speech.

The Booster Club

Having stopped the Republican momentum, the Hillary Clinton Booster Club—also known as the elite media—offered even more of a helping hand.

On August 24, the Monday after the Republican convention, both *CBS This Morning* and NBC's *Today* (for a second time) featured taped interviews with the dynamic duo of Democratic spouses, and both offered themselves as eager and willing forums for criticism of the Republican convention.

CBS This Morning cohost Paula Zahn felt pain for Hillary and Tipper. "I know you both say that these attacks come with the territory. But don't they penetrate you? Does it not hurt anymore?" Hillary felt free to joke: "How could you get hurt by things that aren't true? They might as well say that I'm six feet tall and I have wonderful, beautiful hair." You could understand Zahn's passion for Hillary better when you read the July 14 New York *Daily News*, which reported that Zahn and other TV news women (NBC's Mary Alice Williams and Faith Daniels, ABC's Lynn Sherr, and NPR's Nina Totenberg) were "not afraid to show their political stripes" when they attended a power lunch thrown by *People* magazine publisher Ann Moore for Ellen Malcolm, head of the fundraising committee Emily's List, which financially supports only pro-abortion Democratic female candidates—like Hillary Clinton.

On NBC, cohost Katie Couric declared, "One reason, Mrs. Clinton, you came under attack by not only Pat Buchanan, but by Rich Bond, chairman of the Republican National Committee, and to a lesser degree by Marilyn Quayle and Barbara Bush, was that they claim that you and your husband have predicted that this will be a copresidency." *Claim?* Republicans had *quoted* the Clintons saying it. Had Couric taken the year off up to that point? But Hillary pretended right along: "There's no basis in that." To which Couric said nothing, nothing at all.

Then Couric asked the kind of question that made Republicans wonder why she just didn't go ahead and wear a "Clinton for President" button on her lapel: "Do you think the American people are not ready for someone who is as accomplished and career-oriented as Hillary Clinton?" Conservative arguments that Mrs. Clinton would be both liberal and powerful in the White House were once again being undercut with amateur psychoanalysis that conservatives fear strong women.

Like Woodruff, Couric used her interview with Barbara Bush to discuss . . . attacks on Hillary. In the interview, held four days before her lovefest with Hillary, Couric lectured Mrs. Bush: "Bill Clinton actually says that discussion about Hillary and talk about where she stands on various issues and analysis of some of her previous writings have been really misinterpreted and taken out of context. And he finds it, quote, something like a 'pathetic and desperate effort.'" Notice how Clinton could call Republicans "pathetic and desperate," and yet it was the Republicans whom the press disdained for "going negative."

Time's Margaret Carlson, Hillary's most aggressive booster in the "objective" press, represented the feminist corps of the liberal media when she explained her feelings in a fall Freedom Forum special report on campaign coverage: "There are many women in the press, and you couldn't have fought the battles you have fought to get where you are and not find what the Republicans said about women offensive. . . . It's not possible, you cannot be that objective. When Marilyn Quayle says that I have given up my essential nature as a woman and that I don't take care of my family because I'm working, I cannot help feeling offended by that."

Carlson did her part for Womanhood. In fact, she deserves an award for serving as Hillary's premier national publicist while masquerading as a "news" writer. Her September 14 cover story—remember, this is a *news* report—began, "You might think Hillary Clinton was running for President. Granted, she is a remarkable woman. The first student commencement speaker at Wellesley, part of the first large wave of women to go to law school, a prominent partner in a major law firm, rated one of the top 100 lawyers in the country—there is no doubt that she is her husband's professional and intellectual equal. But is this reason to turn her into 'Willary Horton' for the '92 campaign, making her an emblem of all that is wrong with family values, working mothers, and modern women in general?"

It was only 1992, her husband hadn't even been elected president yet, and the media were already paving Hillary her own path to the White House. The long campaign had begun.

Chapter 4

Hillary Takes Command, the Media "Make Nice"

Feminaut explores gender cosmos. The most fabulous woman in U.S. history?!?!

—*Newsweek*'s "Conventional Wisdom Watch," February 15, 1993

All of this talk about Hillary Clinton being the smartest woman in the world—I'm looking at this and I don't see any evidence of this. The reason Clinton health care is not the law of the land today is precisely because she ran it.

—RUSH LIMBAUGH, in an interview with the authors

The election of the "Buy Bill, Get Hillary Free" ticket kept liberal reporters in euphoria for weeks. Each day was Valentine's Day. In choosing her "winners of the year" on *The McLaughlin Group*, *Newsweek*'s Eleanor Clift gleefully declared victory for "the women of America." With "Hillary Clinton as a role model in the White House," Clift said, it was "the new age of feminism." Former *Wall Street Journal* reporter and feminist author Susan Faludi proclaimed that Hillary had "violated the cardinal trade-off rule of American womanhood" and cast off unhappiness by combining "equality with ecstasy, liberty with laughter."

As Washington giddily prepared for the liberal co-presidency to take over, *Washington Post* reporter Martha Sherrill told the First Lady's life story in a three-part series in the paper's Style section from January 11 to 13 called "The Education of Hillary Clinton." That section was known as the "For and About Women" section until 1969, and Sherrill wrote as if her work was stuck in those less "liberated" days. There was no room during this three-day extravaganza for pioneering-female-lawyer contro-versy. Sherrill didn't even mention Mrs. Clinton's partisan tenure as chair of the federal Legal Services Corporation, devoted only one paragraph to Mrs. Clinton's career at the Rose Law Firm, and included just two about her legal writings. But she did spend twelve paragraphs explaining the various changes to Hillary's hair. Sherrill also wrote that Mrs. Clinton had "provoked a certain amount of weeping" among "old girlfriends" who thought "the world has so grossly misunderstood their warm, funny, smart, tough, loyal Hillary."

In a *Time* magazine cover story naming Bill Clinton "Man of the Year," Margaret Carlson celebrated Hillary and Bill in her article "The Dynamic Duo." Hillary, she said, "is the disciplined, duty-bound Methodist, carrying her favorite Scriptures around in her briefcase and holding herself and others to a high standard." And then there was the open swipe at Nancy Reagan: "Perhaps a First Lady who consults law books rather than astrologers doesn't look so frightening after all. And perhaps Bill Clinton, rather than seeming weak by comparison with his wife, has proved that it takes a solid, secure man to marry a strong woman."

When we interviewed Carlson at the time, she insisted, against all evidence and logic, that her syrupy reporting of Hillary as a Scripture-toting combination of Oliver Wendell Holmes and Mother Teresa was "down the middle. . . . I don't have a brief for Hillary." Perhaps trying to prove her objectivity regarding the incoming First Lady, Carlson pre-dicted that "the minute she stumbles, people [in the media] are going to leap on that, including me."

But the press was nothing like Carlson's caricature, of course—and it wasn't just the females who set out to create a warm, fuzzy media envi-ronment for their feminist icon. According to a study by the Center for Media and Public Affairs (CMPA), from January 20 to July 20, 1993,

President Clinton received only 34 percent positive coverage from the network evening news shows, while during the same time period the new First Lady scored a startling 79 percent rate of positive coverage. Not even a beatified pope scores that well. Mrs. Clinton was frequently praised for her new activist take on the First Lady job and for the example she was setting for women everywhere. In those first six months Hillary had an incredible eighty-five stories devoted to her—more than any other member of the Clinton administration. To put that in its proper context, CMPA noted that only one TV news source evaluated Barbara Bush during the first six months of her husband's term.

All of this glowing coverage came during a time when Hillary Clinton was heading up a massive health care "reform" drive that called for a government takeover of one-seventh of the economy. Despite having a House and Senate with comfortable Democratic majorities, passing a massive new government program wasn't going to be easy, even for the Clintonista zealots champing at the bit to create their own brand of socialist utopia. There would be obstacles, of course, but the liberal news media would not be one of them.

"The President's Wife Is Trying to Do the Best She Can"

Hillary was presented as health care czar on the morning of January 25, 1993, quick on the heels of her husband's inauguration. Just four days later, Paul Bedard reported in the *Washington Times* that Hillary's new task force was facing a little legal problem. She was not a government employee, and the Federal Advisory Committee Act (FACA) requires every panel that includes nongovernment employees to conduct open meetings. This was rich in irony—Hillary Clinton, the liberal Watergate staff investigator, utterly ignoring a post-Watergate reform—but the entire major media, print and broadcast, couldn't be bothered, even after Congressman Bill Clinger, the ranking Republican on the House Government Operations Committee, demanded that the closed meetings stop.

When on February 24 the Association of American Physicians and Surgeons sued to open the meetings, a few media outlets finally sniffed the story—one piece ran in the *New York Times,* one in the *Washington Post,* and one on ABC by Brit Hume. The coverage was inconsequential, but it was enough to send Hillary's journalistic allies rushing to her defense. "I'm all for secrecy," volunteered *Newsweek* bigfoot Evan Thomas. "For one thing, that's the only way they are going to get it done." Ted Koppel, who was so eager to expose Reagan administration secrecy during the 1980s, suddenly had a change of heart with the Clintons. "Seems a little bit—a little bit petty," he lectured conservative activist Peter Flaherty on *Nightline,* who was agitating to have the health care task force meetings opened. "I mean, clearly the president's wife is trying to do the best she can, and if they need to have some meetings in private, does that really matter?"

In March, Judge Royce Lamberth ruled that the task force did violate the FACA, and that while small working groups could meet in private, the full task force meetings would need to be open to the public. Finally the other networks noticed—but only for a few seconds. On CBS, Dan Rather quickly passed along that "the judge said any hearings the full task force might hold in the future must be open to the public to comply with so-called sunshine laws." How rich. With the Clintons in power, media outlets that usually screamed about the people's right to know and darkly warned about government "Star Chamber" secrecy were now dismissing "so-called sunshine laws."

Weeks later, the *Washington Times* revealed that many task force members Clinton claimed as federal employees actually were funded by the private sector, not the government. When the Clintonites released a list of 511 names, the *Times* noted that the list "did not meet the [General Accounting Office] request for dates of employment, salaries, and detailed backgrounds." The network reaction to the abuse of GAO rules? Absolutely nothing.

How hypocritical can you get? The reporters who yawned through controversy over Hillary Clinton's secretive task force to create a health care bill were the same ones who later screamed hysterically over the secrecy of Dick Cheney's task force to create an energy bill in 2001 and 2002. The same Dan Rather who dismissed "so-called sunshine laws" when they applied to Hillary's health care task force would report almost a decade later that "congressional investigators looking into the Bush energy policy say they are now being denied access to key information—namely, who met with and advised the for-a-while secret energy task force headed up by Vice President Dick Cheney, the president's designated point man on energy policy."

Apparently, Democrats hold "private" meetings to form proposals, while Republicans hold "secret" meetings.

When the GAO decided to sue for access to the Cheney records in 2002, CBS gave the story comprehensive coverage, and then leapt to conduct polls, reporting that 58 percent of the public thought the Bush administration was "hiding something." But in 1993, CBS didn't conduct any surveys asking the public about Hillary's secret task force. Instead, it saved its poll money to plug the popularity of Hillary's still-evolving health plan. On April 5, Linda Douglass reported, "Americans urgently want to solve the health care crisis. It is one of their highest priorities. . . . In fact, according to a CBS News–*New York Times* poll taken last week . . . reforming health care is more important than reducing the deficit. The poll shows most Americans would be willing to pay higher taxes for health care reform and they support some government regulation."

CHEERS FOR THE FEMINIST "MASCOT"

While the task force secrecy fight was a whisper in the background, Hillary Clinton was still having her toenails polished by the press. In a famously fawning May 10, 1993, cover story, *Time*'s Margaret "I Don't Have a Brief for Hillary" Carlson relegated the task force to one paragraph out of forty, and left it utterly out of her interview with the First Lady, saving that space for more important questions, like "Do you get a chance to exercise?" And "You give the president lots of support. Who supports you?" Hillary should have replied, "Well, for one—you."

Why didn't Carlson ask Hillary about the task force secrecy suit? In her conversation with the Media Research Center, Carlson claimed that *Time* "looked at that ruling several times in the magazine in different ways." Now, *Time* staffers may have investigated it, but they certainly never did it "in the magazine"—*Time* never covered the issue. She also suggested that the suit was irrelevant, just another lame attempt at politics: "I think people look around for a way to challenge something and they find a statute that might help them." Carlson further explained that having already put "a lot on the record about health care," *Time* chose to "get in stuff that nobody's seen." This sheds light on why, with people's lives and fortunes at stake, the magazine put Hillary on the record with questions about her aerobics schedule.

Carlson's cover story was a dizzying parade of compliments: "Every witness has his or her horror story about getting sick, and Hillary listens as if hearing such woe for the first time. . . . Ever the best girl in class, there seems to be no fact she hasn't memorized. . . . When she briefed the committee, the clarity of her pitch opened a few eyes. . . . When the President's economic address to Congress was scraps of paper on the conference table in the Roosevelt Room, she stepped in and pasted it back together again. . . . She goes through paperwork like butter, scribbling in the margins of the mail, trying not to touch the same piece twice. . . . She has taken to her role like a student, reading 43 White House biographies and numerous histories."

Carlson's conclusion for *Time*'s cover story is priceless. It ought to be framed, because it demolishes, utterly vaporizes, the notion of an objective press capable of distancing itself from the altar of St. Hillary: "As the icon of American womanhood, she is the medium through which the remaining anxieties over feminism are being played out. She is on a cultural seesaw held to a schizophrenic standard: everything she does that is soft is a calculated cover-up of the careerist inside; everything that isn't is a put-down of women who stay home and bake cookies. . . . Perhaps in addition to the other items on her agenda, Hillary Rodham Clinton will define for women that magical spot where the important work of the world and love and children and an inner life all come together. Like Ginger Rogers, she will do everything her partner does, only backward and in high heels, and with what was missing in [former Bush campaign manager Lee] Atwater—a lot of heart."

Martha Sherrill, the unofficial *Washington Post* Hillary booster, returned that spring with another bucketful of sweets. A loving May 4 article on the inner Hillary's political and spiritual influences carried this typically gauzy passage: "In the midst of redesigning America's health care system and replacing Madonna as our leading cult figure, the new First Lady has already begun working on her next project, far more metaphysical and uplifting." Hillary's mission was nothing less than "redefining who we are as human beings in this postmodern age." Sherrill also wrote, "She has goals, but they appear to be so huge and so far off—grand and noble things twinkling in the distance—that it is hard to see what she sees." Goals like the presidency, perhaps? Sherrill went on, "She is both impersonal and poignant—with much more depth, intellect, and spirituality than we are used to in a politician." Hadn't the Clintonites kept insisting that Hillary *wasn't* a politician? The Hillary Rodham Clinton narrative was changing quickly.

Not surprisingly, Carlson and Sherrill reacted hysterically to Hillary's critics. Wrote Sherrill, "All this children business, *children business*—keeps reminding the far right of communist youth camps, early indoctrination, Marxist brainwashing." (Italics hers.) Sherrill would later tell us, "I think [conservative criticism] comes from a lot of emotion and not very much thinking."

Carlson also caricatured the right for the audacity to think Hillary was a lefty: "In a state where Gloria Steinem was considered by some a communist," she wrote in *Time*'s cover piece, "Hillary started out being regarded as a stuck-up feminist from Wellesley and Yale who wouldn't change her name and ended up being a popular and admired First Lady." When we challenged her to name a conservative who had labeled Steinem a communist, Carlson couldn't do it and acknowledged to us that her statement "was overly glib, and I regret it now."

The two reporters later shared the stage on CNN's *Reliable Sources,* and Sherrill confessed her bias. "I think there's an intensity of interest in her," said Sherrill, "and I think it's very hard for career women, working women"—that is to say, Sherrill & Co.—"to not be rooting for her." A few months later in a *Washington Post* piece, Carlson concurred: "As much as we try to think otherwise, when you're covering someone like yourself, and your position in life is insecure, she's your mascot. Something in you roots for her. You're rooting for your team. I try to get that bias out, but for many of us, it's there."

Instead of presenting a balanced picture of the First Lady, reporters were actively assisting Mrs. Clinton politically. As Clinton biographer

Elizabeth Drew explained, "The essence of these articles was a portrait of a whole woman: a working mother who struggled to keep all her roles intact, a normal, warm person. An anecdote about Mrs. Clinton making scrambled eggs for an ill Chelsea was featured in three of the articles, which served only to suggest how rare this kind of thing must have been. The softening of her image from the sometimes chilly and remote person that much of the public had perceived was obviously, and not too subtly, designed to give her more of the benefit of the doubt when the health care plan was unveiled."

HAILING HILLARY ON THE HILL

While conservatives barnstormed the country trying to stop a massive and dangerous government takeover of the most successful health care industry in the world, the Hillary-boosting media were selling the Clinton plan as a moderate solution to a pending catastrophe. As summer vacation ended, the *Washington Post* promoted the "New Democrats" on the front page with the headline "Post-Vacation Clinton Swims Toward Mainstream," while the nationalization of health care decisions was mysteriously described as a step away from "the old Democratic ideology." *Time* declared that since this socialist scheme didn't ban insurance companies altogether, it was "somewhere near the political center." CNN bizarrely categorized Ira Magaziner and other HillaryCare architects as "free marketeers."

The main attraction of this "centrist" circus was Hillary Clinton, who appeared before six different congressional committees in late September to tout her new plan, all 1,300-plus pages of it. Her testimony drew rave reviews from reporters. First it was on account of her liberal trailblazing. On September 24, ABC named her "Person of the Week," with Peter Jennings referring to her as "Hillary, the problem-solver," and adding that she "has been positively liberated" by her experience. ABC aired five sound bites, all of them coddling, at the end of which Jennings oozed, "This particular individual had come a long way in the last year or so. And then we thought—no, maybe it's the country which has come a long way."

ABC was proclaiming its collective appreciation not just for Hillary's historic role, but for her historically huge plan as well. ABC medical editor Tim Johnson, another journalist who clearly saw no responsibility to strike a tone of impartiality, told *20/20* viewers, "I say the Clintons are almost heroes in my mind for finally facing up to the terrible problems we have with our current health care system and bringing it to the attention of the public."

Then there was the acclamation for Hillary's brain, and how it sizzled so brilliantly that a solar system could revolve around it. "There seemed no detail she did not know, no criticism she had not considered," pronounced CBS reporter Bob Schieffer on September 28. "It was a boffo performance. Republicans were impressed, Democrats just loved it." The next day, CNN's Candy Crowley found "more rave reviews for Hillary Rodham Clinton, who put in yet another virtuoso performance. . . . This is a lady who knows her stuff. . . . Pro and con on the issue, lawmakers seem unanimously gaga."

Republicans were *unanimously gaga* over Hillary's brilliance? We decided to check.

Bob Livingston laughed when we read him that quote. "I was singularly unimpressed," recalled Livingston, who was a powerful member of the House Appropriations Committee at the time. "It was an incomprehensible plan."

Congressman Jack Kingston of Georgia agreed. When we asked if he was gaga, he told us, "Not in the least. It was a socialized medicine game. . . . There was a lot of fanfare, but I don't think [many] Republicans were ever surely with her idea of health care. Even some Democrats didn't [want to] run with it."

Conservative commentators were equally uninspired. Ann Coulter told us, "Did I experience a few seconds of panic over the possibility that Hillary's plan, if enacted, would destroy the world's best health care system? That kind of 'gaga'? Yes, I did. Then I calmed down and realized it could never pass. Which turned out to be correct."

Rush Limbaugh was even more blunt when we asked whether conservatives were "gaga" over Hillary: "On my side of the aisle, there was never, never any kind of trust for either of [the Clintons]." At the time, he remembered, he was saying that he didn't understand how people could be won over by Hillary's health care plan "when we don't get the straight skinny from these people on virtually anything, and if you look at the details of this health care plan, it's an abomination."

But the press was tone-deaf to GOP sentiments. In *Time*, three reporters (none of them Margaret Carlson) penned their own tribute: "Perhaps the most striking thing about Hillary Clinton's performance last week on Capitol Hill was the silent but devastating rebuke she sent to her cartoonists. This was not the Hillary as overbearing wife, the Hillary as left-wing ideologue, or even the Hillary as mushy-headed spiritual adviser to the nation." Mrs. Clinton was advocating the single largest transfer of power from the private sector to the federal government in American history—but was no left-wing ideologue? "This was Hillary the polite but passionate American citizen—strangely mesmerizing because of how she matched the poise and politics of her delivery with the power of her position. No wonder some of Washington's most acid tongues and pens took the week off."

One who was strangely mesmerized was CBS anchorman Dan Rather. The night the president unveiled his health care plan, Rather anchored a prime-time *48 Hours* special, with an interview of Hillary Clinton as the main attraction. He tossed the First Lady one slow pitch softball after another. "When you walked in, it was pretty clear you were excited, but also a little nervous. Am I right about that?" And "Are you having fun with this or is it all just hard work? It looks to be very hard work."

During his flattering face-to-face interview with the First Lady, Rather showed no interest in asking tough questions about those irksome little details the Clintons didn't want to discuss. For example: Where the hell were they going to get the *$784 billion*, which is what the (Democrat-controlled) Congressional Budget Office was projecting this monster program would cost over the first seven years?

Rather asked question after question straight out of the Clinton White House Talking Points playbook—and didn't laugh when Hillary gave her preposterous answers: "Let me run down a checklist. . . . [J]ust give me a yes or no answer. Will every resident of the United States be covered under this? [Yes!] Will this entail any major increase in taxes? [No!] Will this help reduce the deficit, perhaps by as much as $91 billion? [Yes!]"

Rather just couldn't stop drooling. "I don't know of anybody, friend or foe, who isn't impressed by your grasp of the details of this plan," he told

Mrs. Clinton. "I'm not surprised because you have been working on it so long and listened to so many people. Is it possible, and I'm asking for your candid opinion, that when this gets through, whether it passes or not, that we will have reached a point when a First Lady, any First Lady, can be judged on the quality of her work?"

Dan Rather had reduced himself and CBS, the glittering "Tiffany Network" of liberal media lore, to something akin to a high school cable-access project. "The interview will be remembered as perhaps the second-most-shameful episode in a career full of such episodes," Ann Coulter said in our interview.

Just one week later, Rather spoke to news executives at the Radio-Television News Directors Association convention in Miami and had the gall to lambaste *them* for soft-pedaling the news: "They've got us putting more and more fuzz and wuzz on the air. . . . [Reporters are driven to] do powder puff, not probing interviews. Stay away from controversial subjects. Kiss ass, move with the mass, and for heaven's and ratings' sake don't make anybody mad—certainly not anybody you're covering, and especially not the mayor, the governor, the senator, the president, or the vice president or anybody in a position of power. Make nice, not news."

Maybe Rather was referring to Larry King. When it comes to "make nice, not news," let's face it: King is king. After he interviewed Mrs. Clinton on October 2, the schmaltzy CNN host salivated over her in his *USA Today* column: "She was funny, charming, sexy—yes, gang, sexy. We are both Scorpios, which tells you a lot." (We don't know about you, but it tells us absolutely nothing.) King also hurled insults toward anyone who dared challenge her leftist agenda: "Meanwhile, she's earned the respect of everyone (except the wackos) with her handling of the health care issue. Indeed, she has gotten everyone (except the wackos) to agree that we need health care for everyone. This is a very formidable idea, ladies and gentlemen."

HILLARY LOSES, MEDIA MOURN

With all the formidable national media in her favor, how was it that Hillary Clinton actually lost the battle? In the spring of 1993 it was virtually

impossible to find a political pundit who thought Hillary would not succeed with her national health care agenda. Behind the scenes some conservative lawmakers were frantically looking for ways to stave off what
they saw as an unstoppable juggernaut. But Hillary, no doubt mesmerized by her own press clippings, registered one of the greatest political
blunders in years when conservatives counterattacked.

Leading the conservative response were people like John Goodman,
whose Dallas-based think tank the National Center for Policy Analysis
outlined the disastrous consequences awaiting the country if socialized
medicine became law; Senator Phil Gramm of Texas, who stood alone in
the Senate and proclaimed that this monstrosity would pass "over my
dead body"; and Bill Kristol, former chief of staff to Vice President Dan
Quayle, who delivered almost daily faxes giving conservatives the strate-
gic ammunition to combat this federal power grab.

No one did more than Rush Limbaugh, who took to his microphone
daily to rally millions of Americans to oppose HillaryCare. "These two
[Bill and Hillary] had just won the election," he recalled in an interview,
and the mood among defeatist Republicans was "'Don't appear to be
mean. Join the chorus of support, the path of least resistance.' But I was
never cowed by any of this."

Rush rallied his listeners to take to the streets. In the summer of
1994, the Clintons planned a big bus trip in support of the health care
plan, beginning in Portland and Seattle and traveling cross-country to
Washington, D.C. Limbaugh looked at the itinerary and began alerting
people in every upcoming city, and "we thoroughly disrupted it. Everywhere they went they were greeted with more protesters and heckling
signs, so that they had to schedule meetings at night and redo their itinerary. It was fun, and we did it in a fun way." Other groups, like Citizens
for a Sound Economy, also brought balance to every bus stop.

In Seattle, when Hillary's protesters could not be silenced, she carped
into the microphone, "You know, there's an old saying . . . if you don't
have the facts on your side, yell! And there's a lot of yelling going on
in America. And the yelling is starting to drown out the majority of
Americans." In Hillary's mind, she had evidence, while the other side
had only the ideology of the rabid minority. She marshaled the majority,
and her foes were corporate pawns.

Throughout, the elite media were still sounding Hillary's alarm and sharing Hillary's assumptions, that the socialist majority was being thwarted and democracy overturned by the lobbyist hordes. None of Hillary's defeat could be blamed on the media being fair and balanced on her health plan.

By the summer conservatives had traction, and by fall the efforts of Limbaugh, Goodman, Kristol, and many others had marshaled public opinion to oppose this nonsense and had stiffened Republican legislative spines. Still, "Hillary Clinton thought she could go up to Congress and ramrod this thing through with the force of her personality," Limbaugh said. "She was horrible at managing the process." Finally in September, the Clinton team—once seemingly assured of passing their health care plan through a Democratic Congress—tabled the initiative altogether. It had become unmistakably apparent they could not muster the votes to win.

"The reason she failed was because of hubris," Goodman told us. "There were moderate Republicans in the Senate who were ready to go with her. . . . She could have gotten the basic things had she been just a tiny bit willing to give over some of the credit and to work with them. I think she wanted this to be her health care plan . . . that they couldn't make any changes, they couldn't compromise anywhere, and that's why it failed."

Republican congressman Dan Burton echoed Goodman's point when we interviewed him: "Had it been that well thought out, they would have done their homework and worked with the legislative branch before the thing came up, and it would have been sure to pass."

The consequences of Hillary's political blunder were enormous. "The result is that they wound up getting a totally unworkable plan that had no basis in support," GOP strategist Frank Donatelli told us. "HillaryCare was such a disaster the Democrats wound up losing control of Congress."

Limbaugh agreed about the costs of Hillary's screwup for Democrats, and offered a sobering reminder to those who today are touting her as the ablest presidential candidate in the field: "What has she done? She botched the health care [plan], which led to the Republicans leading the House for the first time in forty years."

Chapter 5
Style Defeats Scandalous Substance

What happened was a riveting hour and 12 minutes in which the First Lady appeared to be open, candid, and above all unflappable. While she provided little new information on the tangled Arkansas land deal or her controversial commodity trades, the real message was her attitude and her poise.

—*Time* reporter MICHAEL DUFFY on the "Pink Lady"
press conference, May 2, 1994

The Clintons managed to diminish the charges against them to the lowest level of personal self-aggrandizement by those leveling the charges. "They're doing it for jobs, they're doing it for money, they're doing it for their career." They managed to divert attention from the Clintons to that guy—always to the motive of the messenger. They're forever slaying the messenger. The label of personal assault is so petty, it's a new low in American journalistic discourse. There may have been something like this during the Grant administration, but I don't think the level of discourse has been any more infantile than what the Clintons introduced.

—R. EMMETT TYRRELL JR., in an interview with the authors

S o the person now touted in many quarters as the most qualified presidential candidate is the same person who was responsible for one of the greatest political failures in recent memory—a disaster that occurred despite the fact that she was surrounded by helpers. Her party controlled both houses of Congress and had a powerful lobbying group at the ready in the media.

If the true story of the health care fiasco was the only thing that tarnished the record of Hillary Rodham Clinton, it might be enough to disqualify her as a serious presidential candidate. But there's more—much more.

Further problems appeared soon after the Clintons were forced to abandon their health care scheme. Halloween descended scarily on the First Lady in 1993, as the ghouls and goblins of Whitewater resurfaced. The front page of the *Washington Post* carried a story by reporter Susan Schmidt announcing, "The Resolution Trust Corp. has asked federal prosecutors in Little Rock to open a criminal investigation into whether a failed Arkansas savings and loan used depositors' funds during the mid-'80s to benefit local politicians, including a reelection campaign of then-governor Bill Clinton." The words *criminal investigation* proclaimed that this wasn't just a game of political tiddlywinks. Someone could end up in an orange jumpsuit.

Now, let's stop and think about this for a minute. Let's travel back in time to Watergate, and that criminal investigation. The issue was political corruption: Richard Nixon's cronies burglarized his opponents' headquarters in order to gain who-knows-what political advantage in the upcoming presidential campaign, and when caught, tried to cover up Oval Office involvement through lies and deceit. Then there was Iran-Contra, the next big criminal investigation involving a sitting president. The allegation here was public policy corruption, a series of activities that, no matter how noble the ends, were not justifiable means: circumventing the legislative process. In neither case was the president seen as the primary architect of the alleged crime, and yet the press saw it (correctly) as its responsibility to investigate each issue to its fullest. Each of these Republican scandals became a national sensation.

With Whitewater, the issue was rank *personal* corruption, and the primary players in the corruption were the president and the First Lady. But when the *Washington Post*—the same paper that led the investigative pack in both Watergate and Iran-Contra, spurring story after story throughout the rest of the media—dropped its front-page "criminal investigation" bombshell about the Clintons (who were Democrats, of course), almost nothing happened. Only the *Washington Post* and the *Washington Times* stayed on the story. Network coverage was virtually nonexistent, except for one NBC piece on November 11. The news magazines dismissed the story with one page or less each. In *Time*'s only Whitewater story of that year (in the November 15, 1993, issue), James Carney demonstrated the pattern to come, a series of almost desperate attempts to amputate any connection between the McDougals and the Clintons. Carney wrote, "Federal officials insist that the Clintons are not targets of the investigation and that the only link is their coincidental association with McDougal." *Coincidental?* Try imagining this sentence in the early days of Watergate: "Federal officials insist that President Nixon is not a target of the investigation and that the only link is his coincidental association with E. Howard Hunt."

It would take another holiday week to really set the story in motion again. On Monday, December 20, *Washington Times* reporter Jerry Seper wrote that after White House lawyer and close Hillary associate Vince Foster was found dead in Fort Marcy Park, Clinton aides raided his office and removed sensitive documents about the Clinton finances. "The searches included a clandestine visit July 20 to Mr. Foster's office— less than three hours after his body was found about 6 P.M. in a Virginia park—by two Clinton political operatives," Park Police investigators told Seper. How could supposedly skeptical reporters now continue to dismiss the idea that the Clintons were hiding something important?

That wasn't the only bad news in Hillaryland. The night before Seper's story broke, wire services and CNN began reporting that *The American Spectator* had a new exposé out. Four Arkansas state troopers (two of them named for the record) alleged that Governor Clinton had used state police to secure sexual conquests, and that Clinton had dangled the prospects of federal jobs to keep these troopers quiet. On Tuesday, December 21, the *Los Angeles Times* followed with a 4,300-word exposé of its own, complete with phone records of Bill's prowling middle-of-the-night calls to paramours.

But the troopers' story attracted only twenty-two evening news stories in its first twelve days, nine of them on CNN—about the same amount of coverage that Clinton's first widespread "bimbo eruption," the Gennifer Flowers story, drew (only fourteen stories in a six-day period). Ollie North would have been thrilled to get so little attention. What does it say about the media that they downplayed the trooper story so much? Ann Coulter summed it up in our interview: "Most of them are terrific people just trying to do their jobs—i.e., helping the Democratic Party."

The Clintons couldn't ignore the story entirely, though, so Hillary once again played the Tammy Wynette stand-by-your-man role for her scoundrel husband. She used previously scheduled year-end interviews with the Associated Press and Reuters as her platform. George Stephanopoulos loved this approach, which he described in his memoir as "Hillary defending her husband surrounded by mistletoe and holly."

Sure enough, the media took the bait when Hillary savaged conservatives. The *Los Angeles Times*, the media outlet primarily responsible for breaking the Troopergate scandal in the first place, now wrote, "Hillary Rodham Clinton assailed new allegations of her husband's marital infidelity as outrageous Tuesday and charged that they were motivated by hope of financial and political gain by enemies of the President." Hillary didn't use the term *vast right-wing conspiracy*, but she might as well have: "I find it not an accident that every time he is on the verge of fulfilling his commitment to the American people and they respond . . . out comes yet a new round of these outrageous, terrible stories that people plant for political and financial reasons." It took until the sixth paragraph for the *Times* to note, in passing, the meat of the matter: "Mrs. Clinton did not specifically deny the assertions in the story but merely denounced the accounts as terrible."

Look at the transcript of the AP interview and you'll see how easy it was for Hillary to pull off this political gambit. Perhaps fearing that Hillary would storm out of the room at the mention of the word *trooper,* the AP interviewer asked fifteen questions (including gooey questions about Chelsea) before the abuse-of-power angle finally emerged. And even then it was severely downplayed. The interviewer never even pressed Mrs. Clinton to confirm or deny (or even address!) the veracity of the charge. As was now standard operating procedure for the press, they approached this Clinton scandal as an opportunity to question the motives of the Clintons' adversaries, not the Clintons:

- "We've heard the rumors. . . . This time it is two state troopers who are on the record making the allegations. . . . What do you make of all this?" Note the language: These weren't facts. These weren't even allegations. They were *rumors* "we've heard." That question invited Hillary to dismiss the story as a sad attack during the Christmas season, and twice she mentioned "political and financial" motives, for emphasis.

- "Do you think the cops are making money?" Hillary: "It seems to be the story."

- "Do you stand by your husband?" Hillary: "Absolutely . . . the same people are behind it."

- "Is it [Little Rock attorney Cliff] Jackson?" This is where Hillary uncorked the "not an accident" conspiracy talk.

- "So it's no accident?" Hillary: "No. To me, it isn't."

And that satisfied the AP reporter. He moved on to Hillary's support for taxing guns to pay for her health program.

Hillary's handlers must have been thrilled when the media transformed the First Lady's slippery nondenials into full-blown denials she had never made. On CBS the next morning, anchor Giselle Fernandez announced, "First Lady Hillary Rodham Clinton has come out swinging, calling allegations of infidelity leveled at the president garbage." CBS was referring to the Reuters interview, but a review of *that* transcript demonstrates that once again Hillary was not specifically denying Bill's sexual escapades. "I think my husband has proven that he's a man who really cares about this country deeply . . . and, when it's all said and done, that's how most fair-minded Americans will judge my husband, and all the rest of this stuff will end up in the garbage can where it deserves to be." In other words, she had said nothing to deny the specific allegations.

National reporters and editors made no effort to nail the First Lady down on the factual particulars. What they wanted to know was: Who are these haters, and why won't they go away with these ancient stories? And Hillary was happy to oblige them with answers.

The major media completely ignored another bombshell in the Troopergate report, which *American Spectator* editor R. Emmett Tyrrell Jr. feels was "the most newsworthy information in the story": the troopers also claimed knowledge of an affair between Hillary and Vince Foster, the recently deceased White House lawyer. The media made no mention of the alleged affair.

Too Little, Much Too Late

Although the Clintons' allies in the press let Bill and Hillary dodge the most damning parts of the Troopergate story, they couldn't keep the lid on Whitewater forever. In fact, Troopergate may have reinvigorated the old story. Take the example of taxpayer-funded PBS and NPR. According to the Nexis news data-retrieval system, the word *Whitewater* did not appear in an NPR news feature until December 21, 1993—a full 663 days after the *New York Times* broke the Whitewater story, on March 8, 1992. The same is true of *The MacNeil/Lehrer NewsHour;* the word *Whitewater* first surfaced there on December 24, 1993, 666 days after the fact.

As George Stephanopoulos remembered it in his memoir, "The repressed energy stirred up by the trooper story was sublimated straight into the 'Whitewater cover-up.'" Conservatives on Capitol Hill, in the public policy community, and in the world of talk radio would not let up, and the Foster-papers hunt led to growing calls for an independent counsel to investigate Whitewater, something Hillary fervently opposed. As 1994 began, pundits began pressing, and momentum started building. When Stephanopoulos tried to make the case for agreeing to an outside probe, Hillary attacked him for his infidelity, he reported in his book. "You *never* believed in us," he recounted her saying during a White

House meeting. "In New Hampshire . . . you gave up on us. . . . If you don't believe in us, you should *just leave*." (Italics his.) He remembered that it made him cry.

But when Whitewater stories kept coming on a presidential trip to Europe in January, the White House relented. Clinton's attorney general, Janet Reno, named a special prosecutor, Robert Fiske. The media acknowledged, for a short time, that a serious scandal had arrived. On February 10, ABC's *World News Tonight* devoted eighteen of its twenty-two minutes to exploring Whitewater. The Clintonites had to hope the press would move this story to the back burner. They would get even more than they wished for.

Too Much Boiling in the "Lunatic Cauldron"?

After mostly ignoring the Whitewater scandal for nearly two years, the press now began fiercely condemning itself for *over*covering the story. Whitewater coverage was denigrated as a "lunatic cauldron" (*Newsweek*'s Joe Klein), "definitely overheated" (Walter Cronkite), "too much, off-target" (Bryant Gumbel), "unprofessional and distasteful" (Marvin Kalb), driven by "Cotton Mather–ish obsessions with character and morality" (former CBS producer Jon Katz), with the media becoming "a too-powerful amplifier . . . blaring too loud" (*Los Angeles Times* reporter Tom Rosenstiel).

But were the media really consumed with the Whitewater scandal, as so many journalists like to suggest even to this day? How big a story was this, even at its height? A quantitative analysis by the Center for Media and Public Affairs (CMPA) gives some telling facts: the Big Three networks gave both Watergate and Iran-Contra more than *three times* the attention they gave Whitewater. Moreover, as the political turmoil increased, so too did the positive spin control. CMPA found that the percentage of pro-Clinton talking heads actually went up in Whitewater stories. The White House may have preferred no stories, but they were given the next best thing: ample opportunity to air their spin.

Another obvious sign of the networks' comparatively low level of interest in the Whitewater story was the lack of specials on the controversy.

When the Iran-Contra story broke on November 25, 1986, the networks dove in. ABC dedicated its entire *World News Tonight* that night to Iran-Contra and actually expanded its *Nightline* broadcast to sixty minutes. CBS aired a half-hour special. NBC did an hour-long special. On December 18, ABC's *20/20* devoted yet another hour to the story. NBC aired two one-hour specials, on December 15 and January 6. After the Tower Commission's report on February 26, 1987, CBS broadcast a special called "Judgment on the White House."

Whitewater generated one special, on ABC, which aired on *Nightline* on April 19, 1994, an astounding 792 days after the story first broke. While the special was commendable for offering some time to Clinton opponents such as Rush Limbaugh and *Wall Street Journal* editorial page editor Robert Bartley, reviewing the Clintons' behavior in the scandal wasn't really ABC's theme. It apparently was the media's behavior that needed evaluation. The title said it all: "Whitewater: Overplayed or Underplayed?"

In addition to the number of stories, there was also the question of the language used in stories. After Walter Mondale introduced the term *sleaze factor* in the 1984 campaign to savage the Reagan administration in particular and Republicans in general, the media picked up the phrase and used it with abandon thereafter. Fact: Throughout the years 1984–1994, that term appeared no fewer than 114 times in newspapers and news magazines.

Ten years later, how many times did these same journalists use that phrase to describe the Clinton administration, a perpetual motion machine of scandals that could safely be described as "sleaze"? Not once. The phrase was retired.

In mid-March, the White House sought news magazine interviews with the First Lady to spray the fire extinguisher on the flaming scandals. The obvious spin was to admit some error, primarily an unwillingness to be more forthcoming with the liberal media. The *Time* interview was headlined with a quote: "Yes, We Made Lots of Mistakes." *Newsweek* topped its article with "Hillary: 'I Made Mistakes.'"

But both interviews were soft. *Time*'s interview carried the subheadline "Clearing the Air with Hillary Rodham Clinton," but mostly, Hillary was allowed to blow more smoke. When *Time* reporters Ann Blackman and Nina Burleigh tried asking about Whitewater specifics, they drew nothing. When asked if the Clintons invested only $13,000 into Whitewater, Hillary accused her partner Jim McDougal of having a faulty memory. The reporters asked, "How do you respond to questions of conflict of interest raised by your representation of Madison?" Hillary claimed that there was only one tiny "limited representation" on a stock matter and everything else amounted to "lots of illegitimate claims floating around." Note the rope-a-dope evasions here. If the $13,000 figure was inaccurate, what was her actual investment? She never said. Even if her Madison involvement was only a "limited representation," was she suggesting this was unimportant because it was only a limited crime? Normally, seasoned reporters wouldn't let a public figure get away with this, but this was Hillary, and her statements were allowed to go unchallenged.

And like so many others, *Time*'s duo couldn't resist dipping into the syrup bottle: "How do you and your husband explain this to each other?" And then this follow-up: "And Chelsea?" Hillary said stuffily of Chelsea, "She doesn't need an explanation. She is fully aware of what happens in politics. With it comes a lot of the worst that human nature has to offer. We've been telling her that since she was six." Blackman and Burleigh ended with the perfunctory touchy-feely, we-too-feel-your-pain question that has probably never once been posed to Tom DeLay: "What effect does this have on you?" Hillary swung, and hit it out of the park. "People can lie about you on a regular basis, and you have to take it. That's very hurtful."

There was another element to these interviews that separated them from standard journalism fare. Both news magazines had to negotiate into the interviews by accepting conditions. G. Allen Randolph wrote in the *Forbes Media Critic* that Blackman told him she understood they were not to ask questions directly related to Whitewater. It was a condition *Time* broke, to be sure, but the magazine never mentioned these conditions to readers. And for good reason, since the conditions made a mockery of their Hillary-Comes-Clean headline. By contrast, and to its credit, *Newsweek* did disclose that Hillary "agreed to an interview as long as it did not touch on specific issues before a grand jury"—perhaps because *Newsweek*'s adoring Eleanor Clift did a much better job of observing White House stipulations. She didn't so much ask questions as make supportive assertions.

• "The only thing I see comparable [to Watergate] is that a lot of people want to launch careers based on finding something."

• "Sometimes, these investigations take on a life of their own. [Whitewater special prosecutor Robert] Fiske has taken out a lease for three years in Little Rock."

• "You present a rational face to the world. How angry are you, about how the way this has mushroomed from a little land scandal . . . into an allegation that you and your husband are corrupt?" Hillary interrupted in mid-question: "It's not even a scandal. It's not a scandal. A failed land transaction." (Ann Coulter laughed when she read this transcript. "Right," she told us, "that's why more than a dozen people went to prison over it!" But then Coulter put herself in Hillary Clinton's shoes and rethought the issue. For Hillary "it *was* barely a contretemps. To be fair to Hillary, if you were married to Bill Clinton, your scandal bar would have to be set pretty high.")

• "So if there is nothing wrong, why were you so resistant to making records public? My theory is you have a thing about privacy." Hillary replied, "I have a big thing about it," and claimed that Whitewater was something that wasn't "in any way connected with the fact that my husband is in public life."

• "The attacks against you are really about more than Whitewater. They really go to the whole role you're taking on and whether you can be spouse of a president and a policymaker."

• "Edward Bennett Williams used to say that Washington likes to burn a witch every three months." Hillary agreed: "I think that's right." (Coulter laughed again. "There's your double standard, right there! Every time I've called Hillary Clinton a witch I got yelled at.")

Clift told Randolph that her goal was just to gain "some insight into how Mrs. Clinton felt," and employed the ignorance defense on the softball session: "My knowledge of Whitewater goes down a couple of layers, but not that far." Randolph concluded that *U.S. News & World Report* should have been happy it was snubbed over refusing conditions, since "[i]nsofar as Whitewater is concerned, no interview at all would have been better than the interviews *Time* and *Newsweek* offered their readers." In an April 4 *Washington Post* story on Clift's Clinton-apologist reputation, an anonymous *Newsweek* staffer said, "I think she takes it too far. . . . A lot of people find it embarrassing."

One of those embarrassed is Ann Coulter. "Before I read this exchange I didn't think it was possible for me to think any less of Eleanor Clift. Turns out I was wrong."

GOING SOFT AT THE CATTLE CALL

On March 18, 1994, exactly 500 days after the election, another scandal burst—this one centered directly on Hillary. Jeff Gerth's latest *New York Times* scoop was headlined "Top Arkansas Lawyer Helped Hillary Clinton Turn Big Profit" and introduced America to Cattlegate. Starting just three weeks before Bill Clinton was elected governor of Arkansas, "Hillary Rodham Clinton made about $100,000 in one year in the commodities market with the help and advice of a friend who was the top lawyer for one of the state's most powerful and heavily regulated companies." That friend was James Blair, a lawyer for Tyson Foods—who had worked hard behind the scenes to influence Jim McDougal and others in Arkansas to shut down the Whitewater drip-drip to Gerth during the 1992 primaries.

At first, the White House would not release how much money Hillary initially invested, and when it was revealed to be only $1,000, the White House's reluctance was understandable. How did she achieve such an astounding capital gain in a matter of months? Mrs. Clinton first claimed that she just read the financial pages. Later it was discovered that her trades were arranged through Blair, so she changed her story. He selected the trades, and she approved them, she said.

This information was forthcoming only because the Clintons finally had agreed to surrender their federal tax returns from 1978 and 1979, years Bill Clinton was the governor of Arkansas. Imagine if reporters had been more diligent in covering the Whitewater story in the spring of 1992. Had they pushed to discover the real story then, they would have found that these tax returns didn't match the Clintons' publicly stated financial claims about Whitewater—the couple in fact contributed less to Whitewater than advertised. In the process the press also would have uncovered the cattle futures story, which was there all along. It is not idle speculation to suggest that these two stories, coming on the heels of the recently uncovered evidence of Clinton's wretched womanizing, might well have exhausted Democratic primary voters' patience with Team Little Rock and spared the country this eight-year presidency. The very real possibility that serious and timely coverage of the Clintons' scandals would have dealt a fatal blow to the Clinton campaign under-scores the extraordinary role this post-Watergate, post–Iran-Contra press corps played in the 1992 presidential election.

Even when the story finally broke in 1994, major media outlets did little to explore it, despite the screaming red flares of Hillary's shifting stories over the financial windfall. *Newsweek* writer Jonathan Alter sneered, "It was fun to learn about Yuppie Hillary, but the story belonged in the business pages, or perhaps the food section, where the *Times* usu-ally runs its diagrams of cows." None of the Big Three evening newscasts devoted a full story to the mysterious trades until eleven days after the original *Times* scoop. Ultimately, the four networks reported only eigh-teen evening news stories between them on Mrs. Clinton's curious trad-ing. Twelve of the eighteen stories aired on the three days the White House released documents or met the press: March 29, April 11, and April 22—the day Mrs. Clinton decided to hold her famous "Pretty in Pink" press conference to try to put the scandal out. Cattlegate, in other words, merited coverage only when the lead was Hillary's defense of her honor.

Hillary wore a pink blouse and black skirt to the press conference, sat before a fireplace, and calmly maintained that there was "no evi-dence" she'd done anything wrong. During the one-hour-and-twelve-minute-long event she shed no light on the strange affair, saying only that she had left all the troublesome details to friendly men, whether it was Jim Blair on the cattle trades, or Jim McDougal on the Whitewater finances.

Reporters were positively floored by her performance. Immediately after the press conference, NBC's Tom Brokaw pronounced, "She was cool, articulate, and for the most part very responsive to all questions." He asked reporter Lisa Myers if there were any major errors. "No, not a one," Myers declared. He asked Andrea Mitchell for a quick assessment. After Mitchell noted the obvious—Hillary didn't fully answer the questions—she gazed into her crystal ball: "I think you saw the talent of Hillary Rodham Clinton as a politician."

ABC's Peter Jennings repeated Mrs. Clinton's diversionary charge that attacks on her showed that "the country is having some difficulty adjusting to a working woman in the role of First Lady." And then he said something truly laughable: "I think most people will regard this as certainly an enormous effort by Mrs. Clinton to set the record as straight as she can." Later he asked reporter Jim Wooten, "Has she set aside the passion that the Washington press corps particularly has for the details of their life in Arkansas?" Whatever "passion" Jennings was referring to, it certainly hadn't come from him. It had taken him eleven days to arrive on the story, and after Hillary put the pink outfit back in the closet, that's where his interest went as well. But consider this: When *Roll Call*, a small-circulation Capitol Hill newspaper, revealed two months later that Senator Al D'Amato, a Republican, made $35,000 on stock in an initial public offering closed to most investors, ABC reported the story the very next day.

Newspaper reports were tougher on the substance. The *Washington Post* ran an article inside the paper titled "First Lady's Explanations Yield Little Information," and *New York Times* writer Maureen Dowd, who called it "an exceptionally polished and calibrated performance," conceded later in her story that Hillary "never fully resolved the central questions of Whitewater and the commodities trades." Conservative columnist Tony Snow wrote, "She evoked the amnesia defense more often than Ronald Reagan did in the days of Iran-Contra." She said "I don't remember" at least six times. The obvious question emerged: Why would the same media that celebrated Hillary's ironclad memory in testifying (without notes) on health care reform give her a free pass on her slack-jawed amnesia on scandal facts?

On *Washington Week in Review* that night on PBS, *New York Times* legal reporter Linda Greenhouse exemplified journalistic wishful thinking: "About halfway into the hour, somebody asked a non-Whitewater question. Somebody asked a question about health care. And one of my colleagues said, 'That's it. She's exhausted them. Whitewater's over.' And I'd really like to know what you think—is this basically the end of Whitewater?" It sounded like a group of kids in the back of the car asking, "Are we there yet? Are we there yet?"

A new *Newsweek* poll found that 57 percent of the public thought the press was "wallowing" in Whitewater. (Don't bother asking whether liberal media bosses are in the habit of ordering polls to explore media excess when Republicans are in the White House.) Writing in the magazine, Eleanor Clift and Mark Miller said that "the public, if not the press, seems willing to give the vacationing Clintons a break." That supposedly relentless press soon did give Bill and Hillary a break: a month after the Pink Lady press conference, when the White House released documents indicating that the First Lady had received preferential treatment by not being required to post margin (pay cash when her shares' value dropped), the networks were nowhere to be found to report the special handling that she had denied during her star turn.

Such picayune details, apparently, said nothing about government corruption. The Hillary Clinton Booster Club was still wowed by the First Lady. Clift and Miller captured the press's starry-eyed gaze when they concluded their article with this piece of jaw-dropping spin on Hillary's financial scandals: "The public might even be tickled to discover that the prim and preachy First Lady has a gambler's streak. Hillary's brief fling in commodities was possibly reckless, but it shows a glimmering of a more credible, if more flawed, human being."

Not everything Hillary touches turns to gold, certainly, but the media do their best to make it seem that way.

Chapter 6
Big Ugly Men with Subpoenas

One of Chelsea's and my favorite nursery rhymes summed up the absolute unpredictability and frequent unfairness of life:

> *"As I was standing in the street*
> *As quiet as could be*
> *A great big ugly man came up*
> *And tied his horse to me."*

I thought often of that rhyme during our first year in the White House: My father died, our dear friend Vince Foster killed himself, my mother-in-law lost her battle against breast cancer, and my husband and I were attacked daily from all directions by people trying to score political points.

—HILLARY CLINTON in her book *It Takes a Village*

Having been one of Hillary's primary antagonists from '92 to '97 . . . saying sharp but true things about the First Lady on a very regular basis, I am quite familiar with the media coverage on her, and I can't remember a serious question or follow-up question to her from the mainstream media. Of course, she takes no questions from anybody else.

—TONY BLANKLEY, in an interview with the authors

illary Clinton poses a particular challenge for her media boosters: how
to sustain the portrayal of her as a brilliant, sincere, compassionate,
Scripture-toting Methodist when she has been continually mired in
personal, political, and financial scandals.

Case in point: At a time when the media were reluctantly and belat-
edly turning an eye to the sordid business of Whitewater, another
Hillary-created scandal drove the press to develop new and creative
defenses for the First Lady—that is, when they could no longer ignore
the story altogether.

Fortunately for Hillary Clinton, the media have proven up to the
challenge of defending her at almost any cost.

HILLARY'S PUTSCH

Billy Dale's nightmare began on May 19, 1993. Dale had booked flights
for the White House press corps since John F. Kennedy was president,
but that day he and six other White House Travel Office employees were
fired without warning and accused of financial mismanagement, including taking kickbacks. They were told to empty their desks and get out
within two hours, and were spirited off the White House grounds in a
windowless van.

It was unusual and heavy-handed enough that the media, so many of
whom knew Dale personally and had worked with his office professionally, put pressure on the White House to justify the firings. Within a
week, five of the seven exiled employees were given new employment in
the federal government, since even if there was financial mismanagement, none of them had the authority to write checks. That left Billy
Dale as the big remaining target. Then, in July, the White House
released a report based on its own internal investigation. The report
stated that an internal audit of the White House Travel Office, conducted by the Peat Marwick auditing firm, had found evidence of
embezzlement: Dale had failed to record five petty cash checks totaling
$14,000. The Justice Department later charged that he had stolen

$68,000 in money the news media paid to cover costs of traveling with the president, and that he had used it to pay for a house on Lake Anna, Virginia, among numerous other personal items.

Those were the accusations, anyway. Ultimately, on November 16, 1995, a jury took only two hours to exonerate Billy Dale completely. But for the two and a half years between his firing and his exoneration, Dale endured a painful ordeal. He lived under a cloud of embezzlement accusations; the FBI examined every check he, his wife, and their three adult children had ever written; the IRS dissected his finances; his sister, Mildred Wing of Houston, reported receiving a call from the FBI asking if she knew Mr. Dale and why he had given her a check in 1988, and she surmised that the agent thought she was a girlfriend; the FBI grilled Dale's daughter for five hours, reportedly calling her father a thief and asking her, "How can you trust a man who's stealing money?" Explaining the viciousness of the federal persecution, Dale told the *Washington Post*, "I feel like the victims of Ruby Ridge and Waco. The only difference is they didn't use guns on us."

As Rush Limbaugh observed when we interviewed him, this persecution was typical of the Clintons: "They don't just try to defeat, they try to destroy. They don't want just to discredit, they try to ruin people and get them out of the way."

As it turned out, Hillary's fingerprints were all over this particular scandal, though the full extent of her involvement would not become clear until years after the firings.

Why were Billy Dale and the other Travel Office employees unceremoniously dismissed? The first piece of the puzzle emerged with the release of the report from the internal White House investigation. As the *Washington Times* reported, "An internal White House investigation later showed that Hollywood producer Harry Thomason [a longtime Clinton friend], the President's distant cousin Catherine Cornelius, and several other aides improperly schemed to take over the office for personal gain." Thomason wanted a piece of the travel-booking profits. Cornelius wanted Dale's job.

Mrs. Clinton denied any role in the firings when the General Accounting Office investigated. Her lawyers told the GAO, in writing, "Mrs. Clinton does not know the origin of the decision to remove the

White House travel office employees. . . . She had no role in the decision to terminate the employees. . . . Mrs. Clinton did not direct that any action be taken by anyone with regard to the travel office, other than expressing an interest in receiving information about the review."

That was in 1994. Fast-forward to October 24, 1995, three weeks before the Dale verdict. On that day the Republican-led House Government Reform and Oversight Committee released a report that included a May 14, 1993, memorandum from then–White House aide David Watkins. In the memo, Watkins said that the First Lady had told him to replace career Travel Office employees with a private firm partially owned by a friend. Watkins quoted Hillary as saying, "We need those people out—we need our people in. We need the slots."

This was explosive stuff. It not only tied the First Lady to a textbook exercise in the "politics of personal destruction," as her husband might say, but it contradicted statements made by White House officials—and Hillary's lawyers—that Hillary was not a central figure in the firings.

Billy Dale was fired on May 19, 1993, but as early as May 12, Hillary was making it clear she wanted him out. Though she cited concerns over his financial mismanagement, Peat Marwick wasn't even called in until the next day, May 13, as Dale explained in a subsequent *Washington Post* op-ed. He wrote, "I am forced to wonder, what is the 'financial mismanagement' that she was 'concerned with' before Peat Marwick ever began its work?"

The idea that Hillary was a moving force in this issue should not have been surprising. Hillary was busy with a lot of vengeful firings in the early years of the Clinton administration. She fired the chief White House usher, Christopher Emery, after he helped Barbara Bush over the phone with a computer problem. She was also a force in dismissing the entire cast of ninety-three U.S. attorneys, a little-noticed move to get "our people" installed in every state, especially in Arkansas.

But the Clinton White House had attempted to cover up the First Lady's involvement. As Barbara Olson noted in her book *Hell to Pay,* "White House lawyer Jack Quinn even tried to rewrite the factual record, deleting words in the titles of memos, changing 'HRC's Travel Office Chronology' to 'Chronological Analysis of Travel Office Events.' 'HRC's Role' became 'Draft chart analysis and comparison of various

Travel Office investigations.'" Olson quoted House Government Reform Committee chairman William Clinger as saying that there was "a scent of obstruction of justice" about the White House staff's efforts to remove the First Lady's initials from memos.

The title of Olson's book came from another memo by David Watkins. This one, written to Chief of Staff Mack McLarty but never sent, surfaced in January 1996. In it Watkins made clear who plotted the Travel Office firings: "The message you conveyed to me was clear: immediate action must be taken. . . . We both knew there would be hell to pay if, after our failing in the Secret Service situation earlier, we failed to take swift and decisive action in conformity with the First Lady's wishes." (The month before, a leak to *Newsweek* that Hillary had a fight with Bill and threw a lamp at him spurred the Clintons to ask Harry Thomason to look into the bizarre idea of replacing the Secret Service with private security.)

The independent counsel who reviewed the whole Travelgate mess, Robert Ray, would offer this stark conclusion in his final report, issued several years late in 2000: "With respect to Mrs. Clinton, the overwhelming evidence establishes that she played a role in the decision to fire the employees and provided input into that decision. . . . Thus, her statement to the contrary under oath to this Office was factually false."

Why didn't any reporter unearth anything about Hillary's direct involvement in the Travelgate scandal on his or her own? Why did the public have to wait more than two years to learn this critically important aspect of the story? Maybe this will help answer that question: Even after the congressional committee released its report in October 1995, the networks refused to breathe a word about it. They simply didn't report it. Likewise, when Billy Dale was acquitted soon thereafter, the exoneration failed to generate even a mention that night on the news broadcasts of ABC, CBS, NBC, or CNN, although all four networks had, to one degree or another, covered his public humiliation.

Predictably, the media gave Hillary Clinton the chance to spin unchallenged. While promoting her new book in a round of TV interviews in January 1996, Hillary denied the Watkins claim to her role in the firings, and true to form, she turned on associates while admitting little and twisting the truth. "I think what is fair to say is that I did voice concern about the financial mismanagement that was discovered when the president arrived here," she told Barbara Walters. The implication was clear: by replacing Dale, Hillary had nobly and efficiently corrected a problem. But this was not true. As reported by the Associated Press, a GAO audit showed that whatever the situation in 1993, it only worsened after Dale and his colleagues were removed: "The current travel office rarely follows its own policy of paying vendors, such as airlines and telephone companies, within 45 days of the invoice date. . . . Office employees never balanced checkbooks from January through August 1995." The audit also found that the office's accounts receivable had soared to $5.6 million under the new management, while the employees who were fired had only $366,000. The new employees also forgot to enter more than $200,000 in deposits into the office's checking accounts.

Once again, our supposedly vigilant national media went AWOL. The GAO audit drew little national media attention. The *New York Times,* the *Los Angeles Times,* and *USA Today* all failed to report the embarrassing revelations. With the exception of the *NewsHour* on PBS, no network evening news show ran a story, not ABC, CBS, NBC, or CNN. Neither did *Time* or *Newsweek.* They had clear evidence of political and financial corruption that led directly to the First Lady's desk, and they refused to inform the public of it.

Hillary and the "Offensive" Hearings

The driving force behind the unmasking of the Clintons' vast corruption was not the major media; rather, it was conservatives. Were it not for the 1994 Republican Revolution in Congress, there is much we may never have learned. Travelgate, as well as Whitewater, gained steam only when Republican committee chairmen gained the power to subpoena and pressed the Clintons for documents.

In the summer of 1994, the Democrat-controlled House did convene hearings into Whitewater, but these were far too narrowly focused, uncovering very little and resolving even less. The press diligently covered these uneventful hearings.

But when Newt Gingrich and the Republicans took control of Congress in 1995, they organized hearings to investigate the scandal fully. These more comprehensive hearings promised fireworks, so one might expect them to have been of significant interest to a nonpartisan press. This wasn't the case, however. Over two weeks in 1994, the four network evening news shows (on ABC, CBS, CNN, and NBC) devoted forty full stories to the Democratic-run hearings. But in *four* weeks in 1995, the same shows offered only twenty-four reporter-based stories on the Republican hearings. Perhaps the network news bosses agreed with *Newsweek*'s Eleanor Clift, who declared on CNN, "It's not to anyone's advantage to have sleaze on television, and that's exactly what those hearings are."

In a nutshell, coverage was sporadic and often dismissive. For example, on July 17, 1995, CBS's Dan Rather ignored the substance of the hearings while reducing them to political machinations against the sympathetic Clintons. "From another offensive wave on Whitewater to a sweeping rollback of federal regulations on health, safety, and the environment, it's a political carpet-bombing attack, wall to wall, House to Senate," Rather "reported."

While hearings for Watergate and Iran-Contra were presented as grand, serious moments of statesmanship, this time around *Newsweek* portrayed the Republican-run hearings as a damaging distraction. In the August 21 issue, the magazine ran a Whitewater story hopefully headlined "An End in Sight (Maybe)." It began, "The Whitewater scandal occupied key committees in both the House and Senate last week—a two-ring circus whose single goal seemed to be causing maximum embarrassment to Bill and Hillary Clinton and their friends." When reporters extract maximum embarrassment during Republican administrations (see DeLay, Tom; Gingrich, Newt; Bush, George W.; Reagan, Ronald), they are only doing their job. But when the targets are Democrats, it is singularly distasteful.

Had the media bothered to report on the specifics, their millions of viewers, listeners, and readers would have learned of the significant and troubling details investigators were homing in on. For example, Rather, *Newsweek,* and the rest brushed off the congressional hearings even as investigators were highlighting mysterious doings in deputy White House counsel Vince Foster's office in the hours immediately after Foster was found dead in a park outside Washington. Foster and Hillary were former law partners and close friends.

• On July 19, Congress focused on Patsy Thomasson, an Arkansas crony of the Clintons who did not have a security clearance, yet who sat at Foster's desk hours after his death while the FBI and Park Police were denied access to his office. Important? ABC and NBC carried no story. CBS did a story on bungling the night of Foster's death, but failed to note this news. To give you a sense of broadcasting priorities, CNN dedicated two and a half minutes to a photo exhibit of movie kissing scenes, but just eighteen seconds to Whitewater.

• On August 2, former Clinton deputy attorney general Philip Heymann charged that White House counsel Bernard Nussbaum had reneged on a promise to allow a joint review of documents in Foster's office before they were moved to the White House residence. CNN ignored the story, finding time for a piece on the health benefits of tofu. After two weeks without a reporter-based piece, that day NBC aired Jim Miklaszewski's In Depth report on the history and political impact of Whitewater, but relayed nothing about Heymann's testimony.

• On August 10, a second Justice Department lawyer, David Margolis, backed Heymann's claim. Were the Clintons hiding something? CNN and NBC aired no story. CNN felt it more newsworthy to report that Joe Namath had donated the pantyhose he wore in a TV ad to the Planet Hollywood restaurant chain. NBC squeezed in video of a tie-dyed flag flown in honor of the late Jerry Garcia. CBS ignored Margolis and dismissed the findings.

The same pattern repeated itself in the fall. On November 2, senators questioned the First Lady's top aide Maggie Williams and friend Susan Thomases about a raft of early morning phone calls placed two days after Foster died. Phone records showed that Williams called the First Lady in Arkansas on July 22, and that then a call was made from that Arkansas number to Thomases, who proceeded to call Bernard Nussbaum. This was the very day Nussbaum reneged on the agreement to allow Justice Department officials to examine Foster's files. So did Hillary spur the Nussbaum stonewall? And if so, why? The scandal was creeping toward the area of obstruction of justice.

But again the networks were mostly absent. CNN's *World News* ran a brief anchor-read item, but no full story. Nothing appeared on the ABC or NBC evening newscasts. *CBS Evening News* aired a full story, but once more reduced the issue to petty squabbling between political parties. Rather chimed in with the usual lingo, that Republicans "relaunched, again, their Whitewater offensive and took aim at First Lady Hillary Rodham Clinton." Reporter Bob Schieffer, meanwhile, called the hearing "testy" and concluded that it was just "another painful episode" for the White House.

Why did the hearings get "testy"? Because, as Schieffer noted, the two Hillary aides "said repeatedly they could not remember details of what happened." Schieffer also reported that things got "nastier" when Susan Thomases claimed that she "couldn't even recall a White House visit listed in security logs," but he gave no indication of the substance of the senators' response. Most notably, Republican senator Lauch Faircloth issued a devastating rejoinder—that he couldn't believe anyone would "forget" a six-hour visit to the White House.

There was a story in this, had the media bothered to examine it. Thomases had every reason to be a very forgetful witness, as liberal writer Elizabeth Drew revealed in her 1995 Clinton White House chronicle *On the Edge*. Drew quoted a friend of both Mrs. Clinton and Thomases: "Susan gets into everything, protecting Hillary Clinton. She's her campaign manager for President of the United States, and I'm not kidding. Susan believes that somewhere down the road Hillary will be the first woman candidate for President of the United States. She's positioning her. Not that anybody thinks it's a bad idea. It's just a little early."

SURPRISE! WE'VE BEEN HIDING DOCUMENTS

As the election year of 1996 began, Hillary's mysterious Whitewater stonewalling ascended to the top of the news again. On January 5, the White House announced that it had suddenly found and was turning over long-sought Rose Law Firm billing records related to Whitewater. The White House had initially said that they never existed, since Mrs. Clinton did not do the work, and then they acknowledged that they did exist, but were missing. The White House claimed that the records, totaling 116 pages, were found by Carolyn Huber, a special assistant to the president and a former secretary of Mrs. Clinton's at Rose. Somehow these records had been hiding themselves in the Clintons' living quarters, just off of Hillary Clinton's personal office. The discovery came as Hillary was tuning up for the release of her first book, *It Takes a Village.* The round of interviews the networks conducted with the First Lady may have been tougher than the embarrassing fawnings of the past, but left by themselves, they mostly blunted the story's impact rather than heightened it.

Hillary's first stop was ABC's *20/20* with Barbara Walters. Despite her reputation for soapy celebrity interviews, Walters atypically homed in on several fine points of fact. She asked whether David Watkins was lying when he said she had wanted the Travel Office workers fired. Hillary said no in a vague way, then added that while she had expressed concerns, "I did not direct anyone to make the decisions." In one answer she had both denied that Watkins was a liar and again accused him of lying.

To her credit, Walters also asked specifically about "one of the fraudulent loans of Madison Guaranty," a real estate sham called Castle Grande. This project was created by Jim McDougal and Seth Ward, who was the father-in-law of Hillary's law partner Webster Hubbell. As a CBSNews.com report later summarized the case, "Mrs. Clinton's billing records disclosed that she prepared a real estate document valuing a parcel of Castle Grande property at $400,000. The federal government got just $38,000 for it six years later following the S&L's collapse. Federal regulators concluded the S&L used the document prepared by Mrs. Clinton to deceive bank examiners about hundreds of thousands of dollars in commissions paid to Ward."

Despite all this, Mrs. Clinton insisted to Walters, bizarrely and against the black-and-white evidence of the billing records, that she never did legal work for the fraudulent Castle Grande real estate project. Walters didn't press the subject; she moved on to Hillary's relationship with Vince Foster.

As would be revealed when special prosecutor Robert Ray's final Whitewater report came out in September of 2000, Mrs. Clinton told federal regulators in 1996 that she couldn't recall doing work for the S&L. In fact, she said this *ninety-nine times* in the course of one two-and-a-half hour interview with the federal regulators, according to CBSNews.com. There was perhaps a logical explanation for her faulty memory: it's possible that the billing records were inaccurate, that they inflated the amount of hours Hillary billed to her business partner McDougal. But if that was the real story, that wouldn't help her politically, either. Hillary would have to count on a media that often skipped the fine points of fact and preferred a heavily political message of "never mind."

The story of the billing records was one of the unfolding events that caused *New York Times* columnist William Safire to write, famously, "Americans of all political persuasions are coming to the sad realization that our First Lady—a woman of undoubted talents who was a role model for many in her generation—is a congenital liar. Drip by drip, like Whitewater torture, the case is being made that she is compelled to mislead, and to ensnare her subordinates and friends in a web of deceit." Safire added that there was no accountability for her lying: "Therefore, ask not 'Why didn't she just come clean at the beginning?' She had good reasons to lie; she is in the longtime habit of lying; and she has never been called to account for lying herself, or in suborning lying in her aides and friends."

Walters pressed about the blizzard of phone calls between Hillary and her aides on the Foster papers. Hillary claimed that no Foster documents came out of his office the night he died, and "I didn't even know he had documents of mine in his office, so that doesn't make any sense at all." But one Secret Service agent told investigators that they saw Hillary's aide Maggie Williams walking out with her arms stuffed with folders. Another saw aide Craig Livingstone walking out of the White House with a box. Walters should have brought up those charges but didn't, turning instead to the soft book-promoting half of the interview. She concluded the program by bringing Hillary around to "a nursery rhyme in your book. Do you know the one I'm talking about?" Mrs. Clinton said yes, and recited the "great big ugly man with a horse" rhyme at the top of this chapter. Apparently, Republican senator Al D'Amato or the new Whitewater independent counsel, Kenneth Starr, was the big ugly man with a horse.

Two days later on *This Week with David Brinkley*, Walters publicly proclaimed her support for Hillary Clinton. "I think it's been a pretty good week for Mrs. Clinton. I think that a lot of people even listening to the program so much today keep saying, 'What's the crime? What did she do so wrong?' . . . I think there is beginning to be the feeling of she's being harassed too much."

When NPR aired its interview, Scott Simon asked Hillary whether she could put herself in her Watergate-investigator frame of mind. "If the Nixon White House had come to your committee and said, 'Those records you've been asking for, for two years, we found 'em suddenly, we found 'em. And here they are,' would you have accepted that explanation with a straight face?" It was a good question, but Hillary's slippery answer was even better. "I think we would have been delighted," she said. "The problem back then, you'll remember, is that documents were destroyed, tapes were missing—eighteen and a half minutes. The White House was not cooperating. They were claiming executive privilege on every piece of paper. I think the contrast is so dramatic! [Exclamation point in NPR's own transcript.] We want the truth to get out."

On CBS *This Morning*, host Harry Smith was the only interviewer to bring up Billy Dale, but his setup statement on Travelgate was timid at best: "There were very few complaints involved in this. People had the FBI sicced on them. Billy Dale. And it cost him $500,000 to defend himself." Stop the tape. Rewind. *People* had the FBI sicced on them? *Who*, exactly, sicced the FBI on those people? Was it Mrs. Clinton herself, as evidence now indicated? Why did Smith employ the passive voice here and not ask Hillary about that directly? And why didn't he point out, as an essential part of this story, that Dale was an innocent man, found not guilty in two hours, a judicial blink of an eye?

Mrs. Clinton grew impatient, even with Smith's timid introduction. "Now, Harry," she lectured, "there's no doubt there was financial mismanagement. There is no doubt there were financial irregularities . . . there was petty cash left lying around. . . . Now that may not seem like anything to people who spend lots of money, but coming from Arkansas, that sounded serious." The same Mrs. Clinton who found nothing wrong in doing legal work for a failed bank that cost taxpayers $73 million would now have us believe she was so very concerned over the possible mismanagement of a few thousand dollars in the Travel Office? A serious journalist would have to struggle mightily to prevent the eruption of laughter. Harry Smith did nothing.

But the sweetest, most fawning interview came on NBC's *Today* show with substitute cohost Maria Shriver, the Kennedy-family transplant who rarely failed to disappoint conservatives who expected the worst. Before the interview Shriver proclaimed that Hillary's book was "terrific," then telegraphed her support as soon as she sat down with the First Lady: "I know this is an extremely exciting time for you with the publication of your first book, which is really the culmination of about twenty-five years of work on behalf of kids. But it's also been a difficult time with all of the stories swirling around you, from Whitewater to the Travel Office to missing billing records. What's this last week and a half been like for you personally?"

Just for chuckles, let's imagine a similar interview with a conservative. Let's take Ollie North, post–Iran-Contra hearings. "I know this is an extremely exciting time for you given that an entire country has fallen in love with you and your work on behalf of freedom in Central America. But it's also been a difficult time with all the stories swirling around you, from arms-for-hostages to obstruction of Congress to missing financial records. What's this last week and a half been like for you personally?"

But Maria was just warming up. There was much more fawning to go:

- "In the book, you write about preparing your daughter, Chelsea, for the negative things people might say to her about her father, but you don't say in the book about preparing her for the negative things people might say to her about her mom. What's this past week, two weeks been like for her?" Hillary recounted how they told their daughter that people would say mean things about Mommy and Daddy, and "she understands that a lot of this goes with the territory."

- "But this is beyond the territory, I mean, this is tough. This is your mom that's someone's talking about. Is she upset by this?"

Hillary said that Chelsea had the same attitude her parents did. "There is nothing there. There never has been."

• "I think at the root of all of these stories, and I think a lot of them are complicated and people don't understand the ins and outs of all of them, but at the root of it is your credibility, which I know is something that's very important to you. In these polls that we're seeing, more than half the people are saying they don't believe you've told them the whole truth about Whitewater, the Travel Office. What do you, Hillary Clinton, need to do to regain that credibility?" Mrs. Clinton complained, "Of course it's hurtful to have people question your credibility. That never happened to me before my husband ran for president."

• "Whitewater. I know you've been answering questions on this subject for four years. Thousands of documents have been handed over, but they still want even more. As you look back on this, do you wish you'd never worked for Madison Guaranty?" Hillary laughed and said, "I guess I do. . . . I didn't do anything wrong. Everyone who looked at it says there wasn't anything wrong."

• Then came the real God-I-admire-you question: "You also quote a letter in [the book] that Nelson Mandela wrote to one of his daughters while he was in prison . . . that there is no personal misfortune that one cannot turn into a personal triumph if one has the iron will and the necessary skills. You clearly have an iron will, you clearly are skilled. How are you going to turn this personal misfortune into a personal triumph?" Even Hillary was taken aback by that one.

Weeks later on CNBC's *Tim Russert* show, the host asked Shriver how long she had prepared for that interview. "A couple of weeks, about two or three weeks, and I read everything. I memorized that book up and down. I memorized everything that was written about Whitewater, about Travelgate, about Hillary Clinton, about First Ladies. . . . You want to admire her, and yet you're a journalist and you have to ask her these tough questions, you have to be skeptical, and you can't just come on and do this like 'Oh, you're so wonderful' interview."

By her own standards, she flunked.

A New Low

Hillary Clinton's contempt for evidence searches was already evident by the mid-1990s. In *On the Edge,* Elizabeth Drew noted that Hillary "was angry that a report on the travel office affair was being prepared at all and considered it too tough on various people's actions. One White House aide said 'She felt it went way too far.' Members of her staff, who were presumed to be reflecting her opinion, expressed the view strongly that the travel office incident should be dismissed out of hand. Mrs. Clinton argued that there was no reason to apologize for the dismissal of the travel office people." Drew also wrote that Hillary "jumped down" the throat of George Stephanopoulos on the need for a Whitewater counsel. Simply put, the First Lady was opposed to full disclosure—even half disclosure—of politically damaging evidence. And why not? None of these ratings-sensitive (and bookings-sensitive) network interviewers were willing to do what a grand jury or a (serious) Senate investigating committee does: ask tough questions, followed by more tough questions until the truth is revealed.

But Hillary's round of interviews in January 1996 could not contain the suspicions of independent counsel Kenneth Starr and his staff. On January 22, the grand jury subpoenaed Hillary to come to the courthouse and testify on the missing documents. It was a new historic low for First Ladies, but also an opportunity for Hillary's supporters in the press to spin it back against the GOP. As Dan Rather put it, "The Republican Whitewater offensive is taking an unprecedented turn: First Lady Hillary Rodham Clinton has been subpoenaed and now must testify before a Whitewater federal grand jury. That grand jury is led by a Republican prosecutor, Kenneth Starr."

It's almost a surprise that Rather didn't recite Hillary's poem about the big ugly man on the horse.

Chapter 7

Convictions, Conventions, and Conversations with the Dead

"Panel Blasts Hillary for Cover-Up" —WASHINGTON TIMES
"Whitewater Panel Splits on Party Lines" —WASHINGTON POST
"Whitewater Hearing Cleared the Clintons, Democrats Say" —NEW
YORK TIMES

> —Headlines from June 19, 1996, the day after the final
> Senate Whitewater Committee report

*Hillary Clinton's Rose Law Firm billing records were found in the
private residence of the White House. They had her fingerprints on
them and Vince Foster's fingerprints on them. Everyone knows that
she put them there. Everyone knows she left them there, and they
were found by one of their staffers. To the extent she testified before
the grand jury denying any knowledge about them, I feel confident
she committed perjury. We don't have access to any of that testimony.
It went on for hours. But how else would they have gotten where
they were found?*

> —MARK LEVIN on Hillary Clinton's 1996 testimony,
> in an interview with the authors

ate on a sunny afternoon in Little Rock on May 28, 1996, the verdicts
came in at the courthouse from a jury of nine women and three men:
guilty, guilty, guilty, on a pile of felony counts of fraud and conspiracy. Bill and Hillary Clinton's longtime Whitewater Development partners were now felons: Jim McDougal guilty on eighteen of nineteen
counts and Susan McDougal guilty on all four of her counts. They were
criminally negligent in their handling of federal funds—found guilty by
a jury of their peers, not by some Republican conspiracy.

After the verdict was handed down, Democrats entered the spin
room. Senator Christopher Dodd revealed the party line when he weakly
claimed on *Nightline* that "this has nothing to do with Clinton." Amazingly, reporters did not sputter and giggle at such ludicrous spin. In fact,
they helped advance it.

Any conservative can easily ask and answer the following question: If
Ronald Reagan had business partners convicted of multiple felonies,
could the liberal media be convinced that this had *nothing* to do with Reagan? The record shows that idea to be preposterous. Every scandal in his
administration, every allegation of scandal, no matter how bizarre, went
straight to the top. That's how Walter Mondale started the "sleaze factor"
talk. It's why Michael Dukakis said "The fish rots from the head down."

In the case of Whitewater, the McDougal verdicts showed that the
Clintons definitely had something to do with it. Consider: The jury
found, among other things, that Friend of Bill and former Arkansas
municipal judge David Hale had helped secure a $300,000 Small Busi-
ness Administration loan to Susan McDougal's Master Marketing firm,
and that $50,000 of that money improperly found its way into Whitewa-
ter Development, which was co-owned by the Clintons. If nothing else,
Bill and Hillary had benefited from a business defined as a criminal
enterprise.

But even when the guilty verdicts were delivered, the media's reaction
was astonishingly blasé.

Even Ted Koppel couldn't play the bad news straight. His first read
on *Nightline* was to signal the public to wait before making sense of it all:
"Plain, unvarnished truth is likely to be in short supply in Washington

for the next day or so." Wrong. For one day, truth was truth: the jury had defined the crimes.

On NBC, anchor Tom Brokaw said to Washington bureau chief Tim Russert, "Tim, Alfonse D'Amato, the Republican senator who's been running the Whitewater hearings on Capitol Hill, has so much as admitted recently that he didn't get very far. There has been any number of exhaustive journalistic efforts. What do we think may be out there? Anything left?"

Exhaustive journalistic efforts? The Big Three networks had aired only thirteen full Whitewater stories on their evening news shows during the course of the Arkansas trial—an average of only four stories per network over almost three months. Brokaw's *NBC Nightly News* didn't find a reporter to cover the story for two months. Meanwhile, the three network morning shows—despite their growing addiction to celebrity murder trials like O. J. Simpson's, and the trial of the Los Angeles police officers who brutalized Rodney King—aired only fourteen full stories and five interviews in eleven weeks on the Whitewater trial. And the news magazines devoted fewer pages of original reporting to the Whitewater trial and Senate probe than they did to Jackie Onassis auctioning off old Camelot rummage. The notion of "exhaustive journalistic efforts" was pure poppycock.

As for what was "left" to piece together in Whitewater, even if we set aside crimes, there was the matter of the blazing political offense of hypocrisy. Journalists like Brokaw were well aware that Bill Clinton, with Hillary smiling behind him, had made this promise when he announced his candidacy in 1991: "When the rip-off artists looted our S&Ls, the president was silent. In a Clinton administration, when people sell their companies and their workers and their country down the river, they'll get called on the carpet." It turned out Bill and Hillary Clinton were very familiar with "rip-off artists." They called two of them their business partners. That was a bit of a loose end.

Another loose end was the role of Hillary Clinton. The media, though, were shy about reporting damaging developments about Hillary. On March 24, 1996, an ABC News/*Washington Post* poll found that 52 percent of respondents believed the First Lady was not telling the truth about Whitewater and 49 percent said they thought she had acted illegally. The *Post* buried the poll on page A16; ABC never reported its own poll at all. (Had an ABC News/*Washington Post* survey found that half of all Americans thought First Lady Nancy Reagan was a liar and a criminal, is there even a scintilla of doubt that it would have led the ABC broadcast and been the subject of front-page headlines in the *Post*?) Similarly, when word leaked on April 29 that the FBI had found Hillary Clinton's fingerprints on the long-missing Rose Law Firm documents discovered in the White House, it drew only four anchor briefs.

U.S. News & World Report editor-in-chief Mortimer Zuckerman—who penned an editorial titled "The Silly Hillary Pillory"—spoke for the media when he said on Cal Thomas's CNBC show during the Arkansas trial, "The fact that there is a trial going on, I think is not going to be relevant to what the elections are going to be all about. You can't run an election based on attacking the president's wife."

Lost in the furious spinning were some elementary facts that sat plainly in a chronology from James Stewart's Whitewater book *Blood Sport* that was excerpted in *Time* (one of the only substantive treatments of the case to run in the news magazines, and it wasn't written by one of *Time*'s own reporters). Who was responsible for miring the Clinton presidency in Whitewater? See these entries:

- "1985: Hillary angrily rebuffs the McDougals' effort to have the Clintons sign over their interest in Whitewater."

- "1986: Hillary again refuses to transfer the Clintons' interest in Whitewater to the McDougals."

- "1990: Clinton tells McDougal's lawyer he wants out of Whitewater, but Hillary again balks."

- "1992: Hillary again refuses to relinquish the Clintons' interest in Whitewater."

The string of obstinate refusals didn't end until the 1992 campaign ended. Then, after the election, Stewart noted, "McDougal and Vince Foster, representing the Clintons, sign papers selling Bill and Hillary's interest in Whitewater to McDougal for $1,000."

The McDougal convictions changed nothing about the media's need to defend Hillary. They turned from dismissing the jury verdict to dismissing the Senate report on Whitewater. On the June 5, 1996, *Good Morning America,* ABC's Elizabeth Vargas interviewed Michael Chertoff, Republican counsel to the Senate Whitewater probe. She inquired, "It would seem very natural that Hillary Clinton's fingerprints would be on her own billing records. Is this at all significant?" Throughout the interview Vargas sounded like a White House flack: "But, Mr. Chertoff, Mrs. Clinton freely admits she examined those documents back in 1992. How do you know these prints aren't several years old?"

Substitute host Erin Moriarty on CBS's *This Morning* spent three straight days, June 18–20, using the Clinton White House spin to challenge guests. She challenged Representative Susan Molinari (R-N.Y.): "But let's be honest here. I mean, this is an election year. How much of this, as the White House of course says, is just a matter of the Republicans piling on in a presidential election year?" She challenged David Maraniss of the *Washington Post:* "We're talking about transactions that occurred a decade ago. I mean, can't some of this just be simply forgetfulness?" She then turned to Democratic activist Lynn Cutler and simply declared, "You're proud of being a friend of Hillary Clinton. What is your response?"

When the Senate issued its Whitewater probe results on June 18, 1996, CBS's Dan Rather was still at it with his it's-all-about-the-vicious-Republicans theme: "The more-than-year-long investigation ended almost the way it began: A Republican offensive targeted First Lady Hillary Clinton. Democrats claim that it's an all-out election-year political smear attack."

If only the Republicans understood the meaning of the word *attack.* Far from what Rather was telling his viewers, the dead-on-arrival GOP campaign of Bob Dole was determined *not* to pursue the growing buffet table of Clinton scandals but instead to talk only vaguely about "character." After the McDougal verdicts, Dole campaign manager Scott Reed leaked a memo proclaiming their "what scandal?" strategy: "We believe the Whitewater investigation should be allowed to continue without presidential politics playing a role. No members of our campaign staff or official campaign representatives will take part in interviews on today's guilty verdicts."

Dole pollster Tony Fabrizio, who was involved in numerous debates with the campaign over this issue, explained how the Dole team arrived at a position that was roundly condemned by conservatives: "To the extent that this race was about character, it was over," he told us in an interview. "With the voters who were concerned about character, Bob Dole was kicking [Clinton's] ass. The problem was that there was a sizable chunk of America that didn't care about [Whitewater]. . . . It sounded like sour grapes because they had already moved past it." Fabrizio conducted focus group meetings with the same results. "We asked people, 'If you had to describe Bill Clinton as an animal, which animal would you choose?'" The answers were telling: "Ferret, snake, weasel: These are animals that are known to be sneaky," but in the final analysis, these voters had "made their decision and they were willing to accept Bill Clinton with his flaws. Until we could prove that someone actually broke the law, they weren't going to change their positions."

Dole senior adviser Don Devine was also involved in the internal deliberations, and fought to have the campaign focus on Clinton's abuse of power, not Whitewater, "which was too complicated. It was too hard to get people focused" on the details. It wasn't "that they didn't fight enough. I would say they didn't fight it the right way."

But that internal wrangling came at a cost. The ultimate above-the-fray pose only gave the media another excuse to ignore Whitewater as a defining issue determining whether the Clintons deserved another four years to hide things in the White House.

SLOW OUT OF THE GATE ON FILEGATE

In June 1996, one scandal erupted out of another. House investigators looking into the treatment of abused Travel Office boss Billy Dale discovered that the White House had ordered his FBI file, presumably looking for more damaging information to justify sacking him. From there, it only grew worse. The White House admitted on June 7 to collecting FBI reports on no fewer than 338 GOP officials, including former secretary of state James Baker, Bush press secretary Marlin Fitzwater, and even Nixon-era CIA director William Colby. It was a shocking admission, Watergate all over again, but this time orchestrated by the Democrats. News? Not to the networks. ABC, CBS, and CNN failed to mention the revelation that night. NBC's Tom Brokaw, Mr. Exhaustive Journalistic Effort, did a brief item.

ABC aired its first story the next day after Bob Dole raised the Watergate comparison. NBC and CBS used this development to run hit pieces on . . . Dole. "The politics of Campaign '96 are getting very ugly, very early," NBC's Brian Williams warned. "Today, Bob Dole accused the White House of using the FBI to wage war against its political enemies, and if that sounds like another political scandal, that's the point." A Democratic White House raiding confidential FBI reports was something that "sounds" like a scandal; a Republican condemning that action was "very ugly." And on CBS, Bob Schieffer said, "Republican presidential candidate Bob Dole took his hardest swipe yet at President Clinton today." Reporter Sharyl Attkisson echoed him: "Dole used a Marietta, Georgia, campaign rally to launch his most scathing attack yet against President Clinton. . . . Dole is not going to let an issue this dicey die easily." Once again, the center of scrutiny of a Clinton scandal was a Clinton accuser.

The yawns were noticeable. Three days later, only ABC reported that FBI procedures were violated, and the next day, June 12, ABC and NBC didn't even bother to report that President Clinton apologized. On June 13 the networks were again silent, though the Senate announced that hearings would be held and the FBI began an overhaul of procedures. On June 14 FBI Director Louis Freeh charged the White House with "egregious violations of privacy," and the number of purloined files increased to 408. All four networks did reports on this story, and even liberal media icons like NPR's Daniel Schorr caught disturbing whiffs of the Nixon era, but there was no feeding frenzy. By the next day, only CBS was still mentioning the subject.

Liberal journalists dutifully reported it all as an innocent blunder. "The reasons usually were incompetence rather than venality," said NPR reporter Mara Liasson. "I really believe this was a case of general incompetence," echoed *Los Angeles Times* reporter Sam Fulwood a week later. In *U.S. News & World Report,* columnist Gloria Borger put to paper the media's read: "This White House inspires a presumption of incompetence." Oh, so the Clintons were just incompetent? Oh, well then, let's reelect them!

One journalist had the guts to denounce the media's partisanship on Filegate. "There's no question that the press initially blew this story," *Washington Post* media reporter Howard Kurtz declared on the June 16 *Fox News Sunday*. Why? There was a "feeling that . . . a political snooping operation was not the kind of thing they expected from the Clinton White House, whereas if hundreds of files had been obtained by Ed Meese in the Reagan administration on Democrats, I think this story would have rocketed to the front page." But that failed to prod his colleagues. No network noted that day's *Washington Post* report that, in contradiction to White House claims, the Secret Service had not asked the FBI to produce the list.

With the so-called mainstream media shirking its investigative responsibilities, it fell again to Congress and the alternative media to probe the emerging Filegate scandal. The more they investigated, the more the shadowy figure of Craig Livingstone emerged. Livingstone was an advance man for the 1992 Clinton campaign who became head of personnel security for the White House. Joseph Duggan, a speechwriter for President George H.W. Bush who was one of the Republicans whose FBI files had been purloined, told us that Livingstone's background— he used to be a bar bouncer—raised concerns about whether he "should be on the White House staff anyway."

At the White House, Livingstone worked under William Kennedy, one of Hillary Clinton's Rose Law Firm partners. Livingstone accompanied Kennedy to identify the body of Vince Foster. Livingstone was also sighted walking out of the White House with documents at the time Hillary's aides were searching Foster's office. What was he doing? Who was he taking orders from? Was Hillary, a tough political fighter, behind Livingstone's file snooping? Who hired him, anyway?

The White House declared that Craig Livingstone had been brought to the White House by the deceased Vince Foster, and on June 22, *Newsweek*'s Eleanor Clift tried to warn people against those suspicious of this claim: "Hate radio and innuendo is going to put Mrs. Clinton at the center of this, and for a party like the Republican Party that has this huge gender gap, targeting the First Lady on every one of these issues is not going to be effective politics." But days later, former FBI agent Gary Aldrich said William Kennedy had told him that Livingstone got his job, despite security concerns like previous use of illegal drugs, because "Hillary wanted him." Years later, it would surface that the White House had also requested the FBI file of Aldrich (and for good measure, Lewinsky whistle-blower Linda Tripp). But once the FBI-files matter was put into the growing basket of scandals under the purview of Special Prosecutor Ken Starr, the media lost interest in further investigation, presenting us with a rather delicious irony: the man to whom the media would defer to carry forward the investigation would subsequently be vilified for carrying forward the investigation. To this day it is a barely reported fact that Craig Livingstone told both Aldrich and Tripp that it was Hillary, not Foster, who picked him.

HILLARY, PERSECUTED LIKE JESUS, CONVERSES WITH ELEANOR ROOSEVELT

Having passed the Filegate scandal on to Ken Starr, the press turned to Bob Woodward's embarrassing portrait in his book *The Choice,* which came out in the last week of June 1996. Woodward told of the First Lady sitting in the White House solarium for an hour-long session in April 1995 with Jean Houston, a flaky New Age medium and author who claimed to talk to the Greek goddess Athena daily. Houston told the First Lady to close her eyes and talk to Eleanor Roosevelt, and then imaginatively proclaim what words Eleanor would say back to her. Then she encouraged Hillary to talk to Mahatma Gandhi. Mrs. Clinton told him how she, like he, suffered for peace. Then Houston encouraged Hillary to talk to Jesus Christ, but Hillary protested that this was "too personal." (What a lost opportunity. She could have compared herself to Jesus on the persecution scale.)

Why would Hillary bond with this kooky spiritual adviser? Woodward wrote that the friendship clicked when "Houston said Hillary was carrying the burden of 5,000 years of history when women were subservient. . . . She was reversing thousands of years of expectation, and was there upfront, probably more than virtually any woman in human history—apart from Joan of Arc." It grew more ridiculous: "Houston felt at one point that being Hillary was like being Mozart with his hands cut off, unable to play. Though Houston did not articulate the image to Hillary, she felt that the First Lady was going through a female crucifixion." (Another reason to chat with Jesus Christ, no?)

The lesson: Flattery (and some New Age psychobabble) could get you welcomed into Hillary's inner circle. The solarium session was only one of a series of Houston meetings, including a meeting of gurus like Tony Robbins and Houston friend Mary Catherine Bateson at Camp David at the end of 1994 to consider what was going wrong for the Clintons.

Woodward's revelations reminded many political observers of former White House chief of staff Donald Regan tattling in his 1988 book about Nancy Reagan's use of astrologer Joan Quigley to plot President Reagan's schedule. But the liberal media who roasted Mrs. Reagan for her strange behavior were agnostic about Mrs. Clinton's New Age voodoo.

Take, for example, *Newsweek* magazine. In 1988, George Hackett and Eleanor Clift did allow Mrs. Reagan's press secretary, Elaine Crispen, to ask, "If she could get a little comfort and consolation from astrology, why not?" But they also forwarded other spins: "Scientists showed less tolerance for the President's participation in what they consider medieval superstition. 'How can you control a science budget of billions of dollars when you believe in nonsense of this magnitude?' says James Kaler, professor of astronomy at the University of Illinois." Hackett and Clift added, "Criticism also rumbled from fundamentalists, who liken astrology to Satan worship. 'This is the last straw for a lot of religious people who treated Reagan as their political savior,' said conservative columnist and former Moral Majority vice president Cal Thomas."

Newsweek failed to explore how Hillary's séances squared with her professed Methodist commitments. It could have been done: on June 25 *Washington Times* reporter Julia Duin interviewed several disappointed Methodist theologians and evangelicals—and found some eager Methodist defenders. But that might have clashed with *Newsweek* religion reporter Kenneth Woodward's October 31, 1994, verdict that "Hillary

Rodham Clinton is as pious as she is political. Methodism, for her, is not just a church but an extended family of faith that defines her horizons." He called the Clinton era "Washington's Methodist Moment."

Instead, *Newsweek* Washington bureau chief Evan Thomas predictably picked up the old pity song in the wake of the séance scoop: "To many women, Hillary Clinton is not a cold-eyed conspirator, but a martyr." He quoted one fan saying that people, including the press, were out to get Hillary, because "a lot of people don't like a strong woman." Thomas concluded the story by declaring that in the eyes of her followers, "Hillary looks just the way she does to her philosopher friend, Dr. Houston—as a Joan of Arc figure, persecuted for her righteous crusade."

Try ABC for another example. Back in 1988, on the heels of the Nancy Reagan revelations, Peter Jennings had begun by joking, "If today is your birthday, your horoscope says this month should be emotionally varied and your problems seem to involve communication." But he added that "the White House will not take the Regan book lying down" and that "Mrs. Reagan is not easily deterred." Sam Donaldson followed with a straightforward report that quoted both a mocking critic and a Reaganite, and he concluded by emphasizing that this story would have real political repercussions: "Presidents and their wives look to their place in history, and to the Reagans, Regan's book doesn't help."

But with Hillary Clinton in 1996, Peter Jennings began by belittling the story as beneath real journalists: "Mrs. Clinton is all over the headlines today and it is all because of a new book on politics over which some of the tabloids, particularly, are having a field day. In the book, Bob Woodward of the *Washington Post* writes that Mrs. Clinton, apparently as an exercise, conducted some imaginary conversations with, among others, Eleanor Roosevelt. Some flap."

Unlike Sam Donaldson's 1988 story, reporter Jim Wooten's 1996 piece quoted only one side: the put-upon First Lady's. In the story he quoted Hillary, Clinton aide Leon Panetta, and Hillary's guru: "Ms. Houston says that any other interpretation of her relationship to Mrs. Clinton would be merely political. . . . Such role-playing conversations are traditional counseling techniques, and Ms. Houston describes Mrs. Clinton as beleaguered, in pain, and seeking help." Wooten ended by pleading with the audience for sympathy: "The unwritten subtext here, of course, is that even here at the end of the twentieth century there is a political price to be paid for those in public life who seek help for their private problems."

The news reports on the Reagans and astrology were reasonably fair (let's admit that the story did invite humor), but any damaging tidbit on the Clintons, no matter how trivial, drew an entirely different instinct. In Republican presidencies, reporters provoke damage control; with Democrats they practice it.

CONVENTION WISDOM: HILLARY WRONGED BY REPUBLICAN NASTINESS

By the time the Democratic National Convention rolled around in the last week of August 1996, everything that might have embarrassed Hillary was largely forgotten, and journalists gathered in Hillary's childhood home of Chicago to celebrate their favorite revolutionary. The week of strong support began on the Sunday roundtable on ABC's *This Week,* where Sam Donaldson served up the usual liberal line: "I think much of the opposition to Hillary Rodham Clinton is the fact that she is a strong-willed woman doing things in a man's arena, and we men don't seem to like that." After George Will pointed out that politics is the arena of many women, from Margaret Thatcher to Indira Gandhi, Cokie Roberts disagreed: "The world I graduated from college into was certainly a man's world," she said. "That has changed. And one of the people who was an agent of that change was Hillary Clinton and her generation. And it's very difficult for the world to accept people who have been revolutionaries."

Pause for a moment here and contemplate Roberts's words. That is *precisely* how Hillary Rodham Clinton is viewed by most feminists in the national media. Hillary the Revolutionary "is the goddess messiah," as Cal Thomas put it when we interviewed him. "She is the great deliverer." Rush Limbaugh went further: "She spent thirty years eating dirt, thirty years being humiliated, thirty years playing second banana when everybody knows she's the smart one in the family, the smartest woman in the world. . . . She's one of them, one of their generation. She is owed because she is the feminist denied her opportunity by virtue of marriage to a hick who made her live in the swamps of Arkansas and get involved with these trailer-park deals like Whitewater. It's simple to me why she is treated the way she is."

So when the 1996 convention rolled around, the media's whitewash campaign meant not bringing up Mrs. Clinton's roughhouse approach to politics. Her role in firing and lodging criminal accusations against Travel Office workers, her role in urging campaign staff to destroy the stories of Bill Clinton's girlfriends, and her potential role in urging the lifting of FBI files didn't come up. Throughout their prime-time coverage of a convention in which almost nothing newsworthy occurred, networks barely mentioned Whitewater or Travelgate. These issues came up only twice on NBC and PBS, only once each on ABC, CBS, and CNN. The FBI files were utterly ignored. Hillary was ready for the cold drinks and palm-frond breezes offered by her servile corps of television interviewers.

Remember that in 1992, then–PBS anchor Judy Woodruff gave a tissue-soft convention interview to Hillary Clinton in New York, but blistered Barbara Bush about GOP nastiness the next month in Houston. Now with CNN, Woodruff was the first to set the tone on the outrage of Republican criticism. She began by asking Hillary if Bob Dole's convention remarks on her new book *It Takes a Village* should be an issue. This is what he'd said: "We are told that it takes a village, that is collective, and thus the state, to raise a child. The state is now more involved than it ever has been in the raising of children. And children are now more neglected, more abused, and more mistreated than they have been in our time. This is not a coincidence." This wasn't personal, it was political—tough and accurate. But the left, and Judy Woodruff, were outraged.

Woodruff continued, "Former president George Bush told the delegates he 'worked hard'—I'm quoting here—'to uphold the dignity and the honor of the presidency, to treat it with respect.' And then he added, quote, '[I]t breaks his [*sic*] heart, when the White House is demeaned, the presidency diminished.' Does that hurt coming from your immediate predecessor?" Hillary protested, "I don't think that has happened, and it would break my heart if it had, but it hasn't."

Woodruff kept going: "He then went on, Mrs. Clinton, he made a point of saying that his wife, Mrs. Bush, quote, 'unquestionably upheld the honor of the White House.' Is that an insult to you?" When Mrs. Clinton said she perceived that as a compliment to Barbara Bush, Woodruff would have none of it, editorializing that Bush "was clearly drawing a contrast there." She wanted to know Hillary's reaction to Bush's speech—"You're not hurt?"—which allowed our Victim Hillary to rise, rise, rise above the fray: "I'm not hurt by anything Republicans say about me. I don't think there's anything left that Republicans could say about me that hasn't been said, although I'll probably find out there is." This was not an interview, it was a beatification.

On CBS's *This Morning*, cohost Jose Diaz-Balart offered more of the same. "In the San Diego Republican convention, you were the subject of much conversation, and I think the target, I think many would say, of some very serious attacks." He played a snippet of Dole's remarks on *It Takes a Village* and asked, "Do you ever, seriously, in the White House, when all the doors are closed, do you ever say, 'Is this worth it'?"

The only tough questions either Diaz-Balart or Woodruff asked were from the liberal perspective—asking, for example, how she could go along with the president signing a welfare-reform bill. Neither asked a thing about the McDougal convictions or Travelgate or the FBI files or the solarium séance.

Hillary's speech on Tuesday night of the convention was devoid of radical proposals; her socialized health care agenda had been crushed and she knew the country had no appetite for more. Instead she championed relatively modest ideas like creating twenty-four-hour hospital hotlines for new parents, and an expansion of the Family and Medical Leave Act "so that parents can take time off for children's doctor appointments and parent-teacher conferences at school." After the speech ended, NBC's Maria Shriver, so fervent in her partisanship toward the First Lady, was awarded an exclusive interview just under the podium. NBC cut in precisely as Hillary was wrapping up a telephone call with the president, ending in "I love you, too, honey." After asking Mrs. Clinton to repeat the love message the president just proclaimed over the phone, Shriver immediately launched into accolades: "Everybody was nervous for you out there. . . . You are known for your incredible composure, but that standing ovation, that sustained applause, looked like it affected you." Hillary said she was moved by the support.

- "This has been a difficult couple of years for you. Did that applause, the way you've been treated here, the way people have been reacting to you, kind of make it all go away?" Hillary repeated the moved-by-the-support answer.

- "You were credited with really redefining the role of First Lady, and for doing that, you've taken a lot of heat, a lot of criticism." Breaking into a supportive grin, Shriver asked, "As you look back, do you wish you'd redefined it a little less?" Hillary said she had to be true to herself.

- On Hillary's father, Hugh Rodham, who died in 1994: "He's not here this evening. He never got a chance to see this. What do you think he would have thought of you, his little girl, in front of that crowd, that applause?" The only thing missing from the interview was a request for an autograph.

The other reporters were just given a few seconds in a scrum to toss out questions, but they weren't any tougher. CBS's Bob Schieffer inquired of her, "Weren't you a little offended when he [Bob Dole] made the reference he did [to your book]?" CNN's Wolf Blitzer echoed, "What goes through your mind when you hear some of these bitter attacks against you?" Hillary quipped, "Well, it takes a village to spin conspiracy theories. I mean, there are so many of them. They come from all directions. I view it as partisan, politically motivated, and I really don't spend a lot of time worrying about it."

In truth, Hillary had very little to worry about. Regardless of the problem, the press would come galloping to her defense, no matter how egregious the charge or bizarre her behavior. From editors to anchors, from gumshoe beat writers to celebrity television reporters, her legions were manifold, pledging their oaths of loyalty by spinning on her behalf. On September 1, verbose CBS *Sunday Morning* TV critic John Leonard got into the act. "Nancy pushed Ronnie into an arms treaty with the

Russians because she wanted him to win a Nobel Prize. So maybe astrology was healthier than whatever the rest of the nuke-Managua globocops were smoking in the Reagan White House." He concluded, "That Hillary should talk to Eleanor Roosevelt bothers some of us less than the fact that her husband obviously doesn't. . . . Our pathological fear of Hillary and any other uppity woman, whatever her politics, is a form of footbinding as well as a species of hate radio."

Chapter 8
Swatting the Pests

I think what our adversaries, that are almost pathologically obsessed with personal destruction, don't get is that . . . politics is about real people and their hopes and their dreams. So to me, all this [scandal] stuff—you all always say, gosh, I don't know how you put up with it. How do you put up with mosquitoes in the summertime in Arkansas? You just swat them and go on.

—BILL CLINTON in a speech to Arkansas Democrats in Washington,
December 13, 1997

It was a merciless attack on me because I was the investigator. Not only did they try to malign me and tried to make me look like I was an uneducated idiot, a nincompoop. But they tried to make it look like I was a scoundrel to boot. It was very tough on my family and me, but it didn't dissuade us from doing our job.

—CONGRESSMAN DAN BURTON on the attacks he endured for
investigating Clinton scandals, in an interview with the authors

Thanks in large measure to the nearly nonexistent Dole for President campaign, the suspense-free 1996 presidential election ended with another Clinton victory lap outside under the lights in Little Rock, with Hillary standing demurely next to her husband in a milk-chocolate-colored suit. President Clinton thanked his wife for teaching him, over twenty-one years of married life, about how it takes a village to raise children. Al Gore was much more effusive in his victory speech: "On behalf of millions of families in villages throughout our land, a very special thank-you to a woman who has faced extraordinary pressures with grace, dignity, and an unbreakable commitment to serving our nation—America's First Lady, Hillary Rodham Clinton." As fireworks lit up the night sky, TV pictures showed the president with his arms wrapped around Hillary and Chelsea as they all peered skyward, and CNN's Judy Woodruff was touched. "This is quite a picture here. I think we see some teary eyes on the part of the First Lady."

The occasion led to lots of chatter about how the Clintons could now build that promised "bridge to the twenty-first century," about which they'd droned all year, but now that the reelection of Team Clinton was complete, the Clintons instead were preparing to perform the same tired song. Any scandal would be met the same way as in the first term: supporters who could be useful would be called upon for pity, while enemies, and even former friends if they had outlived their usefulness, would be covered in mud. In short, bridges in Village Clinton would be burned, not built. And the media would dutifully carry the gasoline.

The media also diligently pumped up Mrs. Clinton's profile. The pro-Hillary postelection spin began on November 25 in an evening-news story by CBS White House correspondent Rita Braver—the wife of Clinton lawyer and powerful Washington book agent Bob Barnett. Barnett was hailed by James Carville as the ace debate sparring partner/preparer for Democratic candidates, a role that he had played in every presidential election since 1976 (and that he would play again for Hillary Clinton's Senate bid in 2000). Hillary later put Barnett's picture in her memoir and called him a "close friend" who counseled her "in good times and bad." That connection was one of those tight personal relationships between the media and the Clintons that even *The New Republic* mocked in April of 1993 in a cover story titled "Clincest." On this night, Braver supported the First Lady with that now-familiar feminist refrain: critics of the First Lady were uncomfortable with strong women and all that unbreakable grace and dignity.

Casting Hillary as a trailblazer for the oppressed souls of past First Ladies, Braver endorsed Hillary's political spin on her failure to fulfill a promise to monitor (or preferably, strangle) welfare reform: "Perhaps Mrs. Clinton best expressed her own awkward situation when she told an Australian audience that the only way for a First Lady to escape criticism is never to express opinions or ideas." It apparently never occurred to Braver that it was the First Lady's exotic liberal ideas rather than her gender that needed confronting.

Within two months, CBS again came to Hillary's aid, this time on *Sunday Morning,* and this time with another friend, former Wellesley classmate Martha Teichner, holding the microphone. On the morning of January 19, host Charles Osgood hinted at the interviewer's long-standing friendship with Mrs. Clinton when he said, "It happens that Martha Teichner has known the First Lady for almost thirty years and was invited to the White House last week for another of many conversations she's had with Mrs. Clinton." Osgood's approving tone glossed over the fact that this friendship ought to have disqualified Teichner from conducting the interview in the first place.

Teichner didn't disappoint her friend. She made no effort to question the First Lady on unresolved subjects about which Hillary had not been forthcoming—Whitewater, Travelgate, Filegate; missing documents, found documents, and stolen documents; cronyism rampant and careers destroyed. Instead Teichner sought to soothe and sympathize. First she virtually asked her audience to feel the First Lady's pain: "Heat doesn't begin to describe the firestorm that erupted when the president handed over health care reform to his wife. . . . Were you startled by the fact that it was as controversial an issue as it was, and that you became controversial?" The question was disingenuous. The issue of health care reform was not controversial; it was Hillary's radical "solution"—a 1,342-page blueprint for socialism complete with a militant refusal to compromise on any point, along with her scandalous secret task force—that made it, and her, controversial.

Teichner continued with Hillary's woes: "Health care was just the beginning. She has been the subject of a nonstop, time-release litany of investigations. Three at the moment being conducted by Whitewater special counsel Kenneth Starr. Speculation she may be indicted continues." This allowed Hillary to kvetch, "I expect this matter to drag out as long as it is to anyone else's advantage to drag it out and then it will end.

I mean no one likes to be accused of having done anything improper or wrong. It becomes frustrating when you know that people are saying things that aren't true, but you just learn to live with it and you just go on day after day and—"

Teichner interrupted. But interrupted how? She could have directly challenged Hillary on this shameless spin. *Now, wait a minute, Mrs. Clinton. Number one: Who is dragging anything out? The record shows, conclusively, that it is you, along with your husband, who, time and again, have failed or refused to cooperate. And number two: Who are the people who are saying things that "aren't true"? Billy Dale, as one example of many, certainly feels it's the other way around.*

But this is wishful thinking. Instead, when Teichner interrupted, it was only to enhance Hillary's spin: "But how do you do [learn to live with unfair attacks], though, in the climate of a nonstop four- or even eight-year bashing?"

To underscore it all Teichner added that her friend's "biggest gripe is that the positive is never what the public sees; that her media image as a First Lady under fire, edgy and defensive, belies the real Hillary Clinton, who has even been known to laugh." And in another line that would cause eye-rolling everywhere outside of Hillaryland, she stated, "The First Lady has become more and more uncomfortable and wary around the press."

Later that day, C-SPAN aired its own inauguration-eve interview with the First Lady, and she complained about a "very effective, well-organized advocacy press that is, I think, very upfront in its right-wing, conservative inclinations and makes no apologies." According to a story in the *Washington Times,* she elaborated on how "there's not something comparable to that" on the liberal side: "You've got a conservative press and/or right-wing press presence with really nothing on the other end of the political spectrum, so that most of what is left in what you might call the middle or the establishment or the mainstream tries to be objective and tries to be thoughtful."

That statement was as audacious as it was preposterous, but also straight out of the Clinton playbook, a line both Clintons would use whenever a reporter veered from the company line. It was designed to intimidate, to tarnish the journalist with the scarlet "C," the "conservative" or

"Clinton-hater" label, thus threatening to expel him/her from the company of decent society—and time and again, it worked. This time, however, Hillary had every reason to launch an attack on the press. Cracks were developing.

Some reporters, almost exclusively in the print press, just couldn't continue to ignore the mounting evidence of corruption on a wide variety of fronts. Conservative talk radio was booming in the nineties, and everyone was focused on Clinton scandals. The Internet, too, was exploding, with thousands of websites appearing weekly, many focusing on the administration's misbehavior. And with the launch of MSNBC (July of '96) and Fox (October of '96), the very nature of television news was about to undergo a radical change, with the twenty-four-hour cable news format covering the news ignored by the broadcast networks.

Paula Jones Returns

After a flurry of legal motions and appeals in federal courts to delay President Clinton's sexual-harassment accountability until after his reelection, the Paula Jones sexual-harassment lawsuit made its way to a Supreme Court hearing on January 13, 1997. When Jones first came forward to claim that she'd been sexually harassed in February 1994, no one in the so-called mainstream media covered it. They waited until she filed suit in May, when they could no longer ignore it, but when they did give it some coverage, they did so by turning on her with a vengeance.

In the fall of 1996, former *New York Times* legal reporter Stuart Taylor wrote an article for *The American Lawyer* boldly asserting that "the evidence supporting Paula Jones's allegations of predatory, if not depraved, behavior by Bill Clinton is far stronger than the evidence supporting Anita Hill's allegations of far less serious conduct by Clarence Thomas." Explaining that sexual-harassment cases are often strongest when friends or family members of the accuser recount nearly immediate corroboration of the offense, Taylor wrote that he had interviewed two Jones witnesses, Pamela Blackard and Debra Ballentine. Both of them, he said, offered persuasive testimony that "an extremely upset Jones" had told them immediately after the event "that Clinton had supposedly exposed himself and demanded oral sex after Jones had rebuffed his efforts to grope her." Of course, most media outlets ignored the witnesses' accounts. Taylor also noted that "President Clinton has carefully avoided making *any statement whatever*—sworn or unsworn—about what, if anything, happened, between him and Paula Jones." (Italics his.) That fact underlined the media's absolute failure to follow up against Clinton—over a period of years.

Taylor was no conservative activist, and most certainly not in the "Clinton-hater" camp. Indeed, Taylor described himself as "one who voted for President Clinton in 1992 and who may do so again (with multiple misgivings), and as one who lamented Justice Thomas's confirmation to the Supreme Court."

But the media avoided the Taylor article until ten weeks later—after the election, when the political damage was minimal. If these charges were serious, why wasn't it a serious issue for voters to consider before the election? Throughout all of 1996, the networks had aired only eight news stories mentioning the Jones case. The January '97 coverage began when *Newsweek* put Paula Jones on the cover, a remarkable reversal for that magazine, which in 1994 had portrayed her as a "Dogpatch Madonna" who pinched male behinds at the Red Lobster and rubbed her crotch on men at duck hunts. (By contrast, *Newsweek* reported in 1991 that Anita Hill was a "straight arrow" who had been an "unusually bright and determined child.")

Newsweek's Evan Thomas, who apologized on NBC for his "stupid" 1994 remark on TV that Jones was "some sleazy woman with big hair coming out of the trailer parks," now acknowledged that "the mainstream media have been skillfully spun by the White House and Clinton's lawyers. By playing on the class and partisan prejudices of reporters, as well as their squeamishness and ambivalence about printing stories about the sex lives of politicians, Clinton's operatives have done a brilliant job of discrediting Paula Jones and her case." In all of that spin, you could still hear the echo of Hillary's command at the first bimbo eruption: *"We have to destroy her story."*

By June, the Jones suit was threatening the Clintons with so much political trouble that CBS aired two stories hinting that the White

House should settle the suit. One story starred historian and Hillary pal Doris Kearns Goodwin, and the other former prosecutor Greg Garrison, a CBS News consultant who'd convicted Mike Tyson of sexual misconduct. Garrison told CBS reporter Phil Jones that once the president went under oath, perjury was a real danger: "And the judgment day may be in his deposition, it may be in trial. But when it happens, you can't wiggle, you can't move, you can't take a breath. You've got to answer the question, because if you try to dodge, you're dead."

In the October 20 issue of *U.S. News & World Report*, in a piece touting Hillary's newfound popularity, Kenneth Walsh reported that Mrs. Clinton was urging her husband toward a settlement in the Jones case.

THE NETWORKS YAWN AT HILLARY'S PAL
THE MILLIONAIRE THIEF

The Paula Jones complaint wasn't the only scandal news darkening the horizon as the second Clinton administration settled in. Consider the story of Hillary's good friend and former Rose Law Firm partner Webster Hubbell. When Bill and Hillary came to power, this man was named associate attorney general of the United States, the third-highest-ranking law officer in the land, and he was more powerful even than that.

As the *New York Times* noted, "Arriving in Washington months before Janet Reno was nominated to lead the department, he took over the office that is attached to the Attorney General's suite and was, for all practical purposes, running the department." Even after Reno arrived, there was still controversy over whether the White House was running Justice through Hubbell. After the Waco fiasco, for instance, Reno raised eyebrows in the capital by saying that she was communicating with the president—through Hubbell.

Today Webster Hubbell is a person few people remember, and those who do are likely to be dismissed as obsessive Clinton-haters for remembering. Even then, by the end of 1997, *Washington Post* reporter Frank Ahrens profiled Hubbell with this jokey aside: "Hubbell hasn't become a linchpin for history. Hubbell already feels as far away as [Jimmy Carter official and scandal figure] Bert Lance." But Hubbell is still relevant to

Hillary's story, particularly as his case shows how she—with the help of a compliant media—brushed scandals under the rug.

By the summer of 1993, the Rose Law Firm had begun pressing Hubbell to explain some poorly documented expenses, and on March 14, 1994, Hubbell resigned from his powerful Washington position—smack-dab in the hottest month of Whitewater media coverage, and just four days before Hillary's cattle-futures fiasco surfaced.

On December 6, 1994, the real truth of Hubbell's office expenses emerged: he pleaded guilty to two felony counts of mail fraud and tax evasion. Sounding regretful, he confirmed that on more than four hundred occasions between 1989 and 1992, he had submitted bills to cover personal expenses and concealed the theft with phony expense vouchers and inflated accounts of the hours he'd worked for clients. Hubbell had stolen $394,000 from his partners and clients.

But it was not until 1997, after he'd served eighteen months in a minimum-security prison camp, that another, more outrageous story emerged. After Hubbell resigned in disgrace under suspicion of stealing hundreds of thousands of dollars, what did Bill and Hillary Clinton do? They leaned on presidential buddies (and corporations who wanted to get close to the Clintons) to pay him *another* $700,000 for "jobs" that demanded no substantial work.

How did Hubbell go from public servant making $124,000 a year to someone reaping this "consulting" bonanza? Remember that Hubbell was a key figure in keeping the Whitewater story tamped down. In 1994, it had yet to emerge that Hubbell had held Whitewater documents in his possession for the Clintons. It also had yet to emerge that Hillary's billing records suggested she had done her most intense Whitewater lawyering on the phony Castle Grande deal, which centrally featured Seth Ward, Hubbell's father-in-law.

All the payments to Hubbell, which totaled $704,152, came in 1994 and early 1995, with the exception of the $61,667 he received from publisher HarperCollins in 1995 and early 1996. According to the *Washington Post*, House investigators found that Hubbell's records showed he did little or no work for most of the money he received from eighteen companies and individuals, including the HarperCollins money, which was paid for a book that Hubbell never completed. The media company

Time Warner paid Hubbell $5,000 supposedly for lobbying work, except he never contacted a government official. *Time* defensively reported that Democratic lobbyist Michael Berman, who helped broker the Time Warner arrangement, "said the idea for hooking Hubbell up with [Time Warner lobbyist Timothy] Boggs was his alone; no one at the White House, he said, suggested or even knew of the deal." But they also noted that "Berman is in *the first circle of advisers to the First Lady* and talks regularly with Clinton's close friend and aide Bruce Lindsey." (Italics ours.)

Imagine the outrage a thirty-second ad on this could engender with the average American—yes, we know you work hard for $60,000 a year, but if you have good friends in Washington, you can rip off your company and then grab another half-million on your way to prison! This painted a gaudy picture of real Ivan Boesky–style criminal excess. But the TV networks had no appetite for it; they were like a gaggle of vegetarians dragged into a five-star steak house with gift certificates they didn't want to use. Even as their counterparts in the print media reported one scoop after another about the Hubbell payoffs for little or no work, they stayed away from the story.

Had Hubbell been a high administration official and close golfing buddy of a Republican president and guilty of this kind of corruption, the networks would have had a field day with the revelations. (Just consider their treatment of Reagan administration attorney general Ed Meese—and he was innocent!) But from January 1 to May 31, 1997, only ten evening-news stories were devoted to Hubbell on the Big Three, six on CNN's *World News* evening newscast, and just four on the network morning shows—a mere drop in the ocean of network media minutes. While the TV news titans downplayed or outright ignored many hard-hitting newspaper stories about the Clinton administration's handling of Hubbell, of particular interest to us are the substantial number of pieces showing Hillary Clinton's active involvement in the Hubbell case that the networks glossed over in 1997:

1. After Hubbell left prison, the February 25 *Los Angeles Times* noted that "the Clintons have stayed quietly in touch with Hubbell" through aide Marsha Scott, who visited him in prison and later traveled to Little Rock to confer with him as he prepared to give testimony before a grand

jury. Coverage? Zilch on ABC's *World News Tonight,* the *CBS Evening News,* or NBC's *Nightly News.*

2. On April 1, former White House chief of staff Mack McLarty and then–chief of staff Erskine Bowles admitted soliciting deals for Hubbell. Since the White House was putting out the information instead of the newspapers, this kicked the networks into gear. All the networks ran reports on the Clinton staffers' insistence that they were just helping a friend in need. When CBS's Mike Wallace interviewed Hubbell for the April 6 edition of *60 Minutes,* he was quick to cast the First Lady as a victim. After Hubbell denied that Hillary knew of his bill-padding at Rose, Wallace ended the interview by asking, "Did you ever look your former partner, Hillary Clinton, in the eye and say to her, 'I let you down'?" Hubbell replied, "No. I hope someday to say that."

3. On April 6, the same day as the *60 Minutes* interview, the *Los Angeles Times* reported that on March 13, 1994, the day before Hubbell resigned, Chief of Staff Mack McLarty told a group of Clinton inner-circle members that Hubbell would step down. "Based on McLarty's recollection," the *Times* added, "he then told Hillary Clinton, out of earshot of others, that he would seek to help Hubbell financially. The First Lady, according to McLarty, nodded her approval." Network coverage? Zero.

4. The next day, the *Washington Times* published a story on the front page headlined "Hillary Got Formal Warning on Hubbell." Jerry Seper reported that Hubbell's testimony under oath to the federal Resolution Trust Corporation (RTC) probe of Whitewater "was meticulously described in a March 1, 1994, memo written by White House Associate Counsel W. Neil Eggleston and forwarded to Mrs. Clinton by White House Deputy Chief of Staff Harold Ickes." As Seper pointed out when we interviewed him for this book, the memo demonstrated that, through her staff at the very least, Hillary was keeping close tabs on Hubbell's cooperation with investigators. "[Hillary] and her husband had over a long period of time significantly denied they knew anything about Whitewater," he told us, "and I thought this was an indication of her role in this thing. . . . It showed her active participation in what might previously have been described as a cover-up, or at least an attempt to keep herself apprised so that they could do damage control." Network coverage? Zero.

5. On April 10, the *Washington Times* added more detail. The First Lady ordered the RTC in 1993 to "advise her of all media questions about an RTC probe of a failed Arkansas thrift at the core of the Whitewater investigation, including inquiries on Webster Hubbell's ties to suspected criminal wrongdoing." So she wasn't just keeping tabs on Hubbell, but ordering federal officials to keep her updated on the pesky reporters covering Whitewater. Why such concern? For Seper, "this Resolution Trust Corporation [business] was like a screaming missile. I thought it actually portrayed wrongdoing by Hubbell and Hillary Clinton." Network coverage? Zero.

Someone relying on television for his or her news wouldn't be connecting the dots, that Hillary was watching the financial care and feeding of Hubbell—and closely managing the publicity surrounding Whitewater as well. But on April 7, all the networks that ignored or soft-soaped Hubbell's sleazy payoffs jumped to cover a joke Hillary made to poohpooh Hubbell hush-money questions and the whole Whitewater "saga," as she dismissively called it. Just two weeks after members of the Heaven's Gate cult killed themselves in a kooky plot to join a UFO behind the Hale-Bopp comet, Mrs. Clinton told liberal NPR talk-show host Diane Rehm that people with the temerity to keep asking her about Whitewater were part of "the never-ending fictional conspiracy that, honest to goodness, reminds me of some people's obsession with UFOs and the Hale-Bopp comet." Note the dismissive "fictional conspiracy" talk some nine months before the First Lady famously went on the *Today* show to blame the Monica Lewinsky scandal on a "vast right-wing conspiracy."

New House Government Reform and Oversight Committee chairman Dan Burton had pledged to investigate Clinton scandals in the second term, so it was no surprise that reporters picked up the Hale-Bopp crack, attached it to Burton, this conservative for whom they had no use, and ran with it. *Time's* Margaret Carlson smacked Burton on CNN: "The UFO comparison is apt in his case. He is considered flaky and a bit of a crackpot, even though a nice guy. Some crackpots are nice." (Just how well did Carlson know the man she was attacking? Burton told us, "I've never even talked to that woman.") James Warren, Washington bureau chief for the *Chicago Tribune,* added that Burton "is sort of like the Republicans' wacky aunt stuck down in the basement. You don't want to let her out in front of the guests." *Newsweek*'s Evan Thomas called Burton "a car wreck waiting to happen."

6. On April 16, *Washington Post* reporter Susan Schmidt discovered that "Webster Hubbell had more than 70 meetings with administration officials" in the nine months between his resignation and his guilty pleas, showing that "the extent of Hubbell's contacts within the upper reaches of the White House and the administration was much broader than previously known." Network coverage? Zero.

7. On May 3, *Washington Post* reporter Sharon LaFraniere noted that Bill and Hillary met with Hubbell four times in 1994. The White House now conceded this after previously claiming only two meetings. Network coverage? Zero.

How did the networks grade their own miserable performance? Freelance journalist Marc Morano questioned CBS's Dan Rather about the media's lack of investigative energy and drew an amazing response. "There's no question that [Clinton] had extremely intense scrutiny on this issue," Rather said with a straight face. "No one can argue that anybody in the press—right, left, center, above, or below—has failed to cover everything in Whitewater to the maximum extent and continue to do so."

Hillary Clinton had arrived in Washington with three close Rose Law Firm associates. Vincent Foster was dead. William Kennedy resigned in 1994 over his clumsy handling of Travelgate. Hubbell resigned under an ethical cloud in 1994, and was now an ex-convict. The Rose Law Firm deserved to be seen as a disgraceful nest of cronyism and corruption. Yet journalists like *U.S. News & World Report* owner Mortimer Zuckerman continued to make excuses about the Hubbell payoffs, as he did to Chris Matthews: "I think there is at least as much reason to believe that compassion motivated them as much as anything else. . . . This is sort of a group of people who came here as a happy band of brothers and were getting, you know, knocked off one by one."

Some in the media, like CNN talk-show host Larry King, went further, not just running interference for the Clintons but brazenly attacking conservatives. On April 29, King invited the First Lady to the set, offering Hillary a set of puff questions, such as "Have you felt, like with grand juries and the like, beleaguered, put upon?" and "Mr. Hubbell—were you just being a friend?"

Another reporter who felt Hillary's pain was Linda Douglass, who covered the Clintons as both a CBS and an ABC reporter. When Hubbell resigned in 1994, Douglass closed one story for CBS by saying, "This was a difficult day for Mrs. Clinton as she watched another close friend, Webster Hubbell, forced from public life. She had urged him and other friends to join her to serve in Washington; yet despite her power, she's had to watch some of them fall and has been unable to protect them." Protect them? From what? The implication was that Hillary's friends were innocent, which summarily they were not. And if they were guilty, why would it be appropriate for the First Lady to protect them?

Linda Douglass's conflict of interest was profound indeed. In 1998, Byron York reported in *The American Spectator* that Douglass and her husband, John Phillips, regularly welcomed Hubbell and his wife, Suzy, over for dinner. After Hubbell resigned, Phillips arranged for the Consumer Support and Education Fund, which he had helped establish, to pay Hubbell $45,000 to write an essay on public service. The families vacationed together in the Greek islands, with Phillips footing most of the bill. Hubbell never produced the essay, forcing Phillips to pay the $45,000 back to the foundation. But Douglass never told that story on TV. Neither did anyone else.

On April 30, 1998, after independent counsel Kenneth Starr indicted Webster Hubbell for evading taxes on the $700,000 paid to him by Clinton friends and donors for little or no work, Dan Burton's committee released audiotapes of Hubbell's prison conversations in which he suggested he'd have to "roll over one more time" for the Clintons. Even then, the networks tried to bury the incriminating hush-money echo on those tapes, claiming that the Burton committee's highlights were edited to remove references more favorable to Hubbell or Hillary Clinton.

Burton was under attack as a bumbler. "The criticism of Burton is piling up," ABC's Mike Von Fremd contended in a May 3 story devoted to Democratic complaints. "Democrat Henry Waxman accused Burton of selectively releasing portions of the tape just to make the First Lady look bad." On the May 5 *Nightline*, reporter Chris Bury insisted, "Now the tapes will be remembered less for what they reveal than for the controversy they generated, and the president once again has been blessed by the bumbling of his enemies."

That whole Waxman line of selective release of the tapes was false. *National Review*'s Ramesh Ponnuru and John J. Miller revealed that journalists had access to the full tapes, not just the committee highlights. Hillary's media friends buried the story and attempted to demoralize conservatives by denouncing Republicans as incompetent Keystone Kops.

QUIET ON HILLARY'S HANDLING OF HUANG, CHUNG, AND THE COCAINE SMUGGLER

One of the largest payments to Hubbell, $100,000, came from Hong Kong businesses controlled by the Riady family of Indonesia, who, as the *New York Times* reported, "received crucial backing from the Administration [on a $2 billion project in China] about the same time that Mr. Hubbell was being paid." Hubbell's connections to those businesses, the Lippo Group, made more sense as the illegal Asian fundraising scandal began to grow. It all began on October 8, 1996, when the *Wall Street Journal* front page introduced the story of John Huang and his trip through the power elite. It started when he was head of the Lippo Group's U.S. operations, which included ties to Bill Clinton's loose-governing era in Little Rock, and it continued as Huang got a position in Ron Brown's Commerce Department and then moved to the Democratic National Committee, where he raised large amounts from Asian donors.

Before Bill Clinton's reelection, it was too early (and too politically touchy) for the networks to come to conclusions about the manipulations of John Huang and other foreign fundraising figures. But in 1997, as the House and Senate took up investigations of the illegal fundraising, they found nothing but obstacles. One of them was the TV news brigade, which routinely suggested that illegal fundraising was not a Clinton-crony story but a "both parties do it" story, and filed reports insisting that the hearings were expensive and boring and were not accomplishing much.

On the June 18, 1997, edition of ABC's *Prime Time Live,* reporter Brian Ross interviewed Nolanda Hill about her business partner and close friend Ron Brown, the late commerce secretary. She put a lot of incredible charges on the table, including that Brown believed Hillary Clinton had placed Lippo employee John Huang in his Commerce Department slot. Nobody—not newspapers, not magazines, not networks (including ABC's other shows)—followed up.

The Asiagate figure most connected to Hillaryland was Taiwanese-American businessman Johnny Chung. Chung made at least forty-nine visits to the White House, despite the fact that a National Security Council official concluded that he was a "hustler" seeking to exploit his friendship with the Clintons to impress Chinese business associates.

On July 30, 1997, the *Los Angeles Times* carried a bombshell by William Rempel and Alan Miller: "Contradicting accounts by the Clinton administration, one of the Democratic Party's biggest donors, says he gave a $50,000 check to the first lady's chief of staff on White House grounds in 1995 in direct response to solicitations by aides of Hillary Rodham Clinton." If true, this was a violation of the Hatch Act, which forbids the solicitation of political contributions in government buildings. The most memorable line in the story was Chung's maxim "I see the White House is like a subway: You have to put in coins to open the gates."

On *World News Tonight,* ABC's Bob Zelnick called it "a potentially explosive development," but gave it only thirty-eight seconds in a larger story on GOP attacks on Attorney General Janet Reno. On CBS's *Face the Nation,* reporter Rita Braver also called it a "potentially explosive" story, but that night, the CBS anchorman gave it sixty-two words. Only *NBC Nightly News* devoted a full story (its lead story) to the Chung scoop. But by the next morning, the "explosive" story was a dud. It was totally ignored by all the morning shows.

When Hillary Clinton's former chief of staff, Maggie Williams, appeared before the Senate Government Affairs Committee on November 13, she testified that she had not solicited the contribution from Chung. She also said that she immediately forwarded the check to the DNC and that she played no role in arranging for Chung and six Chinese businessmen to attend President Clinton's weekly radio address two days later. In addition, she provided a vivid portrait of Chung as a persistent and at times annoying presence in her office whose "enthusiasm for Mrs. Clinton bordered on the worshipful." But ABC, CBS, and NBC all ignored Williams's testimony.

This might have been a story worth pursuing, given that Johnny Chung later told federal prosecutors, after reaching a plea bargain, that Chinese army lieutenant colonel Liu Chaoying, an executive with a state-owned aerospace company, gave him $300,000 to donate to the Democrats' 1996 campaign, and that from 1994 to 1996, Chung made twelve personal or corporate donations to the DNC totaling $366,000. The DNC returned all of the money after the election, stating that it had had "insufficient information" about its origins.

Then there was Jorge Cabrera, cocaine smuggler. The Cuban-born American citizen was already a convicted drug smuggler when the Democrats solicited him for money. He donated $20,000 to the Democrats in 1995 and gained access to a south Florida fundraiser with Al Gore in November—and a White House Christmas party hosted by Hillary in December. Cabrera was photographed with both Gore and Mrs. Clinton.

Three weeks later, he was arrested inside a Dade County cigar warehouse, in a drug bust that found five hundred pounds of cocaine. Cabrera was charged with trying to smuggle three tons of cocaine and thirty cases of Cohiba cigars into the United States, and was sentenced in late 1996 to nineteen years in a federal prison. The Democrats did not return his money until October 19, 1996, when reporters started inquiring. ABC's Brian Ross filed a story on October 22, followed two days later by reports on CNN and NBC. But this was simply not newsworthy to CBS, which ran nothing on Cabrera.

The CNN story was illuminating. It showed the picture of Cabrera taken with Hillary Clinton, with anchor Frank Sesno explaining, "That's commercial fisherman Jorge Cabrera next to the First Lady last December." *Commercial fisherman?* That's a funny title, as you try to explain all the cocaine seized.

On *Today,* NBC weekend host Jodi Applegate made Cabrera's photos with Gore and the Clintons sound like unintentional fender-bending accidents. She said to Tim Russert, "Jorge Cabrera, a convicted drug smuggler who gave $20,000 to the DNC, wound up at a fancy dinner with Al Gore, wound up at a White House Christmas party with Hillary Clinton. But they gave the money back when they found out about his background. It may not look good, but is there any proof that anything was done wrong?" At least Russert acknowledged that the White House had "no standards when it came to raising money."

THE QUEEN OF QUALITY CHILD CARE

The media's soft treatment of the illegal fundraising charges was nothing unusual. Scandal was simply not a subject for Hillary in the fall. The media were there, as always, to burnish her image.

When Mrs. Clinton pushed for bigger government solutions on child care in October 1997, she drew another round of supportive interviews on the network morning shows. The morning anchorwomen didn't ask Hillary about any of her scandals but instead threw supportive liberal questions her way. Katie Couric said, "Regulations for at-home day care vary so much from state to state in terms of the ratio of children to day care provider, do you think there should be some kind of overall federal regulations?" ABC's Lisa McRee proclaimed, "The experts say that it really costs $6,800 per child for a year to provide quality child care. The average American only spends $4,000. Will this administration provide any funding to help make up that difference if, in fact, it's going to cost more to provide quality care?" CBS's Jane Robelot just focused on the urgency of Hillary's action: "What is the cost of ignoring this issue?" No conservative rebuttal on child care was allowed.

Couric did take time to highlight Hillary's poll numbers. "You continue to talk about issues you care deeply about, particularly regarding women, families, and children. But you certainly have not taken such a high-profile policymaking role since your health care reform efforts were unsuccessful, and your job approval, I understand, is at an all-time high, by one poll a whopping 67 percent. Do you interpret that as Americans simply are not ready to have a First Lady in such a high-profile public policy role?"

The story line somehow always came back to the public's fright at the prospect of a Hillary copresidency. Viewers might suspect that these interviewers saw any obstruction of Hillary's liberal agenda as the work of conservative cavemen who wanted to drag their wives back to the kitchen by their hair, as a discrimination problem that could make Mrs. Clinton's supporters hum "We Shall Overcome."

Chapter 9
Playing the Vast-Conspiracy Card

I guess that will teach them to f— with us.

—HILLARY speaking to friend HARRY THOMASON in the White
House solarium after her "vast right-wing conspiracy" interview on
NBC, as recounted in Jeffrey Toobin's book *A Vast Conspiracy*

*There was no vast right-wing conspiracy. The only conspiracies
were the ones in her head and her husband's pants.*

—MARK LEVIN, in an interview with the authors

Hillary Clinton looked tired and puffy under the lights on the *Today* set,
six days after the Monica Lewinsky story broke, and the day after
she stood behind her husband and applauded after he wagged his
finger and insisted, "I did not have sexual relations with that woman,
Miss Lewinsky. . . . These allegations are false." A squadron of TV satellite trucks waited to capture her arrival at the NBC studios at 5:30 in the
morning. "She knew the stakes for this first interview," author Jeffrey
Toobin reported, "and she reveled in the action."

It was the morning of Clinton's State of the Union address, which he
refused to cancel or postpone despite the emerging story of the forty-
nine-year-old president's illicit affair with a twenty-one-year-old intern.
Hillary had booked her interview weeks in advance to publicize the
speech and talk about her latest safe First Lady cause, preserving the

nation's historic treasures, but breaking events called for a different message. As aide Sidney Blumenthal, a lover of conspiracy talk, wrote in his tome *The Clinton Wars*, he advised her instead to take the offensive and hit conservatives with the message that there were "professional forces at work whose only purpose is to sow division by creating scandal."

NBC's Matt Lauer tried to begin gently, asking whether the president had described his relationship with Monica Lewinsky to her in detail, to which Hillary answered, "Well, we've talked at great length, and I think as this matter unfolds, the entire country will have more information." That was no answer, so Lauer tried again, a different way. "But he has described to the American people what this relationship was *not*, in his words. Has he described to you what it *was*?" Again Mrs. Clinton replied with a creepy nonanswer: "We'll find that out as time goes by, Matt. But I think the important thing now is to stand as firmly as I can and say that, you know, the president has denied these allegations on all counts, unequivocally. And we'll see how this plays out."

Notice the double-talk here. Hillary had spoken with her husband "at great length," but "we'll find out" what the truth was. And she could "stand as firmly as I can and say" . . . that *her husband* had denied the allegations. Would any wife who wasn't so graspingly ambitious, so politically calculating, respond to charges she thought were outrageously false by suggesting so impersonally "we'll see how this plays out"? Would any normal wife tell millions of American women the answer was unimportant, that "We'll find that out as time goes by"?

Next Lauer asked whether she knew that her husband had given gifts to Lewinsky, to which Hillary answered, "I've seen him take his tie off and hand it to somebody. . . . He is kind. He is friendly. He tries to help people who need help, who ask for help." She wanted to change the subject: "But I'm very concerned about the tactics being used and the kind of intense political agenda at work here."

Lauer said he would get to independent counsel Kenneth Starr, but had a few more questions about Monica Lewinsky. Did she know, or had she ever met, Lewinsky? Hillary didn't think so. Had White House aide Evelyn Lieberman, who forced Lewinsky out of the White House and into her Pentagon job, warned her of the intern problem? No again. Wasn't it odd that Lewinsky, as an intern, would be interviewed for a UN job by the UN ambassador, Bill Richardson, and helped with job interviews by presidential pal Vernon Jordan? Hillary spoke again of the great kindness of the people she knew.

When Lauer turned to the subject of Starr, the tone of the interview suddenly changed. The tough questions stopped, replaced by an avalanche of sympathy: "So if what you have heard is something you can believe, and if what the president has told the nation is the whole truth and nothing but the truth, then you'd have to agree that this is the worst and most damaging smear of the twentieth century?" Hillary vaguely resisted. "Well, I don't know. There have been a lot of smears in the twentieth century. But it's a pretty bad one."

And then the moment arrived. Lauer quoted James Carville—"Great American," Hillary interjected—declaring that this was now a war between the White House and Ken Starr. This allowed Hillary to pull the pin on Sid Blumenthal's grenade and deliver what would become one of the most infamous lines of the Clinton presidency: *"This is—the great story here for anybody willing to find it and write about it and explain it is this vast right-wing conspiracy that has been conspiring against my husband since the day he announced for president. A few journalists have kind of caught on to it and explained it. But it has not yet been fully revealed to the American public. And actually, you know, in a bizarre sort of way, this may do it."*

The last creepy section of the interview came when Lauer asked, point-blank, "If an American president had an adulterous liaison in the White House and lied to cover it up, should the American people ask for his resignation?"

Hillary wanted to duck: "Well, they should certainly be concerned about it."

Lauer asked again: "Should they ask for his resignation?"

Hillary the defense lawyer erupted with "Well, I think that—if all that were proven true, I think that would be a very serious offense. That is not going to be proven true." Across the country, skeptics of the Clintons had their faces screwed up, repeating, *"Proven true"?* If it wasn't *proven* true, it was okay?

Interviewed for this book, Landmark Legal Foundation president and popular syndicated radio host Mark Levin seized on Hillary's last answer. As Levin pointed out, Hillary told the American people innumerable times that "it was a personal matter," and yet there she was on national TV saying "if it can be proven"—thus inviting, or at the very least recognizing the necessity for, public scrutiny. And then Levin demolished Mrs. Clinton's argument: "It *was* proven and he didn't resign, did he?" But the most troubling aspect of that line, Levin astutely noted, is what it revealed about Hillary herself: "She knew it was true, so she was misleading Matt Lauer and the American people."

Fox News host Sean Hannity agreed. "Considering what we now know about Bill Clinton, for her to turn around and blame everybody for Bill's problems, indiscretions, and lies says a lot about her," he told us. "She's an enabler. It reeks of somebody putting her ambition above everything else, including the truth, and the ability to tell the truth to the American people."

Hillary wasn't going to play defense. As we'd already seen the Clintons do numerous times, it was incumbent to put the accusers on trial, and what she said next was, almost unquestionably, a threat: "I think we're going to find some other things. And I think that when all of this is put into context, and we really look at the people involved here, look at their motivations and look at their backgrounds, look at their past behavior, some folks are going to have a lot to answer for." What was Hillary implying? Had she already seen the files on Republican foes Henry Hyde and Dan Burton, whose reputations and credibility were ultimately dealt damaging blows when their own extramarital affairs were exposed?

Within hours of the interview, reporters would be leaping not to demand a documentation of this bizarre accusation of a "vast right-wing conspiracy"—but to advance it as credible.

Although few remember it, Mrs. Clinton also granted an interview to ABC's *Good Morning America* the day after the State of the Union speech, and cohost Lisa McRee made Matt Lauer look like a pit bull by comparison. McRee asked apologetically, "We have to ask the Monica Lewinsky questions. You've said that you heard of the allegations as the story hit the press last week, as most of the nation did. Did you privately ask your husband if it was true?"

Mrs. Clinton stayed vague again: "I have talked to my husband about everything. But I don't, you know, ever talk about my conversations with my husband. But I can state unequivocally that, as my husband has said, these are false allegations." Again the qualifier: *as my husband has said.*

McRee followed up: "Do you believe he's told you the whole story?"

Hillary boasted, "I know he has. And I know that the American people will eventually know the story. And"—time to go on the offensive—"I guess my attitude about all of this is that because I have seen so many false accusations against not just my husband but myself, I really just want everybody to take a deep breath and relax and just, you know, sit back, because here they come again. We're going to have to just ride through this, as we have so many of these other false accusations."

McRee took the bait. "What is it about your husband, Mrs. Clinton, that seems to make him a lightning rod for these types of allegations? . . . You've also talked about your husband's generosity and his warmth, and his, you know, his warmth with people even, you know, people he hardly knows." Hillary said, "He just is that kind of human being that reaches out to all kinds of people. . . . He is who he is. I mean, he is a happy, friendly, loving, kind, good person."

McRee moved on to questions so soft that they polished Hillary's pumps: "Did you want him to come out fighting earlier, though? Because you are known for your political wisdom as well as your legal skill." She continued, "In the last few days, you, other members of the president's team, have been talking about a right-wing conspiracy. Kenneth Starr last night said it's nonsense. Your reaction to his comments?" For this interview, Hillary repeated the Blumenthal professional-forces line: "I don't think there's any doubt that there are professional forces on the right at work for their own purposes and profit. There are just so many curious relationships among a lot of people, and various institutes and entities. And I think that that deserves thorough investigation. All these relationships should really be looked into."

"That's a scary quote," Hannity said. "That is a chilling quote, a threatening quote. The very thing she was accusing people of is the very thing she and her husband were guilty of." Hannity continued, "They're the ones who investigate and attack other people. Go talk to Kathleen Willey, or Paula Jones, or Gennifer Flowers, or Monica Lewinsky, or Dick Morris, or any number of critics of the Clintons, and you'll see that if someone dares oppose them, that person can expect some type of retribution."

Eagle Forum's Phyllis Schlafly agreed. "Yes, I think it was a threat," she said of Hillary's comments. Mrs. Clinton was declaring that "the right-wingers were doing something that was criminal and secret and she could use the power of government to investigate it."

Congressman Dan Burton, whose House Government Reform and Oversight Committee investigated the Clintons, certainly feels he was targeted for reprisals. "They sent people out that were not officials but people sent out as investigators for the White House, and they went through everything I did," he told us in an interview. "They went through tax records, real estate, they even called, I believe, the captain of my golf team. They also went after me, saying I tried to solicit an illicit contribution and twist some guy's arm that used to be head of the DCCC [Democratic Congressional Campaign Committee] and also worked for the Carter administration for a $5,000 contribution." Burton gave us more examples but asked that they remain confidential because of their personal nature. "The reason I'm telling you this story is that they were merciless. I had to spend over $100,000 on two lawyers to make sure I wasn't railroaded."

For *The American Spectator*'s R. Emmett Tyrrell Jr., who was intimately involved in the investigation of so many Clinton scandals, Hillary's comments came straight out of the Clinton playbook. "They manage," he told us, "to diminish the charges against them to the lowest level of personal aggrandizement by those leveling the charges—'They're doing it for jobs, they're doing it for money, they're doing it for their careers.' They manage to divert the attention from the Clintons to that guy, always to the motive of the messenger. They're always slaying the messenger."

Sean Hannity saw in Hillary's threat frightening implications for the future. "It's a reminder of what we're dealing with, and I think it ought to be a motivation for those of us who believe in freedom of the press and free speech, of what we would be up against should Hillary Clinton become the president."

THE CONSPIRACY BELL RINGS, AND THE NEWS HOUNDS BARK

When Mrs. Clinton called for journalists to hunt down the "great story" of a vast conservative conspiracy, they obliged with an enthusiasm that surely brought beaming smiles of satisfaction to "great Americans" like James Carville and Sidney Blumenthal.

That night, *CBS Evening News* listed a handful of Ken Starr's alleged conflicts of interest in the Clinton investigation. Reporter Phil Jones made sure the right wing was described with extreme adjectives: "Hillary Clinton linked Starr to a conspiracy that has even suggested the president was involved in the murder of a former campaign worker. . . . It is Starr's past and continuing connections with *very conservative* organizations and causes that have brought him into the crosshairs of the First Family. As their evidence they point to his very appointment as independent counsel by a three-judge panel headed by Judge David Sentelle, who is a close ally of *ultraconservative* North Carolina senators Jesse Helms and Lauch Faircloth."

Dan Rather had already been banging the conspiracy can before Hillary started her cycle of interviews. On the night before Hillary hit NBC, Rather announced, "A CBS News/*New York Times* poll indicates a majority, 51 percent of Americans, feel the president's political enemies are *more to blame than he is* for creating the current situation." (This underlined another trend that the networks unloaded all year: regular poll questions asking the public to question the motivations and competence of Starr. They never dreamed of asking the public to assess the job of Reagan's supposedly spotless Iran-Contra prosecutor, Lawrence Walsh.)

Ted Koppel's *Nightline,* which couldn't find Whitewater for 688 days after the scandal broke, would air two Hillary-pleasing programs within a week, one on the motives and methods of Starr, and another on the tentacles of the "far right."

CNN, by this time run by Bill Clinton's friend Rick Kaplan, was especially friendly to the VRWC trend. Kaplan leapt into action at CNN with two-hour specials attacking any and all Clinton critics. The programs included "Media Madness," which asked the media on behalf of the public, "What the hell are you people doing" probing Bill Clinton's sex life? "Investigating the Investigator" came next, which described Ken Starr as "suspect" over his "religious and Republican roots." In May, Kaplan devoted an hour to demonizing Congressman Dan Burton, whom reporter Bruce Morton compared to English despot Oliver Cromwell.

NBC's Lisa Myers was the only network reporter on VRWC night who put a little brake on the First Lady's bandwagon, calling the charge a "favorite Clinton tactic" and labeling Starr one of the "so-called chief conspirators."

The Clinton strategy was to refocus the debate from Bill Clinton to Kenneth Starr; from a discussion of the president's legal and moral problems to a discussion of Republican dirty tricks; from a legal crisis to a political war. And the press went along gleefully. The news magazines prominently featured the war theme on their covers the next Monday. "The Secret Sex Wars," screamed *Newsweek*. "Starr at War," blared *Time*. Inside, the magazines lent credence to Hillary Clinton's bizarre charge of a vast right-wing conspiracy by publishing graphs detailing links between Starr and different figures and groups in the conservative movement. Oddly, with an O.J. Simpson trial link, *Newsweek* included former LAPD officer Mark Fuhrman in their anti-Clinton conspiracy graph. Big Tobacco was linked through tobacco lobbyist Bill Hecht helping Linda Tripp get a job in the first Bush White House.

When we asked Rush Limbaugh about his reaction to Hillary's "vast right-wing conspiracy" bombshell, he zeroed in on the response of the elite media, or the "drive-by media," as he calls them. "I thought it was hilarious, because what it spawned . . . is the drive-by media then doing exhaustive examination reports on the existence of the vast right-wing conspiracy and how it works." He added that "they actually did stories on how there is [a conspiracy]," because that's how elite journalists think: "They all think there is one, anyway."

Dispatches with this tone erupted all year long, many from Dan Rather, who announced typically on April 2, "On another front, there could be trouble for the Ken Starr Whitewater investigation. Reports continue to surface that this key witness for the prosecution, David Hale, may have been secretly bankrolled by political activists widely regarded as Clinton opponents, people that Clinton supporters call Republican haters from the far right."

Haters. It was a word millions of Americans would hear applied to Clinton's opposition over and over again throughout the presidency. *Republican haters. Clinton-haters.* Bill Clinton had his detractors, to be sure, and many conservatives couldn't stand him—just as many liberals disliked Ronald Reagan with every fiber of *their* being. So if *hater* was an appropriate adjective to apply to Clinton's critics, wouldn't it follow that a dispassionate press would apply this term as much to liberals during the Reagan era? To find out, the Media Research Center used the Nexis news data-retrieval system to find all mentions of the term *Clinton-hater* compared with the term *Reagan-hater* in *Newsweek, Time, U.S. News & World Report,* the *New York Times,* and the *Washington Post.* For Reagan, we reviewed stories from 1981 through 1988; for Clinton, from 1992 through mid-April 1998. These publications contained sixty-three uses of *Clinton-hater.* We found just one use of *Reagan-hater.* When the target was Reagan, every investigation (and critic) was idealistic, motivated only by the noble pursuit of justice. When the target was the Clintons, every investigation was cynical, hurtful, with "haters" out to destroy their opposition for political gain.

The Clinton marriage was beginning to look like the ugly highway accident it is, with President Clinton careening from one sexual "mis-understanding" to the next, but that's not how the press saw things. Reporters continued to embarrass themselves by insisting that the Clin-ton marriage was fraught with romance and passion.

Beginning his career as a Clinton courtier in 1992, Sidney Blumen-thal boldly declared in *The New Republic,* "While George Bush—all whiteness—talks about 'family values,' the Clintons demonstrate them by confessing to adultery." (Hearing this quote, columnist Cal Thomas laughed. "If confessing adultery is pro–family values, then I guess a con-victed murderer who confesses on the stand could be said to be pro-life.") The next year, *Time* White House reporter Margaret Carlson rapturously declared the Clintons so much more loving and carnal than those repressed Bushes. In both *Time* and *Vanity Fair,* Carlson set the stage: "Finally alone, they . . . exchange gifts and touch each other more in two hours than the Bushes did in four years." It just couldn't get better for the Clintons than this: a media demanding their infidelities not be investigated while simultaneously gushing over their marital fidelities.

In March 1998, *Newsweek's* Karen Breslau and Matt Cooper (mar-ried to Clinton spin controller Mandy Grunwald, the first paid TV dis-misser of the Gennifer Flowers story) embarrassed themselves with paragraphs of absurdity. After repeating Hillary's mantra that "the only people who count in any marriage are the two that are in it," they proclaimed, "There is a simple alchemy to their relationship: she's goofy, flat-out in love with him and he with her. 'They don't kiss. They devour each other,' says one aide. He needs her—for intellectual solace, political guidance and spiritual sustenance." The *Newsweek* duo wasn't done: "Clinton-haters"—here we go again—"and even some supporters wonder whether their marriage will end with the presidency. That seems wildly unlikely. Neither Clinton plans to trade in a public career for shuffleboard. As long as they're in the limelight, their turbulent partnership seems certain to endure—for better or worse. That's because they see themselves in almost Messianic terms, as great leaders who have a mission to fulfill."

For conservatives—and anyone else who has watched this couple over time—this is sheer nonsense, so outrageously inaccurate as to be a parody of the "news" media. "[Bill and Hillary] don't behave that way, never have," Mark Levin declared emphatically in our interview. "[These journalists] wrote that knowing full well that Bill Clinton is a serial adulterer who may well have forced himself upon at least one woman." As for Hillary, she "doesn't behave that way. She's not a very passionate person unless she's yelling at somebody, so that's just pure propaganda."

Cal Thomas agreed. "This is a marriage of enablement. . . . I think Hillary knew, cynicism notwithstanding, that there was no way she could get to the top without Bill, and for Bill there was no way he could become president without Hillary remaining supportive during all of his extramarital affairs."

In midsummer 1998, NBC's love affair with Hillary Clinton had another rendezvous. On July 16, the aggressively fawning Maria Shriver presented *Today* show viewers with a taped Hillary interview from a tour bus promoting historic sites, but instead of focusing on museums, Shriver smothered the First Lady with accolades. "Four states, ten or eleven stops! Four days! This is a real commitment for you. What do you get out of that? It is exhausting, it seems to me." And "Do you feel physically, emotionally, spiritually different when you get out of Washington, get on the road?"

Shriver steered clear of any hint of a controversy: "You and I spoke right at the beginning of this second term. Now with two years left, is it something you look forward to? Do you get out there and say, 'I want to keep going out, I want to meet people, I have more stuff I want to do?' Or do you look and go, 'Oh, my gosh, two more years'?"

But what about the next job? Shriver wanted to know. "There's so much speculation now about what you're going to do, what Hillary Clinton's life is going to be like after the presidency. Do you find that that takes away from what you're trying to do? Or do you just, like, slough it off or take a look at it?" Mrs. Clinton denied any ambitions.

Shriver wanted the First Lady to know how terribly misunderstood she was. "See, I talked to several people, and they came up to me and said, 'You know, she's so different than I thought she would be. She's so much more of a people person. She's funny. She's nice.' Do you think that people, like, don't get you? I mean, you get out there—you get out there and people see a different side of you." Hillary could only respond in kind: "People tell me that all the time, you know?"

THE TRUTH GOES AGAINST HILLARY, BUT THE JOURNALISTS DON'T

The ground really began to shake for the Clintons on July 30, when ABC reported that Monica Lewinsky indeed possessed a blue dress that could have President Clinton's bodily fluids on it. When President Clinton was finally forced by DNA evidence to admit an affair with Lewinsky, and as a consequence his false testimony, again the networks came to Hillary's side.

For the most part, they channeled the ridiculous story that Hillary was surprised and crushed just days before Clinton's testimony to learn the Lewinsky story was—gasp!—true. Almost nobody believed that. As *Newsweek* reported, "Only 11 percent of Americans believe that Hillary Clinton found out about her husband's affair just days before his speech; 84 percent think she had known for some time."

And yet that bizarre story was accepted by those same reporters who liked to portray themselves as hard-boiled skeptics, people who boast of goofy slogans like "If your mother says she loves you, check it out." It was at this point that pro-Clinton reporters looked truly ridiculous, impossibly dim, and naïve beyond belief—if they truly believed what they were saying, and writing.

You could actually hear journalists on television trying to talk themselves into this fatuous story. On the talk show *Inside Washington*, *Newsweek*'s Evan Thomas was lining up with the hard-core 11 percent of Kool-Aid drinkers: "I couldn't believe it when I first read that she didn't hear about it till Thursday. It seemed improbable to me, because she's so smart and because she's been here before. But I am beginning to believe it now. I mean, our reporting indicates that she, it sounds implausible, but marriages are complicated things and she may have just willfully decided she didn't need to hear it straight from Clinton and Clinton may have held out to the last minute before telling her."

On August 14, just three days before Bill Clinton testified before Ken Starr's deputies and committed perjury on the Monica Lewinsky matter, ABC, CBS, and NBC all filed sympathetic Hillary profiles. NBC's Andrea Mitchell defied reality in her ode to the First Lady. "Politician, strategist, lawyer, protector—in a marriage that friends say is based on brutal honesty and unconditional love." *Brutal honesty?* If Hillary really, really didn't know, then Bill really, really had lied to his wife. If Hillary did know, she had helped him lie to America. *Unconditional love?* Mitchell asserted, "Close friends say she knew everything from Day One and still went on NBC in January to deny all." What a trouper.

Wait a minute. If we are to believe she advanced her husband's dishonesty out of marital loyalty, it follows that she had conjured up that vicious "vast right-wing conspiracy" distraction for the same reason. And that charge, like her husband's denial, was also a falsehood. But Mitchell ignored it all and instead jumped to offer her sympathies. "So how does she cope? What other wife would tolerate so much embarrassment? Two clues to Hillary Clinton's character: friends say she is deeply religious and incredibly angry, blaming Ken Starr, not her husband."

ABC's Juju Chang joined in on *World News Tonight*, with more Orwellian journalism focusing on how Hillary's "unflinching loyalty has earned her a new level of respect" in high approval ratings. "Hillary Clinton has used her fierce determination, which used to be seen as a negative, to turn what could have been a humiliating experience into a position of strength."

CBS followed suit, also finding a way to blame Republicans for the Clintons' now-documented dishonesty. Reporter Eric Engberg opened by noting, "Hillary Clinton has made it clear publicly and repeatedly that she does not regard herself as the wife betrayed. As the subpoenas, allegations, and whispers have piled up against her husband, Mrs. Clinton has grown more steadfast in asserting he's a victim of a political vendetta. At a glitzy fundraiser on New York's Hamptons, she ridiculed the scandal culture of Washington." Engberg said that Hillary now blamed the scandal on a bias against "our state" of Arkansas, even though, he noted, ahem, she's from Illinois. Engberg concluded by emphasizing public support: "A new CBS News poll shows she's viewed favorably two-to-one." The only people quoted in the story were Hillary herself and friends or admirers of the First Lady.

In our interview, Mark Levin dismissed Engberg ("a well-known lefty") and denounced this kind of journalism ("obviously propaganda, not reporting"), but Cal Thomas saw a deeper problem. "It's one thing to confess and say 'I was wrong' according to biblical and other standards that have lasted for thousands of years," Thomas explained. "It's quite another thing to say, 'It's part of a conspiracy to get me; I'll play the victim.' That's not repentance. That's spin." But it's spin that has succeeded—with devastating cultural results. "Now society only disapproves of those who disapprove of behavior of which they *used* to disapprove," Thomas remarked. The only moral stand is against moralists.

Sean Hannity commented, "The Clintons could be caught redhanded on tape committing an armed robbery, and I believe a large percentage of the public would come up with some excuse to justify their support for the Clintons. For years I've called these people 'Clinton Kool-Aid Drinkers.'"

MAKING LEMONADE OUT OF SCANDAL LEMONS

The media's bouquets to Hillary kept flying as Bill Clinton's lies finally caught up with him. On August 17, the day Kenneth Starr's team questioned President Clinton on Lewinsky, CBS's Bill Plante declared on the August 17 *Evening News*, "Bill Clinton stands to be embarrassed by what he says today, but Hillary Rodham Clinton stands to be humiliated." He showed the January *Today* interview and proffered the ridiculous notion that "[f]riends of Mrs. Clinton say that she probably didn't know back then whether Lewinsky's story was true. Now, however, sources say the First Lady is aware her husband is changing his story." Eric Engberg chimed in before the president's posttestimony speech, "Had she not done her job so well, it's not likely the president would have stood up so well in the opinion polls." Engberg noted that the new family counselor, the Reverend Jesse Jackson (who, we would learn later, was well versed in matters of infidelity), "pointed to the fact that Hillary Clinton took part in strategy sessions at the White House as further evidence of her grace and devotion. Referring to the president, he said, 'The good news for Bill Clinton in this is that he learned that Hillary's love is unconditional.'"

Over on NBC on August 17, Andrea Mitchell backed off her talk of Hillary knowing everything from Day One. "Friends say she's known all along something happened, but no details, so chose to believe her husband's early denials." So much for that "brutal honesty."

Have you noticed the common denominator here, how heavily these reports relied on cheery "friends say" testimonials? In *Newsweek,* a prominent caption was emblazoned over a photo of Hillary whispering in Bill's ear as she holds him with both hands: "Friends scoff at theories that the Clintons' marriage is a sham, saying that the affection and intimacy the Clintons display in private can't be faked." But they didn't note that it was also those anonymous "friends" who said the marriage was peachy and blissful and love-drenched over and over again in Bill-and-Hillary stories starting in 1992.

The wave of media affection crested again with the September 9 delivery to Capitol Hill of a truck holding thirty-six boxes comprising the Starr Report listing of impeachable offenses. (NBC's Gwen Ifill called it a "truck bomb" and "a very violent action.") The drums of impeachment were pounding, and though Hillary was ruthlessly orchestrating a White House campaign to smear her husband's critics and had been a coperpetrator of seven months of lies, NBC chose to praise the First Lady for what the network considered a remarkable performance in the role of wronged spouse.

On the September 11 *Today*, cohost Matt Lauer enthused to *Newsweek* writer Jonathan Alter, "Extraordinary performance from the First Lady in the last couple of days. Last night she introduced her husband. . . . Here's what she said with her husband sitting right next to her." Viewers watched the "extraordinary" clip: "I know that all of you are proud of what has been achieved in this administration, and I'm very proud of the person I'm privileged to introduce. I'm proud of his leadership. I'm proud of his commitment. I'm proud of what he gives our country and all of us every day by his commitment. And I'm proud to introduce my husband and our president, Bill Clinton." At least Lauer noted what couldn't be said: "Very supportive, but dealing only with the professional. She certainly didn't say, 'I'm proud of what he's done to our family.'"

That night, Tom Brokaw continued the charade: "Still ahead tonight, NBC News In Depth. How's she coping with this personal betrayal? . . . The First Lady, caught up in the President's lies. Now where does she turn?" Andrea Mitchell played a clip of a minister at a prayer breakfast praising Hillary's grace and courage, adding, "Enough grace and courage to be her husband's chief cheerleader at a political event last night." Mitchell worried, "How can she carry on now that the entire nation can learn the sexual details?" She answered with "friends and former aides who have been with the First Lady," including former Hillary spokesperson Lisa Caputo, and Mandy Grunwald, the Gennifer Flowers attacker.

Jane Pauley picked up on Mitchell's theme the next night in a two-hour *Dateline* special titled "The President and the People." Pauley dutifully endorsed the 11 percent Hillary-was-oblivious view, claiming that Hillary unquestioningly accepted her husband's denials: "She had believed his denials and indeed last January, as she told the *Today* show's Matt Lauer, he seemed to take for granted that she wouldn't believe everything she read in the papers. . . . Then silence. As the investigation turned up the heat on friends and colleagues, even as he testifies under oath before a grand jury, she says nothing. Balancing a threat to her marriage against the assault on his presidency, she does what she does best, she goes to work."

After noting the irony that the woman who said in 1992 she was no

Tammy Wynette just standing by her man, now was doing precisely that, Pauley spun it back in Hillary's favor: "Once vilified for ambition and political overreaching when she took on health care, now she's admired for being the faithful, loving wife."

What the media didn't know (because they refused to investigate) or did know (and refused to report) was that maybe, just maybe, Hillary was far from being that shocked, wronged victim. They refused to entertain the far more plausible theory that rather than being a clueless First Defender who hadn't figured out what all of America had come to learn over the years—her husband was a serial philanderer—Hillary had known, and allowed, the infidelities, and then callously defended her husband by slandering his opponents.

Some Clinton experts suspect that she knew exactly how much fidelity she would get as a wife before she was married. In his Clinton biography *First in His Class*, *Washington Post* reporter David Maraniss told the story of Hillary Clinton's decision to send her father and brothers from Illinois to Arkansas in the spring of 1974 during Clinton's campaign for Congress, about a year and a half before their wedding. "One of the worst-kept secrets at headquarters was that Clinton had become involved in an intense relationship with a young woman volunteer. . . . Aside from the Fayetteville woman, the staff also knew that Clinton had girlfriends in several towns around the district and in Little Rock. Perhaps they could disregard his rambunctious private life, but could Hillary? There was some suspicion that one of the reasons she sent the men in her family to Arkansas was to put a check on her boyfriend's activities." Maraniss also explained about their wedding: "She understood his talents and his flaws. He might not be faithful, but together they could be faithful to their larger mission in life."

"She's the Person of the Year"

Regardless of what Hillary had really known about Bill's infidelity or how she might have lied to the American people right along with her husband, the confession of the Lewinsky affair proved to be a turning point for Mrs. Clinton. Perhaps spooked by the feeling that Bill Clinton's best days might now lie behind him, the media boosters began to buzz about a topic that until then had been rarely and only obliquely discussed in the national press: Hillary's own bright political future.

On the December 3 *Larry King Live* on CNN, Dan Rather began the Vote for Hillary campaign. First he declared his passionate hatred for the Lewinsky story: "I have hated it from the very beginning and I have hated it right through. . . . I have no apology. I hate it. I have hated it all the way through." Then the man who asked the president in 1993 to "tell Mrs. Clinton we respect her and we're pulling for her" showed he was still pulling for her five years later. He told King that she should be *Time*'s "Person of the Year," and perhaps much more: "I would not be astonished to see Hillary Clinton be the Democratic nominee in 2000. . . . Here we are talking about a race almost two years away. Hillary Clinton, as far as I'm concerned, she's the Person of the Year. . . . You talk about a comeback kid. She makes her husband look like Ned in knee pants in terms of comeback from where she was early in the Clinton administration. You know, you add it all up, and you can make a case that Hillary Clinton might, might—mark the word—be the strongest candidate for the Democrats."

This was among the earliest detailed public discussions of Hillary's aspirations and opportunities for national office. Many more would follow.

Even when media figures weren't stumping for Hillary, they were helping her cause by blocking out the ugly parts of her record. Two years after his famous interview with Mrs. Clinton, Matt Lauer was a puppy dog again. He told *USA Weekend* in 2000 that he didn't believe Hillary had been deliberately lying to him in that conversation. He was sure of what he saw in her face: "She was in denial, hoping against hope. Absolutely." He expressed great pride in how he handled that show. "I heard through the grapevine she felt it was a good interview for both of us. That's the best kind of interview. You don't want to feel like you crushed someone, or they crushed you. That interview gave us both something to walk away with."

Huh? But wasn't it Lauer's goal—his journalistic responsibility—to get at the truth? Hillary Clinton had used his show to deny her husband's guilt while defaming conservatives everywhere with her shrill and ugly charge of a "vast right-wing conspiracy." On both counts she was wrong: she was either seconding a lie knowingly or forwarding a falsehood of her own without checking. Where was even the whisper of a suggestion that she needed to apologize? Instead, we are to believe, this was the essence of "a good interview."

Chapter 10
"Queen of the World"

[W]e are in the middle of a primal American saga and the important part is yet to come. Bill Clinton may be merely the prequel, the President of lesser moment—except, so to speak, as the horse she rode in on. . . . I think I see a sort of Celtic mist forming around Hillary as a new archetype (somewhere between Eleanor and Evita, transcending both) at a moment when the civilization pivots, at last, decisively—perhaps for the first time since the advent of Christian patriarchy two millenniums ago—toward Woman.

—*Time* magazine essayist LANCE MORROW, July 12, 1999

If you look at all of them, they came out of the same culture. They're all baby boomers, they're all children of the sixties. All were part of the East Coast elite, either the intellectual left elite or the moneyed liberal elite. They basically came out of the same gene pool, so why wouldn't you expect them to think alike, act alike, walk alike? They're essentially interchangeable. Hillary Clinton might as well have been Katie Couric's long-lost sister, or one who was switched at the hospital.

—CRAIG SHIRLEY on the media-Democrat complex,
in an interview with the authors

E ven as her husband faced impeachment, Hillary Clinton's own political standing grew stronger. In fact, while the president's impeachment was being tried in the United States Senate, the whispers about
her soon joining that august body became roars. And only weeks after
the trial ended, ABC's Barbara Walters was able to offer this glowing
tribute in a special titled "A Celebration: 100 Years of Great Women":
"Hillary Clinton has found her own approval ratings soaring," even
though Walters was quick to point out that "no First Lady has been more
investigated or scrutinized."

The serious scrutiny Walters referred to (but, of course, did not
examine any further) came not from the major media but usually from
the alternative media and congressional committees. This was all in the
past, in the eyes of the so-called mainstream media, who wanted to celebrate Hillary's triumph over her sinister opponents. The coverage of the
Clinton impeachment saga was a good example. The Center for Media
and Public Affairs studied evening-news coverage from September to
December of 1998 and found that nearly every figure in the Monica
Lewinsky scandal drew negative coverage. Ken Starr drew just 13 percent
positive coverage and 87 percent negative; Lewinsky had a similar count
of 14 percent to 86; both Bill Clinton and his White House team drew
37 percent positive coverage, 63 percent negative; congressional Republicans had a 28/72 split. The one exception to this rule? Hillary Clinton.
Her evaluations were *96 percent positive.*

It wasn't only the evening-news programs. On December 9, as the
House Judiciary Committee was hearing the last White House defense
against impeachment, *Today*'s Katie Couric presented a sugary pretaped
interview with the Clintons in which she talked about how popular the
First Lady had been during a recent trip to New York: "Everywhere you
went you got such an incredibly positive response. That's sort of an early
Christmas gift. Are you grateful or gratified by that display of affection
that you really see wherever you go now?"

On a December 28 CBS special, "The *Ladies' Home Journal* Most Fascinating Women of '98," *60 Minutes* reporter Lesley Stahl praised Hillary
for standing by her man: "Why were we so riveted by her performance?

Was it that we expected to see her crumble, cry, agonize? And how do we explain her spike in popularity in the face of her husband's scandal? Part of it was surely sympathy, maybe even pity, and she became more human, more vulnerable. There's also something appealing about her loyalty, her standing by her man, and the dignity with which she has comported herself. We are all grateful for grace in the midst of disgrace."

Nothing is more presumptive than the media's use of the royal *we* to describe what is supposed to be general consensus. *We* were not riveted by her performance, though surely her defense of her husband's innocence was certainly that. *We* did not find dignity in her slash-and-burn politics. *We* did not see grace in her dishonest attempts to introduce a "conspiracy" undermining the White House. And *we* were not grateful for her efforts to malign conservatives as a way of distracting the public from the corruption of her husband's administration.

The *we* in Stahl's paean was the media whose ardor for praising Hillary never waned.

The media never seemed to care that it was Hillary who kicked off a seven-month avalanche of lies by pointing the finger at the "vast right-wing conspiracy." They didn't care that the White House Stonewaller-in-Chief was Hillary more than Bill. They didn't mind that Hillary lied about her Rose Law Firm income and then had those documents shredded, or hidden in the homes of her law partners. They didn't care about evidence showing that Hillary was the force behind firing the Travel Office staff, and the personal destruction of the innocent Billy Dale with a bunch of phony charges of fraud. They didn't mind Hillary giving one fanciful explanation after another (but never the truth) about how she came to make $100,000 in the commodities market virtually overnight. They ignored testimony that it was Hillary who hired Craig Livingstone, the bar-bouncer-turned-librarian of the Republicans' FBI files. None of this mattered to the media. *There's also something appealing about her loyalty . . . and the dignity with which she has comported herself. We are all grateful for grace in the midst of disgrace.*

Just look at *Time* magazine's syrupy year-end article titled "The Better Half: During her husband's greatest crisis, Hillary has come into her own." The title was superimposed over a flattering black-and-white photo of Hillary with a steely look, and the word "Better" was in red for emphasis. In the article, reporters Karen Tumulty and Nancy Gibbs cast the First Lady as a visionary leader: "All through the year, as she pursued the private rescue of a marriage and the public rescue of a presidency, she was the one person who seemed to see the larger story and shaped its telling." The larger story, presumably, was that this was all about Ken Starr and not Bill Clinton—and she shaped its telling by inventing a conspiracy. All this was praiseworthy?

Tumulty and Gibbs added that when the president's confession "finally confronted her and us with the truth" *(finally?)*, "she led the way, from denial through fury to a grudging acceptance." And here we go again with that royal *we*—"The code was always clear: if she can stand by him, she who has been so directly wronged, so should we. . . . She was his salesman, but also our surrogate." They even employed the saccharine spin that the train-wreck Clinton marriage was "a shortcut for two stars in a hurry to reach heaven."

In that same issue of *Time*, the magazine's managing editor, Walter Isaacson, wrote about how much he and his staff had wanted to choose Hillary as Person of the Year: "For a while . . . she was our leading contender. Her strength and her almost surreal ability to assert her dignity were remarkable to some and mystifying to others. She also, for many months, helped determine how the nation framed the scandal debate by portraying it as a partisan battle and disgusting prosecutorial invasion of personal privacy. . . . Sentimentally, a lot of us wanted to [choose her]; I personally was fascinated and impressed by her."

The year-end issue of *Newsweek* pondered Hillary's future with two experts. Talk about stacking the deck. It wasn't so much a story as a transcribed chitchat between two loyal partisans, her historian friend Doris Kearns Goodwin, who was one of the many Clinton pals who stayed overnight in the Lincoln Bedroom, and her former press flack Lisa Caputo. Caputo claimed, "I think it's safe to say that no matter what she chooses to do, there will continue to be a public fascination with Hillary Clinton. . . . She represents so much of what people mean when they talk about the role of women in modern life. And the interest in her will remain alive well after she leaves the White House." Goodwin agreed, making the inevitable Eleanor Roosevelt comparisons, and concluding, "For Mrs. Clinton, too, the richest chapters may still lie ahead."

With such overwhelmingly positive press coverage—*96 percent!*—is it any wonder that Hillary's prospects looked so bright?

"The Abuse and Mistreatment of Women"

It's a good thing Hillary had the media on her side, because still another scandal emerged in 1999 that threatened her blossoming political career. Early in the year, Juanita Broaddrick, a former Clinton supporter, and previously known to the press as "Jane Doe #5," had stepped forward to confirm to NBC's Lisa Myers that in 1978 she had been brutally raped by then–Arkansas attorney general Bill Clinton. But NBC sat on the interview for five weeks until the impeachment trial fizzled. Finally Broaddrick gave her story to the *Wall Street Journal*'s Dorothy Rabinowitz, who published it on the editorial page on February 19. Later that day, in a brief press event with three questions allowed to U.S. reporters, no one asked President Clinton a single question about Broaddrick.

Six days later, NBC finally relented to public outrage and presented Broaddrick's emotional testimony and the Myers investigation that placed Broaddrick and Clinton in the same hotel on April 25, 1978. The evidence was as incriminating as the details were horrifying. How did the public react? A *USA Today*/CNN poll found that fully 66 percent of Americans found the rape allegation to be "no big deal," perhaps because 54 percent of them didn't believe Juanita Broaddrick. But look a bit more deeply into that same survey and another number appears: 44 percent of the public, almost one-half of those polled, had never heard of the story. In other words, that survey was useless. Nevertheless, the media used the "no big deal" results to justify not covering the story. Polling expert John McLaughlin, the founder of McLaughlin Associates, told us that this survey was an example of how pollsters can "manufacture polls to create outcomes they want to happen. They manufactured that result to say, basically, 'Nobody cares, so we're not going to cover this.'" Republican strategist Frank Donatelli dismissed this poll altogether: "It would be like asking people who don't intend to vote if they have an opinion on the presidential race."

MSNBC conducted another survey. It asked people *who were familiar with the report* to call in and register their opinions. An astonishing 30,000 called. Eighty-four percent believed Juanita Broaddrick's story; only 16 percent were swayed by Bill Clinton's "denial"—an interesting observation given that Clinton had yet to publicly deny it.

Broaddrick's story was indeed credible, as Craig Shirley of Shirley & Banister Public Affairs, who has been in the public relations field for more than thirty years and knows the press well, explained when we interviewed him. "This woman comes forward with a credible story about a president who has already established a pattern of serial bad behavior toward women," Shirley noted. Her story was even more credible in that she had turned down many interview requests over the years: "She didn't just come out of the woodwork in 1999. Reporters had been hounding her for years because they had heard the rumors, and she had turned them down. So this wasn't a woman who was seeking the limelight, but someone who was shunning it."

Sean Hannity flew to Arkansas and spent a number of hours with Broaddrick, interviewing her for his radio show. "You can't spend time with this woman as I did," he told us, "and not walk away realizing you have just spoken with a very, very credible person." Broaddrick was "smart, poised, calm—and told one of the most horrific stories you could ever hear about a man's mistreatment of a woman. [She was] brutalized." Hannity found the interview "brutal. It was very difficult to hear. Anybody who has a wife, a sister, a daughter, a mother . . ." His voice trailed off momentarily. "It breaks your heart."

Ann Coulter pulled no punches. "Bill Clinton is a rapist and should be in prison."

If members of the national media were among the 84 percent who believed this woman's story, then they believed that President William Jefferson Clinton was a rapist, and an extraordinarily savage one at that. Just the image of him biting down on this poor woman's lip while he violated her . . . Broaddrick in shock, her face bloodied and swollen, her underwear torn to shreds . . . Clinton nonchalantly putting on his sunglasses while dismissing the victim's agony with "You better put some ice on that" . . . If that doesn't make you sick, then check your heart for a pulse.

If the media did believe the Broaddrick story, they nonetheless ran from it. *Time* ran only a one-page article on Broaddrick's rape charge, in which the writer, Adam Cohen, noted that the "vociferously conservative" *Wall Street Journal* editorial page had printed it first and argued that "the story seems unlikely to have much traction." In *Newsweek,* the only mention of Broaddrick came in the snippy "Conventional Wisdom Watch" feature. The "CW" writer—usually wisecracking Jonathan Alter ("the son the Clintons never wanted," quipped Craig Shirley)—called Broaddrick simply by her Starr Report name, "Jane Doe 5," and declared, "Should have leveled (unproven) assault charge in '78, or '92. But sounds like our guy."

Sounds like our guy? "Callous, callous," said *National Review*'s Kate O'Beirne when we asked for her response. "He had decided Bill Clinton was a lovable rogue with an eye for the ladies. So, rape? *Come on.*" Coulter was simply disgusted: "Mrs. Broaddrick was violated twice. Once by Bill Clinton, and again by Jonathan Alter." Hannity was incredulous and saw hypocrisy in the dismissiveness: "Aren't liberals the ones who are always telling us there's a reason why women don't come forward with allegations of rape?"

So while the media were ignoring what should have been an explosive revelation, what were they focusing on? The covers of *Time* and *Newsweek* tell the story. The issues that arrived the Monday after NBC's Broaddrick segment featured as their cover subject . . . Hillary Clinton. *Time*'s cover read, "Senator Clinton?" and featured a painting of a dignified, smiling Hillary in a black pantsuit. *Newsweek* was gushier: over a head shot of a twinkly, smiling Hillary, the cover read, "Her Turn: Senate or world stage? Either way, Hillary's ready for her own run at history."

Both magazines carried nine pages or more of heavy-breathing coverage. *Time*'s story was illustrated with a huge, flattering cartoon of Hillary standing over the New York skyline, large enough to dwarf King Kong. The headline read "A Race of Her Own: Hillary ignites the country with talk of a New York Senate bid. But will she do it, and with the media and maybe Rudy lying in wait—can she win?" *Newsweek*'s story had a two-page photo of a smiling Hillary handing back a child with the headline "Hillary's Day in the Sun: Now it's her turn. After a quarter century of standing by Bill Clinton—and rising to power with him—the First Lady is ready for a run of her own. Where will she make her mark? In the Senate or on the world stage? The road ahead is risky, but at the moment Mrs. Clinton is the hottest commodity in American public life." Even photo captions betrayed their enthusiasm: "At last, a role reversal. . . . Hillary's fierce devotion to service was forged early."

While the media rushed to cover Hillary as a rising political star, no reporter sought the First Lady's comment on the Broaddrick assault. They even stayed quiet on the Broaddrick subject when the White House was shameless enough to speak out on violence against women. On February 26, just two days after the NBC interview, Vice President Al Gore held a White House event on domestic violence in which he proclaimed, "Physical brutality at the hands of a partner or spouse is not simply love gone wrong, or someone needing to blow off steam at the end of the day. It is criminal assault, pure and simple. We don't do anybody any favors, least of all the abusers, when we ignore it." Then, on March 4, Hillary Clinton declared in a speech at the United Nations, "It is no longer acceptable to say that the abuse and mistreatment of women is cultural. It should be called what it is—criminal." Given that her own husband now stood accused of abuse on a monstrous scale, the connection should have been unavoidable. But nobody in the media cared.

The *Washington Times*'s Tony Blankley aptly summarized the situation when he said in our interview, "It was evidence of how supremely confident [Hillary Clinton] was that reporters would not do with her what they would do with virtually any other president's wife similarly situated."

ENDLESS FASCINATION WITH HILLARY

Just how enamored was the press with the prospect of a Hillary Clinton Senate campaign? The Center for Media and Public Affairs studied the evening news shows for the first five and a half months of 1999 and found that presidential candidate George W. Bush attracted 20 network stories. Presidential candidate Elizabeth Dole drew 14 stories. Presidential candidate Al Gore was the subject of 14 stories. But Hillary Clinton trounced them all, with 33, or almost the same as Bush and Gore combined. What does it say about the networks that they found her campaign more interesting, more important, than a presidential race?

The media didn't just cover the anticipated Senate race; media personalities all but fell at Hillary's feet. On March 12, cohost Diane Sawyer of ABC's *Good Morning America* replayed the spin from inside Hillary's camp: "She clearly hated being thought of as just Bill Clinton's wife. But ironically, it would take his scandals, finally, to free her. Finally, last November 1998, Hillary Clinton showed the world what she could do on the campaign trail without him. Political mastery, every bit as dazzling as his, the thoughtful speech, unapologetically strong, emboldening Democrats, electing senators. So her friends say she has really earned this campaign, this moment, if she chooses, earned it by changing herself, searching, stumbling, and at the end, by standing, not by her man, but by herself." As the Media Research Center's Brent Baker quipped at the time, "Hillary's Senate campaign won't have to produce a promotional video. They can just borrow Sawyer's."

Putting forward the sappiest tribute to Hillary became a competition. CNN's *Inside Politics* presented a daily Hillary update for weeks on end. One show began with her face superimposed on the Statue of Liberty, no less.

On April 1, *Washington Post* reporter Peter Baker grew rhapsodic in recounting the First Lady's trip to Africa and declared that she was too grand for the mere Senate. "Forget the Senate. Over the last 12 days, Hillary Rodham Clinton has looked and sounded more like a candidate for Secretary of State. There she was in Egypt, gently urging tolerance for the minority Coptic Christians. There she was in Tunisia, lashing out at Islamic radicals in other countries who oppress women. And here she was in Morocco, speaking out on everything from the Middle East peace process to the NATO air strikes in Yugoslavia."

But the *Post* reporter was worried. "How does a woman who eagerly told an audience this morning about education and economics in Guatemala and Uganda turn her attention to the pork-and-potholes issues that arise in places like Utica and Ithaca? How does a woman whose international profile is so high that bystanders in Africa two years ago referred to her as 'the queen of the world' adjust to becoming a low-ranking member of the seniority-conscious Senate?"

Queen of the World: now that's a job Hillary could embrace.

In May, after touring Macedonian refugee camps to commiserate with Kosovo's expelled masses while denouncing the "ethnic cleansing" policies of Slobodan Milosevic, Mrs. Clinton joined CNN's Christiane Amanpour for some televised girl talk. Amanpour preceded her question with a statement—a speech, really—that was as preposterous as it was shamelessly self-serving: "A lot of the women that I meet from traveling overseas are very impressed by you and admire your dignity. A lot of the people you meet are people who suffered, people you saw today, and who believe that they identify with you, because they have seen you suffer. And in a speech in Africa last year, you spoke about living for hope and reconciliation, living for forgiveness and reconstruction, and living for a new life." *(And now, the hook.)* "Have you been able to apply that to your own circumstances? Have you been able to forgive your husband?" It was a disgraceful performance by Amanpour, who one year before had married Jamie Rubin, the top State Department spokesman for the Clinton administration, but no one at CNN saw any appearance of partisanship.

Hillary Clinton credited her and Bill's "very strong" marriage in part to "our religious faith," certainly a peculiar religious faith in that it seemed to countenance her serial lying about his serial adultery.

Hillary continued with the devout-Christian line on May 24 in her interview with Dan Rather for *60 Minutes II,* the deceased show that will be remembered for its fierce and dishonest Bush-bashing. This segment, produced by Mary Mapes, that supposed hard-bitten investigator at the heart of the Memogate mess, was reserved for softballs.

Rather emptied his encomiums out like a waterfall: "Once a political lightning rod, today she is political lightning. A crowd-pleaser and first-class fundraiser, a person under enormous pressure to step into the arena. This time on her own." He also puffed, "Polls show she is one of the most admired women in America. But even after seven years in the spotlight, she remains a riddle for many people. It's hard to know what keeps her going through marital problems made public, political fights turned ugly, through triumphs, disasters, and always, the demands of her work. Tonight we get some answers about how she does it from the only person in the world who really knows."

The hard-nosed *60 Minutes* format was nowhere to be found during the interview. Rather did not ask about Hillary's role in a presidency filled with inflicting pain and suffering, inflicting cynicism on politics, showing contempt instead of gratitude for the democratic process that allowed her to be criticized. No, this time it would be pure *Oprah*. Rather asked probing questions like these:

- "We've talked about the possibility of you running for the Senate. You've said that you're obviously interested in it. What are the possibilities that one day, someday you'll run for president?"

- "Let's pretend for a moment it's 2050. There's an encyclopedia and it has a picture of Hillary Rodham Clinton, onetime first lady of the United States. What do you think the caption under that picture will be? . . . What would you like it to be?"

- "Of all the allegations, accusations, charges made, what do you consider to be the most unfair attack?"

At the end of the interview Rather said, "You mention you're a religious person. Did you find yourself praying more over the most difficult period?" This allowed Hillary to give a little sermon about how she survived her ordeals: "You can let it break you and embitter you, or you can take away whatever you've experienced, whatever pain or suffering, and decide you're still gonna have faith. You know, your faith in God, your faith in your fellow man, that you're still gonna believe that you can make a contribution to a better life. It's a choice. Every single day we wake up, you can choose to be cynical or hopeful. You can choose to be grateful or contemptuous. You can make all those choices. And for me, it's not a very hard choice."

Cue the tick-tick-tick closer.

The attempt to cash in on the victim status could go too far. On a Monday morning, August 2, ABC's *Good Morning America* promoted a Hillary Clinton cover story in the new *Talk* magazine, which was published by Miramax, an arm of the Disney company, which also owned ABC. Diane Sawyer asked *Talk* editor Tina Brown and Hillary's interviewer Lucinda Franks to elaborate on how Hillary had claimed in that interview that Bill's rough childhood, "scarred by abuse" from conflicts between his mother and grandmother, had caused his pattern of adultery. Sawyer didn't ask for a reality check. She cued up Brown and Franks to praise the Clintons' relationship. Franks claimed that Hillary's marriage was "quite wonderful in its, you know, in its interdependence of conversation, of ideas, of excitement, of chemistry, sexual chemistry."

Reflecting the softness of the *Talk* interview, Franks answered no when Sawyer asked, "Did you talk to her about any specific women and specific allegations? Kathleen Willey?" Franks justified the omission by saying that "ethically, as a journalist . . . this has been covered and covered and covered and covered," and that it would have been an "invasion of her privacy." Besides, "women would throw themselves at him. Even at Yale, I mean, he's a very handsome man, and he looked like a Beatle back in Yale, you can see pictures of him, I mean, he was gorgeous." It was a staggering statement. Kathleen Willey claimed that she was assaulted near the Oval Office by this allegedly gorgeous man, yet it was "ethically, as a journalist," wrong to raise this issue.

The other networks insisted that Hillary's *Talk* interview was "frank" and "candid." Only reporter Jim Angle, on Fox's *Special Report with Brit Hume*, pointed out the obvious: "The First Lady is now admitting a history of infidelity by Mr. Clinton, something that both of them have sought so often to deny." Wasn't that the real story, Hillary acknowledging that she had known for years—not learned only recently—that her husband was an unfaithful charlatan? Despite this knowledge of his adultery, she joined him in those public denials. But only Angle was willing to state any of this.

THE BUNGLED CLINTON PUERTO RICO TERRORIST PARDONS

Hillary's partisan press also supported her by silencing or downplaying other stories that could threaten her Senate campaign. On August 11, the Associated Press reported on Bill Clinton's decision to offer clemency to eleven members of a militant "Puerto Rican independence group if they sign agreements renouncing the use of violence. Their group staged some 130 bomb attacks on political and military targets in the United States from 1974 to 1983." The article quoted an administration official claiming that "the prisoners were not involved in any deaths." However, the article added that the group FALN "killed six people and wounded dozens" during that ten-year period.

This was a huge issue for Hillary Clinton's Senate campaign. The political facts of life in New York state politics are that a Democratic Senate candidate must carry New York City by a sufficiently wide margin to offset the Republican vote in upstate New York. To accomplish this, Hillary Clinton needed a strong inner-city minority turnout. Some 900,000 Puerto Ricans live in New York City. She needed them, specifically, and as with all things Clinton, ends justified means. As the *Washington Times* editorialized at the time, "Would anyone who has endured the past six years of the Clintons' gross political expediency, his and hers, be shocked—shocked!—to learn that the FALN pardons are expected to energize Puerto Ricans and other Hispanic voters?"

"It was perfectly timed to get the Puerto Rican vote in New York State," Phyllis Schlafly told us. Cal Thomas concurred: "This was another cynical misuse of the power of the presidency to advance the Clinton political and personal agenda." Floyd Brown, the founder of the conservative Citizens United, added, "The truth is that they would let murderers go free if it would help them and give them political advantage and help Hillary get elected."

Imagine the press reaction had either President Bush pardoned terrorists to help a family member's electoral chances. But this was Hillary Clinton. Network coverage on ABC, CBS, or NBC? Zero. Not even CNN, the twenty-four-hour cable news network, saw fit to report this, not even in a snippet. Only Fox did.

Even as the print press, to its credit, pursued this story, the TV news blackout continued:

• August 13: A *Wall Street Journal* editorial underlined the rarity of Clinton's offer: "From the time he took office in 1993 until April 2, the date the Office [of the pardon attorney at the Justice Department] prepared its last report, Mr. Clinton had received 3,042 petitions for clemency. Until Wednesday, he had granted a total of three." Big Three coverage? Zero.

• August 19: The *Washington Times* reported that the president of the Fraternal Order of Police had sent a letter to President Clinton in which he called the offer "a slap in the face" to all police officers. He also cited three New York City police officers who had been maimed in the FALN bomb attacks. Again, not a single mention in the broadcast media.

• August 23: The New York police commissioner, Howard Safir, held a press conference featuring police officers injured by FALN attacks to criticize Clinton's offer. Richard Pascarella, a blinded and retired NYPD detective, refused to hold back his fire, and unloaded: "This is really truly pandering to the Hispanic community, the Latino community, for their vote when Mrs. Clinton runs for the vacated seat of Patrick Moynihan in New York State." Another maimed detective, Anthony Senft, added, "I have a life sentence. I lost an eye. I have a severe case of vertigo. I lost 16 percent of hearing on one side and 40 on the other side." Big Three coverage? Nothing.

• August 27: The *New York Times* reported that before President Clinton made his decision, "a wide range of federal law enforcement agencies that were asked to review a clemency petition filed by imprisoned members of a Puerto Rican nationalist group unanimously opposed any leniency." Big Three coverage? Zero. This time CNN mentioned the story, briefly.

Finally, on Monday, August 30, the networks began to come to the story. Both CBS and NBC featured week-old footage in their pieces. Hillary Clinton had kept silent on the subject, tacitly signaling an endorsement of her husband's pardons, but now that the networks were on the beat, she stepped forward with a statement. On September 4— more than three weeks after the fact—she denounced the clemency offer, but with a trademark Clintonian twist: It wasn't that her husband's commutation offer was improper, it was that the prisoners had not renounced violence as a condition of the pardons. Oh, and one more thing: She hadn't had any idea her husband was going to do this. Once again, the scandal was someone else's fault.

Brit Hume couldn't believe the flip-flop. "Mrs. Clinton comes forward and says, I didn't know, my husband never told me, I didn't know," he said on *Fox News Sunday.* "And so, and now she gets to, and she's going to back out of the deal, expecting that first, we'll believe it was a clean thing the first time, and second, we'll believe that she didn't know anything about it. I can't imagine people being gullible enough to buy any of it."

But the networks did. On Friday, September 9, the House of Representatives voted 311 to 41, with about 70 Democrats voting "present" instead of standing with the Clintons, to condemn the clemency offer. Big Three coverage? Zero, even though ABC's and NBC's morning shows mentioned the next day that the Puerto Ricans would be released that day. CBS's *Saturday Morning* mentioned the release the next morning. On September 14, the Senate followed, voting 95 to 2 on a resolution calling Clinton's clemency offer "deplorable." Big Three coverage? Zero, except a sentence previewing the vote on *Nightline.*

On September 15, the Senate Judiciary Committee held hearings into Bill Clinton's clemency decision. It was criticized by senators from both parties, including committee chairman Orrin Hatch and liberal Democrat Robert Torricelli. Victims of the FALN's bombings spoke emotionally about their outrage over the release. How much ABC, CBS, and NBC coverage? Zero.

If the media knew of the age of terror to come, do you think they would have done more?

House Hunting with Millionaire Lobbyist Friends

Back in May 1997, the weekend chat shows had lit up with outrage. Former senator Bob Dole had agreed to lend money to House Speaker Newt Gingrich for a $300,000 ethics penalty assessed by the House. On CNN's *Late Edition,* journalist Steve Roberts noted Dole's job with a law firm lobbying on the tobacco settlement and asked, "Do we really want a speaker of the House who owes $300,000 to a guy who's a principal in a major lobbying firm?" On the TV show *Inside Washington, Newsweek's* Evan Thomas bemoaned that Dole had retired from public service to "become an influence peddler so he can post bail for Newt Gingrich."

If that outrage was valid then, where were those reporters in September 1999, when the Clintons accepted a much larger loan of $1.35 million to buy an address that would make Hillary a New Yorker? No one really wanted to discuss how the loan provider—political fixer, major fundraiser, and future Democratic Party chairman Terry McAuliffe—was under investigation in several parts of the government. No one wanted to ask whether Americans wanted a president who owed a million-plus to some lobbyist. Few cared to note that McAuliffe had provided the booty in cold, hard cash to evade any messy financial disclosure requirements. ABC and NBC said nothing in their newscasts. Diana Olick yawned through her story on the September 3 CBS *This Morning:* "The Clintons will put $350,000 down, the rest will be mortgaged, and that mortgage will be guaranteed by Terry McAuliffe, a veteran Democratic fundraiser. But the real value of the house is to Mrs. Clinton's potential Senate campaign."

On the staid network TV talk shows like ABC's *This Week,* supposedly committed to the sober discussion of the important issues of the day, and all of which had covered the Dole-Gingrich affair ad nauseam, pundits now labored *not* to raise the controversy. Gruff, liberal columnist Jack Germond, a political analyst renowned for his fierce honesty, was the exception. On *Inside Washington* he suggested that Mrs. Clinton was "going to start to get a little static from the Republicans on Terry McAuliffe putting up the $1.3 million for their house. No other Senate candidate could do that and get away with it. If that were a Republican we'd all be screaming at the press." He then dropped the hammer on his fellow pundits: "[If a conservative] were getting that kind of money we'd all be saying that's illegal." In response, the pride of National Public Radio, Nina Totenberg, tried to correct Germond but only revealed what would be the media's precise pose of hypocrisy. "Well, that's not illegal. We'd all be saying it smells."

For "tough" coverage of the newest emission of Clinton impropriety, ABC turned to its political analyst, former Clinton spinner George Stephanopoulos. On *Good Morning America,* cohost Elizabeth Vargas asked, "Why do you think the Clintons picked this house?" He responded . . . like a former Clinton aide. "Oh, I think it fits on a lot of different levels. It fits their personal taste, it's a nice traditional house, it's private, near a lot of golf courses for the president, and finally they've got a swimming pool. . . . Hillary has wanted a swimming pool for a long time." On CBS *This Morning*, cohost Thalia Assuras was positively giddy. "Do you expect them to participate in, oh, let's say, stoop sales and bake sales?"

In *Newsweek*, Newt-basher Evan Thomas gave McAuliffe's role the glib once-over: "An amiable Clinton golfing buddy who, perhaps as much as any friend, stood by the President during the Lewinsky scandal, McAuliffe is also raising money for Hillary's Senate campaign. While unorthodox, McAuliffe's sugar-daddy role on the Clinton house appears to be perfectly legal." In Thomas's eyes, Dole had been an "influence peddler," but now McAuliffe was an "amiable friend."

Generating outrage over perfectly legal activity was a media specialty during the Reagan years. Remember how back in those days reporters expressed a positively punctilious outrage over the "appearance of impropriety," over anything Reagan-related, and how not only facts, but pure gossip, would trigger it? The Clintons' cozy arrangement with McAuliffe might well have gone beyond simply the appearance of impropriety. On conservative talk radio, switchboards were blazing with the question: Didn't McAuliffe's loan represent an actual campaign contribution, and an illegal one at that? Potential GOP opponent Rudy Giuliani also began questioning the deal. The networks, predictably, ignored them all, but by month's end the Clintons were attempting a more conventional loan. That generated applause from the *New York Times*, and on October 15, NBC anchor Tom Brokaw reported that the Clintons had come up with a new financing plan through PNC Bank after some "tough criticism" of their original plan, "tough criticism" neither Brokaw nor NBC had ever relayed to viewers.

But there was more to the story. The networks were still yawning when *Washington Post* housing columnist Kenneth Harney explained eight days later in the Saturday Real Estate section that the new loan was *also* a sweetheart deal. A super-jumbo loan with a zero-points transaction that the Clintons had arranged usually requires 30 and even 40 percent of the money down. The Clintons had acquired it with a 20 percent down payment. It was, Harney reported, "[n]ot one that most of us—even if you're in their income bracket—could dream of walking away with. Though on the surface it appears to be simply an extra-large version of a garden-variety mortgage that thousands of home buyers negotiate every week, in fact it has some unusually generous terms." "Nobody can get that deal off the street," a Maryland banker told Harney. Another bank president interviewed was more direct: "If he were Joe Blow, he'd have had a hard time getting that loan. Did he get special treatment? Absolutely."

But the bankers were being at least as nice to Bill and Hillary as reporters, anchors, and editors, none of whom cared. In every Clinton financial scandal, large and small, we have seen incredible arrogance fueled by the belief that they simply did not need to abide by the same ethical rules governing mere mortal politicians. And why not? To the media, money scandals were truly scandalous only when committed (or even allegedly committed) by distasteful right-wing defenders of greed like Newt Gingrich. If you were a liberal who came to Washington for The Children, then sweetheart deals and aggressive, even unethical corner-cutting did not meet the definition of "news."

Chapter 11

Building a National Juggernaut

It was hard in the summer of 1992 for a young woman to stay objective and not become enchanted by the promise of Hillary. I had spent my formative professional years undercover in the dark age of Reagan-Bush. Those were the days when women were not allowed to wear pants in the White House. Anita Hill had just been whomped. Anti-abortion judges were packing the Supreme Court. And here was a woman who had kept her own name! . . . I'll be voting for her just to make sure Trent Lott doesn't get another foot soldier for his holy war.

—Former *Time* reporter NINA BURLEIGH, who once said she would give Bill Clinton oral sex for keeping abortion legal, in the February 14, 2000, *New York Observer*

Why ask conservatives to question the Clintons when they're already being grilled by tough, no-nonsense journalists like Dan Rather and Eleanor Clift?

—ANN COULTER, in an interview with the authors

A fter a month of backstage begging and on-air joking, David Letterman was rewarded with a Hillary Clinton appearance on his January 12, 2000, *Late Show. Washington Post* reporter Dana Milbank explained her decision to grant the interview. A Marist poll had found she should accept Letterman's invitation by a margin of 58 to 24 percent. "Clearly, she had no choice," Milbank wrote. "The poll was completed Monday. She announced her acceptance Tuesday. And tonight she pulled up at the *Late Show* studios on Broadway at West 53rd Street, accompanied by a 10-vehicle motorcade—and joined by her pollster."

In the middle of Letterman's opening monologue, former CBS News anchor Walter Cronkite walked out with a warning for the comedian. "David, you're really a dear old friend, so could I suggest, tonight you're interviewing Hillary Clinton, the First Lady of our nation. Try not to be a jackass, will you?" It was a funny, scripted line—and Cronkite was also the perfect metaphor for a compliant national press corps.

That press corps was so compliant that many in the media elite blew gaskets days later when someone in the New York media actually asked Mrs. Clinton a tough question. On Buffalo radio station WGR, host Tom Bauerle asked, "Mrs. Clinton, you're going to hate me. You were on television last night talking about your relationship with the president, Bill Clinton. Have you ever been sexually unfaithful to him and specifically the stories about you and Vince Foster. Any truth in those?" Hillary shot back, "I do hate you for that, because you know, those questions I think are really out of bounds, and everybody who knows me knows the answers to those questions." When Bauerle asked, "Is the answer no?," she answered, "Well yes, of course it's no, but it's an inappropriate question."

Some reporters mocked Bauerle. "There he is, Mr. Self-Appointed Edward R. Murrow of Buffalo," joked *Chicago Tribune* editor James Warren on *The McLaughlin Group*. On CNN's *Reliable Sources*, reporter Bruce Morton pronounced Bauerle "out of bounds," and added, "If she confessed infidelity, half the country might have cheered and said good for you." CBS's Bob Schieffer quoted *Washington Post* media writer Howard Kurtz claiming that the interview "underlines just how rough modern politics has become," and labeling the quiz "completely salacious, appalling, and shouldn't be part of what we call journalism." Schieffer testily concluded, "There is an old saying among reporters that there are no bad questions, just bad answers. But today even some veteran reporters are shaking their heads and wondering what will someone ask next." CBS ignored Bauerle's asking Hillary whether she had used drugs, the very "rough politics" this network and many other national reporters had hurled at candidate George W. Bush. Nor did the network explore Hillary's own standards, such as her asking in *Vanity Fair* in 1992, "Why does the press shy away from investigating rumors about George Bush's extramarital life?"

The quickest route to creating an aura of victimhood around Hillary was to ask her if she'd committed marital infidelity with a man who was dead. But the media routinely failed to ask her any tough questions about anything regarding the Clinton scandals, ignoring serious issues that raised questions about her credibility and judgment. On Fox News, Bill O'Reilly chided Bauerle for not asking instead about what Hillary's aides were doing rummaging through Foster's offices right after Foster's death. But the media seemed incapable of holding her accountable, choosing instead to wax rhapsodic about her outsized compassion and brains, building an intimidating national juggernaut that was just getting started.

FREE TIME FOR THE FIRST LADY

Hillary Rodham Clinton officially launched her New York Senate bid on February 6, 2000, on the campus of SUNY-Purchase, a college just ten miles south of her Chappaqua home. In a twenty-eight-minute speech, Mrs. Clinton announced that she would oppose "the divisive politics of revenge and retribution," the very signature of Team Clinton politics, as so many critics, former supporters, and past lovers have maintained. There was a certain awkwardness in the ceremony as the president stood silently behind the new candidate, uninvited to say a word. The show began with a new promotional campaign film by Hollywood TV producer and longtime Clinton choreographer Susan Bloodworth-Thomason. According to the *New York Times*, the film portrayed Hillary lovingly as "an aggressive advocate for children, a lawyer, and finally, a standard-issue suburban mother, notwithstanding where she has spent the last seven years of her life."

The campaign now a reality, the media expanded into more long, promotional segments to further the cause—free of charge, of course.

On April 24, CNN held a town meeting for Hillary in prime time, at

10 P.M. Eastern at the State University of New York at Buffalo, and Wolf Blitzer claimed, "The format is open-ended." But it was not. *Buffalo News* Washington bureau chief Douglas Turner reported that university officials submitted to CNN all the names of students attending, and that "questions from university students have been screened by CNN staff members." University administrators gave CNN students' phone numbers. Turner called CNN's behavior "slippery," especially CNN's calls for student questions on Tuesday afternoon for a Wednesday night broadcast. Although no one found evidence that Hillary received questions in advance, Turner suggested, "That's an embarrassingly long period of time for mischief to occur." Even if, as CNN claimed, Mrs. Clinton had no control over the questions asked or which students were admitted into the audience, it seems odd that there were zero questions from students about any Clinton scandal. No student at the State University of New York at Buffalo was at all interested in scandals, so many of them salacious, swirling around the Clintons?

In comments before, during, and after the event, Blitzer never explained that the questions and questioners were screened in advance. CNN's Frank Buckley ended a story the morning after the town hall meeting with a very vague reference that Giuliani's campaign, "in a statement issued earlier, described Mrs. Clinton's event as carefully scripted, totally contrived, and utterly fake." Surely it was that, but since Blitzer hadn't mentioned the screening, CNN viewers didn't have the information to fairly judge Giuliani's contention.

CNN did more stage management still, excluding all reporters, with the exception of an Associated Press reporter and photographer, from the auditorium. Even the SUNY-Buffalo student newspaper was barred. In all of the overnight dispatches filed, the AP reporter, Marc Humbert, never mentioned the screened questions or the exclusion of his colleagues.

CNN wasn't the only network playing this game. On May 11, NBC's *Today* promised, "We've invited 60 New Yorkers from all over the state with all kinds of interests. They're Democrats, Republicans, and independents. And they've come here to ask Mrs. Clinton whatever they want." They vowed that Hillary's campaign had had no input, but here's how NBC's "all kinds of interests" played out: of the fifteen questions from audience members, eleven (three out of four) came from the left or far left. These questioners demanded government money to pay for nursing education, attacked the insurance industry for "killing" mental health patients, blamed diesel fuel for "killing" people in poor neighborhoods, and denounced the "national frenzy of standardization and high-stakes testing that's robbing our students of their childhood." They touted ultraliberal role models, from author Jonathan Kozol to Senator Paul Wellstone. This was representative of the average New York State voter?

Throughout all this, cohosts Katie Couric and Matt Lauer failed to pick up the latest scandal news involving Hillary. Two months after the Monica Lewinsky story broke, Kathleen Willey publicly spoke on *60 Minutes* about an incident that occurred in a private study off the Oval Office in 1993, when she was a White House volunteer aide. She met with President Clinton to ask about a paying job, she said, and he fondled her breasts and placed her hand on his genitals. In typical Hillary-style destroy-the-accuser fashion, the White House went public with complimentary private letters to Clinton the day after Willey came forward with her story about the assault. Then, in May, her lawyers filed papers claiming "spousal privilege" for both Clintons as the reason why they would not answer questions about the release of Willey's personal letters to the president. But the *Today* show was uninterested in discussing a federal judge's ruling that release of the letters had violated the Privacy Act. Instead of exploring this legal entanglement, Couric opened by pressing Mrs. Clinton to comment on the breaking story of . . . Rudy Giuliani separating from his wife. When Hillary declined to address that issue, she looked so sensitive—the opposite of the treatment the White House had meted out to Kathleen Willey.

The media not only failed to ask Hillary about her new "spousal privilege" claims, but also failed to ask how the same Hillary who had hailed all of womanhood's debt to Anita Hill before the American Bar Association in 1992 could be so confident that the woman charging sexual harassment in this case was a two-faced liar.

On June 28, CBS's *Early Show* went to its affiliate in Syracuse for about forty-five minutes of audience-participation chat with Mrs. Clinton. Most of the questioners asked seemingly objective policy questions, but there were no conservatives to be found. CBS did produce a man who said he was a Republican, but who sued HMOs for denying health care and gave

Hillary credit for trying to nationalize health care, but most questions were like the one from a woman who said she had hosted a women's show on the local NPR station asking about the gap between the rich and the poor. Bryant Gumbel asked one question that might be classified as conservative, asking why she called school vouchers "gimmicks." Because they don't work, she answered. Her statement went unchallenged.

Embroiled in a crumbling marriage and diagnosed with prostate cancer, Rudy Giuliani, who had never been given the opportunity for a televised town hall meeting of his own, pulled out of the Senate race on May 20. In June, Congressman Rick Lazio entered the race tied, 42–42, with Hillary. A victory for the First Lady still was far from certain. "She certainly had a vulnerability that she was from out of state," political consultant John McLaughlin, a veteran of many campaigns in New York, told us. "I thought that she was definitely beatable." Which is not to say that Hillary lacked confidence, as pollster Tony Fabrizio explained in our interview: "I'd be willing to bet my right arm that before Hillary Clinton decided which state to run from that she'd surveyed in several different states and run simulated campaigns [there] to find the best state from which to run, not only for her Senate ambitions, but her presidential ambitions. She didn't enter that race not knowing her chances of victory were not 70 percent or better."

SOFTENING MOTHER HILLARY'S HARDER EDGES

Back in Washington another political firestorm was raging. Following the lead of thousands of predecessors, Elián González and his mother boarded a rickety boat to leave Cuba behind in the hope for a life of liberty in the United States. Elián was rescued at sea on November 25, 1999, but his mother had drowned. A story that began tragically would end tragically, with the boy having his freedom taken away by the Clinton administration in a predawn raid on a Miami family's home that would have made Joseph Stalin proud.

On Sunday, April 22, 2000, eight SWAT-equipped immigration-service agents burst into the home of little Elián's uncle Lázaro González. A Pulitzer Prize–winning photograph by Alan Diaz of the

Associated Press, which screamed the horror of the moment on virtually every major print and television news outlet nationwide, showed an INS agent with a MP-5 submachine gun pointed toward a terrified Elián and Donato Dalrymple, one of the men who had found him at sea. It was an especially shocking raid considering that Elián's Miami relatives had been on the phone negotiating with Attorney General Janet Reno to hand over Elián when the raid occurred. (Reno insisted that talks had "broken down.")

Where was Hillary Clinton, Defender of the Children, now?

For many years, the liberal Children's Defense Fund has posited itself as the caretaker of children's rights and has featured as a sort of logo a children's crayon drawing with the scrawled-out words "Dear Lord, be good to me, the sea is so wide, and my boat is so small." For many of those years, Hillary Rodham Clinton chaired the group's board of directors. It was striking that neither the Children's Defense Fund nor Hillary Clinton could now be found to defend the rights of the little boy found in a boat out at sea, even after Elián González stated in court documents that he wanted to stay in America. Once the Clinton administration's INS commissioner, Doris Meissner, declared that the six-year-old was too young to file an asylum claim on his own, the stage was set for the raid and, ultimately, sending Elián back to Communist Cuba. That's where the little boy went on June 28, at which point dictator Fidel Castro declared him the official property of the state.

Clinton campaign spokesman Howard Wolfson explained that "Hillary Clinton knows that we must take politics out of this decision." But this clashes mightily with her law review articles in the '70s and '80s, which complained, "The pretense that children's issues are somehow above or beyond politics endures and is reinforced by the belief that families are private, non-political units whose interests subsume those of children." Hillary had spent years championing the belief that the child's interest can rise above the parent's in the eyes of the government. But now her husband's administration, led by an attorney general she helped select, had raided the González home in Miami with guns drawn and dragged Elián González out. Dick Morris joked that Hillary's next book could be titled *It Takes a SWAT Team*.

In all three of the town meetings we've discussed there were questions about Elián's case, with varying degrees of sharpness. CNN's Wolf Blitzer was most blunt, perhaps because the raid had occurred just days earlier. "We've all seen that very dramatic picture, Elián in the closet—he looks terrorized by what is going on. Can you condone that kind of tactic?" Hillary called the raid "unfortunate," but understandable "when faced with continuing recalcitrance and opposition to obeying the rule of law." In May, NBC's Katie Couric ignored the raid—it was unimportant?—asking only whether the U.S. embargo of Cuba should be relaxed. By June, the injustice was only a faint memory. CBS's Bryant Gumbel asked if the Miami relatives who wanted to keep the boy free were "way out of line" and whether the embargo was "antiquated."

The pundits saw nothing but positives for Mrs. Clinton after the raid to seize Elián. After a clip of Hillary's response to Blitzer on ABC's *Good Morning America*, Hillary's usual supporters among female journalists were raving. "I think she handled that just perfectly," clucked *Time*'s Margaret Carlson. *New York Times* columnist (now editorial page editor) Gail Collins cooed, "This has been her really good month. . . . The Elián González thing is working real well for her."

Newsweek put the haunting photo of a hysterical little Elián in the arms of federal agents on the cover of its May 1 issue, but made no connection in print between Hillary and the boy. In the very next issue, however, as part of a cover package on what teenagers think, this time they did want to focus on Hillary Clinton, and awarded her a page-long editorial on "Parenting a Teen." Mother Hillary was allowed to tout how she and Bill had stayed up all night helping Chelsea with a high school research paper. (She graduated from high school in 1998, the Year of Our Intern.)

Time and *U.S. News & World Report* also failed to connect the dots between Elián and Hillary's campaign, but *U.S. News* columnist Michael Barone did note that neither she nor Al Gore were holding press conferences on the campaign trail. "Evidently, neither feels comfortable facing questions from competent, well-prepared, and unawed reporters. Indeed, Hillary Clinton will not venture out except in Potemkin-like campaign events or on programs with Rosie O'Donnell, who gushes over her, or David Letterman, who quizzes her on New York State trivia after providing the questions and answers in advance."

DEFENDING THE DOORMAT FROM
FEMINIST EXPECTATIONS

On June 7, NBC's *Today* interviewed conservative author Laura Ingraham on her book *The Hillary Trap*. Katie Couric made sure to label Ingraham a Clinton-hater in her promo piece before the interview. "Coming up in this half hour, when it comes to Hillary Clinton, people either love her or hate her. Conservative political commentator Laura Ingraham pretty much falls into the latter category." True to form, Couric stuck up for Hillary throughout the segment. She first suggested it was just unfair to criticize Hillary, asking her guest, "But don't you think there's an awful lot of projection that goes on in terms of how people view her, placing their own confused states or their role in society, or how powerful should women be, and it's sort of projected on—upon her as an individual?" What in the world did *that* mean? To question Hillary is to concede one's psychological problems?

Ingraham denounced Hillary for sticking with her husband as he humiliated her with his affairs, so Couric offered another classic Hillary spin line. In fact, if you closed your eyes you might think it *was* Hillary: "I mean, can you really pretend to understand the complexities and dynamics of someone's marriage? And certainly, she's not the first woman who has stayed with an unfaithful husband." The interview ended with Couric dismissively asking, "Quick question. Have you ever met her? Have you ever so much as shook—you know, shook her hand?" Apparently, to know her was to love her.

When we interviewed Ingraham for this book, she commented, "It's likely [Couric] was irritated that I was booked on the show at all. That's how they get back at you." Ingraham added, "It was clear to me that she hadn't even cracked the book. So that's kind of how it is, they really don't cover conservative books at all, rarely."

The next Hillary-book hubbub occurred in mid-July with the arrival of Jerry Oppenheimer's book *State of a Union*, which accused the First Lady of an anti-Semitic slur. Former Clinton campaign aide Paul Fray told Oppenheimer that the night Bill Clinton lost his race for Congress in 1974, Hillary had greeted Fray's arrival at campaign headquarters with the epithet "You fucking Jew bastard!" Among themselves, reporters quickly tabbed this the F.J.B. story.

The networks went on their usual run of disassembling the accuser. CBS and NBC aired full stories, with NBC's Andrea Mitchell curiously noting that NBC had heard the allegation the year before and decided not to report it. "Fray and his wife made the same charge last year to *Dateline*. . . . But *Dateline* never aired the interview. Too many questions about Fray's credibility." She added that Clinton biographer David Maraniss had spoken for hours with Fray and his wife, and the story never came up.

But Mitchell's claim of not using the Fray interview because of credibility issues was not quite true. On the November 29, 1999, *Dateline*, in a long-drawn-out sales job for Gail Sheehy's book *Hillary's Choice*, NBC let Sheehy describe Fray's account of the battle—leaving out the ethnic slur. "Sheehy says Bill Clinton sat in silence as his then-girlfriend Hillary Rodham blamed campaign manager Paul Fray for the defeat, and Fray's wife blamed Clinton, accusing him of sexual escapades with more than one campaign worker. . . . And [Hillary] goes back at Paul Fray: 'You were setting Bill up with loose women!' They are throwing books, ashtrays, furniture. Window breaks. The guy standing outside guarding the door says he heard cussing like he'd never heard before."

ABC tried a more interesting route. It ignored the anti-Semitism flap for two days, then put Fray on *Good Morning America*, only to have Diane Sawyer promise a different kind of fireworks: "A lot of people say his credibility should be under attack. And this morning we put him in the hot seat." Reporter Terry Moran did exactly that, charging that a 1997 letter from Fray to Mrs. Clinton that Hillary's campaign produced showed that "you have falsely accused her before." Fray said, "Yes, I have. Yeah. I was extending the olive branch. I expected her to reciprocate and say, 'Hey, let's, you know, bury the hatchet and go on.' She never responded to me." Moran then underlined that Fray admitted "having legal and medical problems," and asked, "What are we to think of somebody who had to surrender their [*sic*] law license for altering a court document, who was drug-dependent, who the Supreme Court of Arkansas said doesn't have the moral character to practice law in this state? Why should people believe you?"

The irony of that was inescapable. At the same time, the Arkansas Supreme Court had declared that President Clinton didn't have the moral character to practice law in the state; ultimately the president accepted disbarment in a plea bargain with special prosecutor Robert Ray on his last full day in office. We are still waiting for Moran to ask Bill Clinton why anyone should believe him.

The brief Fray flap was all forgotten by convention time, when the networks once again proved their "news judgment" was judgmental indeed. Future First Lady Laura Bush's Monday night speech to the Republican convention in Philadelphia was ignored by NBC and CBS, but First Lady Hillary Clinton's Monday night speech to the Democratic convention in Los Angeles drew live coverage from all networks.

Dan Rather was faced with charges of a double standard for breaking into *48 Hours* to show fifteen minutes of Hillary Clinton's eighteen-minute speech. He conceded that CBS "made a mistake" in not carrying Laura Bush's speech on the first night of the GOP convention—but with a caveat. Rather told Ed Bark of the *Dallas Morning News* that "Laura Bush is not a candidate for anything. . . . I'd be surprised if Mrs. Bush or anybody else didn't agree that to compare the two is a little bit like comparing watermelons with turnips. I don't think anybody would want us to say, 'Well, okay, we made one mistake so we're gonna make another.'" So it was okay to grant candidate Hillary more free airtime? CBS apparently thought so, as did NBC, which ran the drama *Third Watch* instead of Laura Bush but bailed out of its regular programming in order to catch the last twelve minutes of Mrs. Clinton's speech. ABC aired both spouses.

The First Lady was interviewed by all three anchors in time for their evening newscasts on the night of her speech. As usual, most of the questions were more personal than ideological. Dan Rather ended by observing, "Everyone who runs for office has fears." She replied that she feared a prosperous nation "can so easily be lulled into a sense of complacency" and make a "very bad decision" in voting.

Peter Jennings pressed her somewhat on her marriage, asking if she was hurt by her husband's public admission of infidelity. Hillary dodged, but Jennings persisted, leading her to shoot back, "Well, I'm—I think my business and my family is really to be kept private. I don't think it is anyone else's business." The next morning, ABC's *Good Morning America* ran more of the interview, showing how the ABC anchor had unloaded with sensitivity. "He's leaving the greatest thing in his life and you are about to meet the challenge of the biggest thing, certainly, in your political life," Jennings asked. "What if he needs you?"

Only the perpetually starstruck Maria Shriver secured a postspeech interview, perhaps because no network sycophant could ever outperform Shriver on this score. Just listen to this kissy-kissy question, which didn't even pretend to be objective: "You find yourself going to the final home stretch of your own campaign. You've spent a million dollars, worked very hard, and you find yourself neck and neck with a candidate who has nowhere near your stature. How frustrating has that been?"

SETTING UP RICK LAZIO FOR A FALL

Even network media stars could get roughed up if they crossed the line with Hillary Clinton. On September 13, Tim Russert moderated a debate between Mrs. Clinton and Rick Lazio at the PBS station WNED in Buffalo, and which was later rebroadcast nationally on MSNBC. Russert shocked viewers (and from the looks of her reaction, Hillary as well) by pressing Hillary about her shameless declaration that the story of her husband's intern Olympics would not be "proven true," and that the media should investigate "the vast right-wing conspiracy" instead. He asked if Mrs. Clinton would apologize for misleading the country. Apologize? Of course she wouldn't. Instead she insisted, somehow, that the jury was still out: "I wish that we all could look at it from the perspective of history but we can't yet. We're going to have to wait until those books are written." And in typically Clintonesque fashion, she claimed, "I didn't mislead anyone," because she herself, she alleged, was ignorant of the truth.

Lazio's response was deadly. He characterized Mrs. Clinton's attitude as "somehow that it only matters what you say when you get caught. And character and trust is about well more than that. And blaming others every time you have responsibility? Unfortunately that's become a pattern, I think, for my opponent." That wasn't only a Hillary pattern. It was a Hillary-adoring media's pattern as well.

Washington Post columnist Richard Cohen promptly savaged Russert for his inquiry. "Not since the old Saturday night fights has TV seen such a low blow," he complained. Continuing the poor-Hillary line, Gail Collins wrote in the *New York Times*, "All of us have moments in our lives that we prefer not to recall even while cowering in a darkened closet. Mrs. Clinton's just happens to be stored in the files of every news bureau on the planet."

Wait a minute. Aren't journalists supposed to revere the truth and revile political figures who mislead? Any dignified human being who cared about the truth would have apologized not just for being wrong but also for having cast aspersions on her critics. Besides, you don't have to know you're misleading someone to be guilty of misleading someone. And if she didn't know, why did she resort to Clintonian legalisms like it would not be "proven true"? Rather than seek the truth, she spent month after month urging the same old daily strategy: stonewall, lie, rain fire on Ken Starr. She owed Mr. Starr and the nation an apology. She does still.

On CNBC Geraldo Rivera wondered if Russert actually generated "sympathy" for her among viewers. Old *Washington Post* hand Carl Bernstein was most impressed with Hillary: "I thought Hillary Clinton tonight looked like a thoughtful grown-up and Rick Lazio looked, to me, like a high-schooler." (Bernstein's sympathy for Hillary would ultimately appear in his book *A Woman in Charge*, published in 2007, though Clinton supporters would try to dismiss his treatment as an "attack" on Hillary.) On ABC's *Good Morning America* the next day, George Stephanopoulos agreed with the sympathy line and added that Lazio should have lain low.

The media elite also savaged Lazio for being so rude as to "invade her personal space" and ask her to sign a no-soft-money pledge during that debate. No doubt influenced by some of John McCain's advisers now working on his campaign, Lazio tried to make an issue out of Hillary's use of "soft money" corporate contributions. In a bit of staged theater, Lazio strolled over to Hillary's podium with a piece of paper and pushed her to sign a pledge to eschew such financial sustenance. "I'm not asking you to admire it," he challenged. "I'm asking you to sign it. Right here, right here. Sign it right now." Mrs. Clinton smiled and said in response that he would need signatures from his conservative allies and they would also need to abide by this pledge. Photographs of the exchange adorning newspapers across the country showed Lazio standing over Hillary, pointing a harsh finger at her.

The press went ballistic. *Newsweek* editor Evan Thomas called Lazio "a bit of a punk" and compared him to a "puppy dog when he's got his teeth in your ankle." Female columnists were especially distressed. The *New York Times*'s Gail Collins began by calling Lazio "Darth Vader with dimples" and "The Long Island Lex Luthor," making Hillary Princess Leia and Supergirl simultaneously. But her colleague Maureen Dowd topped everyone by relaying one woman's claim that Lazio seemed like "her husband, waving a credit card receipt in her face, yelling at her that she had overcharged, his eyes bulging, his veins popping, screaming at her to return everything to the store." So whatever happened to I-am-woman-hear-me-roar feminism? These allegedly feminist pundits were making it sound as though Mrs. Clinton had arrived to the debate with a parasol, a frilly bonnet, and a hoop skirt.

Dowd used the same domestic-violence theme to urge the public in advance to ignore independent counsel Robert Ray's final Whitewater report. "If Hillary's luck holds, it will be the October surprise she needs to cinch the women's vote. One more brute slapping her around and she may be home free."

Every so often during 2000, Ray had been closing his investigations quietly, to very little media coverage. On March 17, he announced that he would file no charges in the purloined FBI files case. On June 22, he said he would indict no one on the manipulations of Travelgate. Then, on September 21, he announced the effective end of the Whitewater probe, with a flaccid report that reported no plans for further indictments. The media heaved a sigh of relief, and began to lecture.

ABC and CBS worried about the length, cost, and preelection timing of the Whitewater investigation. NBC's Tom Brokaw snidely suggested that Whitewater "may never die in the hearts and minds of hard-core Clinton-bashers." While NBC's Andrea Mitchell acknowledged that Ray was critical of Clinton team delays, like the eighteen-month disappearance of Hillary's law firm billing records, later in her story she wondered, "Was it necessary for Ray to make the critical comment if there was no reason to prosecute? Was that a political statement?"

On *Good Morning America* the next day, September 22, legal correspondent Jeffrey Toobin crowed, "The bottom line is there is nothing on the Clintons in this investigation." Elizabeth Vargas added, "Certainly, after all this time and money, it is considered a huge victory for the president and the First Lady." Toobin agreed: "Absolutely . . . Starr and his successor never issued any verdict on Hillary Clinton's conduct until now . . . with no charges ever filed against Hillary Clinton. . . . The Starr and Ray investigations alone cost more than $50 million and as it turned out, it was much ado—two decades' worth—about not very much." Exaggeration was ABC's breakfast special: the independent-counsel probe began in 1994, which is hardly "two decades" removed from 2000.

But Robert Ray's final report on Travelgate on October 18 certainly did make a statement about Hillary Clinton's conduct. This was the report in which Ray concluded that "the overwhelming evidence establishes that she played a role in the decision to fire the employees and provided input into that decision" and that her testimony was "factually false." Although Ray's report stated that there was "insufficient evidence" to indict Mrs. Clinton in a court of law—which is hardly an exoneration—it also declared, "Mrs. Clinton's input into the process was significant, if not the significant factor influencing the pace of events in the Travel Office firings and the ultimate decision to fire the employees." There was little ambiguity in the independent counsel's assessment.

So how did *CBS Evening News* and *NBC Nightly News* report this report? They didn't. ABC's *World News Tonight* gave it 20 seconds.

In the campaign's last few days, reporters rushed to Hillary's aid one last time after the stumbling, hopelessly inept Lazio campaign and the New York State GOP tried to make radical Islamic terrorism an issue. On Wednesday, October 25, the New York *Daily News* reported that Islamic foes of Israel had given Hillary $50,000 in contributions at a Boston event, including $1,000 from Abdulrahman Alamoudi of the American Muslim Council, who had boasted of his influence with the Clintons: "[W]e are the ones who went to the White House and defended what we call Hamas." (Hillary had also invited Alamoudi to draw up a guest list for the first White House celebration of Ramadan in 1996.) The networks ignored the story from every angle, but when a major New York paper finally covered it, she had to respond.

The day the story hit, she announced that she would be returning the $50,000, including Alamoudi's $1,000. The New York State Republican Party, seeing the opportunity to score points, unloaded—and badly overshot. Their callers began making phone calls telling voters that Hillary was supported by a "terrorist group" like the terrorists "that killed our sailors on the USS *Cole*," where a terrorist bombing in a harbor in Yemen had killed seventeen U.S. sailors just two weeks before. When stories about the calls hit the newspapers on Saturday, Hillary saw her opening. Arriving to campaign in Ithaca, New York, she turned the focus on the GOP: "They have stooped to a level I never thought we'd see." And suddenly, the networks were interested.

When Mrs. Clinton appeared on CBS's *Early Show* on Monday, October 30, Bryant Gumbel didn't ask her about the *Cole* calls or the American Muslim Council ties. But when Lazio was a guest on that show the next day, cohost Jane Clayson ripped into Lazio: "Do you regret that that phone campaign happened?" Lazio said no, and tried to argue that "Mrs. Clinton had invited people to the White House who espoused terrorism and violence as a political tool, people that believed in Hamas, which is a terrorist group." Clayson acted as if she'd never read a newspaper: "You really believe that?"

On the Halloween edition of NBC's *Today,* Katie Couric began with this softball to Mrs. Clinton: "I know that you were outraged last week" about the GOP calls. Couric did press Hillary . . . for being too fast to knuckle under to conservatives. Referring to the fact that Mrs. Clinton had returned the cash from self-professed supporters of anti-U.S. terrorists, the *Today* cohost asked, "But don't you think it might have been helpful for you to find out exactly what this group was condoning or promoting before giving them back the money?" She had nothing to say about Hamas talk at White House events. Couric continued the apology theme by asking Hillary if her husband was right that the Republican Party ought to apologize for impeachment proceedings.

The next morning, it was Matt Lauer's turn to take out a paddle and whack Lazio about charges that "seem to have gotten out of hand." Of the USS *Cole* calls he too asked, "Isn't that outrageous?" In another question, he repeated the call script and proclaimed, "Now, that's obviously exploiting a national tragedy for political gain." When Lazio tried to defend himself, Lauer, well, grew more outraged: "What you're doing is you're saying that it's not coming out of your campaign. But you're not backing away from it at all! . . . Mrs. Clinton has demanded an apology. You're not apologizing!" Throughout the hammering, Lazio kept noting the White House event with the Hamas supporters, and adding that the Clinton campaign had disguised a donation from the American Muslim Council by misrepresenting it on finance reports as the "National Museum Council." Lazio needn't have bothered showing up that day; no one was in the least bit interested in what he had to say.

Hillary's lead had opened up after her victimhood reemerged in the first debate and Tim Russert's request for an apology, and thereafter she was never forced to leave her media comfort zone of soft, female-focused morning-show interviews and tender, scripted town hall moments. The press was giving her a Get-into-the-Senate-Free card. "If the media had been fair . . . she would have lost," John McLaughlin told us. "Her negatives would have been developed and the undecided would have voted for Rick. They didn't hold her to a standard. They gave her a free pass."

Here's a point to consider: Throughout a year and a half of campaigning, Rudy Giuliani and Rick Lazio subjected themselves to nineteen tough interviews with the Sunday morning pros. Hillary Clinton, by contrast, never once appeared on a single one of them. A few weeks before Election Day, AP reporter Beth Harpaz put the question to Hillary, who replied, "I'm going to be talking to the voters of New York and the press of New York." And to Katie Couric. And to Bryant Gumbel. And to Wolf Blitzer. And if all else failed, there was always Maria Shriver.

Chapter 12
Seizing the Senate with Media Sizzle

What an exhilarating moment it must have been for her—the first First Lady in history to be elected to public office. There, for all the naysayers to see, was the woman who had finally come into her own, free at last to be smart, outspoken, independent, and provocative, all qualities she had been forced as First Lady, to "hide under a bushel." Still she was voted one of America's most admired women. Just wait. You ain't seen nothin' yet.

—ABCNews.com commentary by ABC weekend anchor
CAROLE SIMPSON, January 7, 2001

I've lived through so much unending press hostility, so many one-sided descriptions. Just put in parallel the coverage we got for the offer of a $4 million advance for a book, which by the way was a number one bestseller for seven weeks, and compare that with total lack of concern about Hillary's books. . . . My working assumption is the news media will use anything they can to defame Republicans, conservatives in particular.

—NEWT GINGRICH, in an interview with the authors

S he won. Hillary Clinton seized her new power with symbolic aggression, horning in on Rick Lazio's attempted concession speech. Who was Lazio to interrupt her prime-time real estate on the 11 o'clock local news? Lazio was about one minute into his speech when the pictures of Hillary waving and mugging with Bill on stage overtook him. "What we're watching here in New York is a bit of a violation of an unwritten law in politics, not to come out on camera while your opponent is conceding," MSNBC anchorman Brian Williams said over the split pictures. "Not a First Family known to take others into consideration often when planning their own personal moves."

When the returns tumbled in on Election Night, the formerly tight and edgy race between Mrs. Clinton and Congressman Lazio had turned into a cakewalk. She won by 12 points, 55 to 43 percent. But was that win over "Little Ricky," as AP's Beth Harpaz and other reporters called him in public and behind his back, all that impressive? For all her massive celebrity and corps of media sycophants, Hillary drew 5 fewer percentage points than Al Gore did in New York—and had almost the same victory margin as her fellow New York senator Chuck Schumer two years before. Still, as America tangled for a month over Democratic complaints about butterfly ballots and dimpled chads in Florida, the media had something here they could loudly celebrate to the skies.

On November 28, Mrs. Clinton invited in two network morning shows to fawn over her new book on White House entertaining and decorations, *An Invitation to the White House*. She was the perfect combination of Martha Washington and Martha Stewart. Neither ABC nor NBC had any tough questions for Mrs. Clinton, but both made lots of room for compliments. Katie Couric spent most of a half hour on air with Hillary. She began the girl talk by congratulating Hillary and asking, "What are you most looking forward to? Obviously getting to work. But when—when you think of the array of possibilities before you . . ." The real warmth came in the decorating segment of the interview, when Couric fawned, "You obviously also enjoy the domestic aspects of your role of First Lady. But wasn't it hard to balance being an activist First Lady and the responsibilities of a more traditional First Lady?" After asking about the Clinton family's best moment at the White House (it was Christmas with relatives, Hillary answered), Couric followed up with this: "And you have had, Mrs. Clinton, some painful experiences here, as well. And—and how have you grown from—from those experiences?" Whoa! Was Katie slipping into . . . substance? Not to worry.

Couric quickly added a caveat: "And I don't need you to be specific." Hillary answered vaguely by talking about being an author and "I think that I am a—you know, today I'm a different, and in some ways, you know, in my own personal view, a stronger and better person because of what I've gone through for the last eight years."

The comfort level of the duo was revealing at interview's end when Katie said "Thank you so much," and Hillary replied, "Thank you. Thank you. Thank you. For the last eight years, Katie. Thanks." *Thank you, Mrs. Clinton. No, thank YOU, Katie. No, no, thank YOU, YOU, YOU, Mrs. Clinton! No, thank you, Katie, you, you times two!* Couric added later that "we had a great time" and that Mrs. Clinton was "very candid" about the tough times. Candid, and yet not at all specific.

The most gushing press booster of Hillary's decorating-and-recipes book was Ann McFeatters, then a White House reporter for the Scripps Howard newspaper chain. Since Hillary's publisher, Simon & Schuster, was donating profits to the National Park Service, she proclaimed, "It seemed like a civic duty to buy this book. And am I glad I did!" While she joked that all the pictures of the Clintons "hugging, kissing, dancing, laughing, joking, caressing" did not include "pictures of anyone throwing anything," she gave it a rave review: "The dictionary just doesn't have enough superlatives for this book." She lauded Hillary's daily grind: "The First Lady's energy level is superhuman."

Female reporters often sounded like they were watching some sort of movie romance unfold, with Hillary in the role of Cinderella. NBC's Andrea Mitchell was wowed on December 5. "It's a modern fairy tale. From First Lady entertaining 20,000 guests at twenty-six Christmas parties to just another freshman senator today arriving for orientation in an SUV, no limo. From America's finest antiques to unpacking boxes in a basement office. From *foie gras* to Senate bean soup. The senator-elect goes to the Capitol."

THE EIGHT-MILLION-DOLLAR WOMAN

On December 16, 2000, the Saturday papers reported that Hillary had negotiated a stunning $8 million advance for her memoirs from

Simon & Schuster, which had published her other three books. It was one of the richest advances in publishing history. Although even liberal groups like Common Cause made a little noise that Senator Clinton should take customary royalties and not a huge advance, for appearances' sake, the media merely shrugged at the news. The *New York Times,* while noting in its headline that the payout was a "near record," put the story on page B5.

You could bet money that Newt Gingrich probably winced. The double standard was glaring. When incoming Speaker Gingrich accepted a $4.5 million advance from Rupert Murdoch's HarperCollins almost exactly six years before, it became national news in minutes and a scandal overnight. The next day, the *New York Times* ran an outraged editorial titled "Mr. Gingrich's Foolish Book Deal." The *Times* took six days to condemn Hillary—reminding readers of the Gingrich hubbub—in an editorial more blandly titled "Mrs. Clinton's Book Deal."

The TV networks were energized about Gingrich's deal. "We'll hear more about this one," CBS reporter Bob Schieffer promised, and how right he was. One news reporter after another hammered away at the "controversy" they had created themselves, while pundits like Al Hunt on CNN quickly called for Gingrich to dump the advance or donate it to an orphanage. Media pressure took its toll, and Gingrich surrendered his advance within a few days. A lot of good that did. The press kept hitting him. In the first six weeks of the controversy, the network evening news shows aired twenty-seven negative news stories—seven each on ABC, CBS, and NBC, and six on CNN. In all there were hundreds of media stories raking Gingrich over the coals, an avalanche of "absolute hatred," in the words of Congressman Jack Kingston, a fellow Georgian. "They vilified the guy," Kingston told us.

The media went so far as to suggest that Gingrich's book advance might represent an attempt, on the part of a businessman with interests before Congress, to bribe the Speaker of the House. CBS's Dan Rather proclaimed, "More tonight about whether Australian-born and -centered communications billionaire Rupert Murdoch is trying to buy influence with politically connected authors."

Hillary's publisher, Simon & Schuster, was owned by Viacom, which also owned . . . Rather's CBS. Would Rather have the guts to repeat his sentence about "buying influence"? Of course not. He never mentioned the story. Nor did attack-dog reporters like CBS's Eric Engberg fulminate on this arrogant, unethical power broker, as he had when Gingrich's book deal was announced. CBS touched on the story only once, when reporter Kendra Farn pointed out the comparison to Gingrich, the complaints of the liberal ethics groups, and the fact that the publisher also owned CBS. But she ended on a light note: "The First Lady does have some big expenses, including millions in legal bills, a $1.7 million mortgage on her New York home, and a husband who is about to be out of work." That's too cute. This out-of-work husband was set to make millions on the rubber chicken circuit, not to mention his own book deal, which called for a whopping $12 million advance.

Here's another level of hypocrisy: When Gingrich gave up his advance, CBS *Face the Nation* fill-in host Rita Braver asked Bob Dole on January 1, 1995, "You don't think he'll be called the Four-and-a-Half-Million-Dollar Man anymore?" The man behind Hillary's book deal was her friend and agent Bob Barnett, who is . . . Rita Braver's husband. Hillary was never mocked by network reporters as "the Eight-Million-Dollar Woman." The Clintons were never called "the Twenty-Million-Dollar Couple."

The other networks were no better. NBC gave Hillary's big score a few seconds on that Saturday morning's *Today* show. ABC offered one story by John Martin that calmly covered the bases on Friday night, with no time for comments from conservatives. On Friday morning, before the deal was struck, *Good Morning America* cohost Charles Gibson discussed the emerging deal with a publisher's representative and a media reporter. Neither objected to the double standard, even when Gibson raised the Gingrich issue. On ABC's *This Week*, ex–Clinton aide George Stephanopoulos explained that Hillary's book deal was completely legitimate, even if it caused a "PR problem," because the poor dear had so many expenses. "She has to buy a house in Georgetown, she has to pay her legal bills, she's willing to pay." Cokie Roberts couldn't let that shameless spin go unchallenged: "Nobody has to buy a house in Georgetown," she shot back. (The Clintons didn't, ultimately. They "settled" for a $2.8 million, five-bedroom house later in Washington's exclusive Embassy Row neighborhood.)

CNN featured one prime-time debate moderated by Greta Van Susteren, who set aside impartiality to argue that conservative Keith Appell might be seen as sexist when he said Republicans were sick and tired of the ethical double standards. "Some of the women in this country may think you have a huge double standard, because, you know, here's a woman who has obviously been able to go out in the marketplace and command a huge amount of money, and a lot of people are squawking." Van Susteren tried to compare Hillary's big score to Senator Orrin Hatch's songwriting royalties, and to book advances for Senators John McCain and Joe Lieberman, none of which were anywhere near as lucrative as the First Lady's deal.

So Hillary kept her $8 million advance, and once again, the press bailed her out of a situation that could have hurt her reputation. Yet Newt Gingrich was forced to give up his advance and still he faced recurring charges of corruption. The media's hounding of Gingrich was "extraordinarily damaging," according to Tony Blankley, who worked for Gingrich from 1990 through 1997. "All these corruption charges were ultimately unsupported by the evidence and rebutted by the evidence, but it set a tone, a sort of template for every two-bit journalist around the country to trace their stories on Gingrich."

Did Gingrich wince at the double standard? He denies it. "I'm not sure I had a reaction as such," he told us. "I've seen so much, I've lived through so much nonending press hostility, so many one-sided descriptions. My working assumption is the news media will use anything they can to defame Republicans, conservatives in particular."

For reporters, ethics questions about Hillary would only get in the way of the celebrations. NBC's Andrea Mitchell broke out the fairy-tale tone again on January 3, 2001, for Senator Hillary Rodham Clinton's swearing-in. "For this political wife, friends say, a dream come true," Mitchell proclaimed. "Today he holds the Bible for her, trading places from when they first came to Washington eight years ago. From the health care fiasco to the Monica humiliation to the campaign many said she would never win, Hillary Clinton is now the most admired woman in America, beating Oprah by a landslide in the latest Gallup poll."

Mitchell was getting carried away here. First, Bill Clinton didn't hold the Bible for her at the actual swearing-in, where he was banished to the gallery because he was not a senator. The Bill-holding-the-Bible moment was for a swearing-in ceremony staged by a photographer. More significant, the most-admired-woman-in-America Hillary garnered only 19 percent in the Gallup poll. And it wasn't too tough to beat Oprah, who got only 4 percent. It was more a measure of fame (and perhaps great devotion on the left end of the political spectrum) than favorability. It was also probably true that Hillary Clinton was the most hated woman in America. Gallup's Frank Newport told CNN that day that while 82 percent of Democrats liked her, 70 percent of Republicans disapproved. No network coverage there.

Pardon Me, Boys, and Phooey on Hughie

Bill and Hillary Clinton departed the White House with none of the customary style and grace. It had a Beverly Hillbillies ending (the Arkansas power couple struck a publishing gusher and even bought a "cee-ment pond" like Jed Clampett, as Hillary finally got that swimming pool she wanted). On his very last day (make that half-day) in office, President Clinton issued 140 pardons and 36 sentence commutations. He pardoned his own brother Roger. He wiped out several of Kenneth Starr's Whitewater convictions—most notably that of Susan McDougal. (Now that her electoral privileges were restored, Katie Couric asked the former Mrs. McDougal if she'd follow Hillary into politics: "Do you have any interest in running for Senate?"—as if anyone would ever vote her into that, or any other, office.) President Clinton pardoned convicted cabinet member Henry Cisneros, as well as his mistress Linda Jones, for lying to the FBI about hush-money payments he made to her. But the most notorious pardon—and one in which Hillary was implicated—was awarded to businessman Marc Rich, an action that drew negative news coverage for more than a month.

Marc Rich was an American fugitive living in Switzerland who had made a fortune trading with rogue regimes from Cuba to Iran to Libya to apartheid-era South Africa, routinely violating United States embargoes. He fled the United States after committing what prosecutors called the largest tax fraud in the history of the republic. His campaign for a Clinton pardon was facilitated in part by campaign contributions from his former wife Denise Rich. In her book *The Final Days,* the late Barbara

Olson reported that Mrs. Rich's donations included more than $100,000 to the Democratic National Committee and more than $100,000 to the Senate campaign of one Hillary Rodham Clinton, as well as paying $40,000 for entertainers to perform at Hillary's birthday party fundraiser at New York's Roseland Ballroom on October 25, 2000. In response to questions about this very smelly pardon, Senator Clinton very typically denied knowing anything about it before it was announced.

On February 5, the *Washington Post* reported that the Clintons had lifted furniture out of the White House that donors thought would stay in there, not end up in Chappaqua. Within two days, the Clintons returned $28,000 worth of purloined furniture.

Pause here and contemplate: What would have been the media reaction had it been the Reagans making off with White House furniture? You can just imagine the stories that would be filed, day after day, night after night, with no end in sight. What did they make off with? Who was responsible? What does it say about the Reagans that they would do this? Are these criminal offenses? Should the Reagans be indicted? Should a special prosecutor be enjoined? It is standard fare for this avalanche to follow when Republicans are accused of improper behavior.

But not Democrats. It is true that CNN gave the story continuous (if not comprehensive) coverage. But ABC felt this story was so unnewsworthy that it reported nothing. On CBS, Dan Rather touched on it only once, for nineteen seconds—with the cursory announcement of the Clintons' decision to return items.

For its part NBC was schizophrenic in its coverage. When the initial *Washington Post* report came out February 5, NBC's Lisa Myers gave it a full *Nightly News* story, but by the next morning, *Today* cohost Matt Lauer was already tired of it. "Is this a big deal or are we in the middle of Pick-on-the-Clintons Month?" he asked *Newsweek*'s Howard Fineman, who mourned in agreement, "Well, it's always Pick-on-the-Clintons Month." Lauer continued his damage-control efforts. "But isn't there a kind of large gray area here? This isn't black-and-white. First of all, other presidents have taken gifts from the White House, and some of the donors say here, by the way, they're honored if the Clintons took these gifts. So why is it a big deal?"

Not only was this a big deal, but it became even uglier when it emerged that the Clintons actually had been helping themselves to White House furniture for quite some time. On Saturday, February 10, a follow-up *Washington Post* front-page story, headlined "Clintons Shipped Furniture Year Ago," recounted how chief usher Gary Walters objected when the Clintons shipped furniture to their Chappaqua home in early 2000, arguing that the items had been donated to the White House after the Clintons took office, but the White House counsel's office told him he was wrong. ABC's evening newscast on that Saturday night had no story, but had time for a full story on the rap-music star Eminem's popularity in Britain and a piece on the rising interest in toy pianos. CBS ignored that *Washington Post* front-page article, but aired a full story on another development on the *Post*'s front page: the EEOC's suing to stop Burlington Northern Santa Fe Railway from performing genetic tests on its employees. NBC ran another pardon story on Denise Rich's donations to Clinton's presidential library, but nothing on the Clintons' itchy furniture fingers.

Two days later, on February 12, Lisa Myers returned with another *NBC Nightly News* story: "In more damage control today, Senator Hillary Clinton blames a bookkeeping error for the fact that sixteen pieces of White House furniture, all government property, were sent to the Clintons' New York home, then had to be returned." In this report Hillary blamed the situation on "some cataloging errors made seven or eight years ago."

But a week later NBC's Katie Couric was back to damage-control mode, picking up her colleague Lauer's lament in an interview with Chris Matthews and columnist Mike Barnicle: "With the exception of the pardon of Marc Rich and some other moves that probably were somewhat questionable, would you concede this morning that it's gotten to the point where there is a bit of piling-on going on here? I mean, it seems to me that he has done some things that other presidents have done in the past. I mean, you look at other presidential libraries, they are filled with things that those presidents got during their, their years at the White House. And yet somehow it's become a high crime for Bill Clinton to take some of these things with him to put in his presidential library."

The next day, February 21, more bad news emerged—believe it or not, from the *National Enquirer*. Hillary's brother Hugh Rodham had

earned a quick and cool $400,000 for lobbying the Clinton administra-
tion, helping arrange the pardon of herb-cure swindler Almon Glenn
Braswell along with the sentence commutation of drug dealer Carlos
Vignali. The coverage devoted to this bombshell was nothing less than
shameful.

On that night's *CBS Evening News*, a sympathetic Phil Jones insisted
that "this latest scandal involving the former First Lady's brother is
viewed by friends of the Clintons as disastrous." And then he began to
spin. Jones went out of his way to note that Braswell "has also been a
problem for Republicans," since the Bush campaign and the Florida
GOP returned donations after they learned he was a convicted felon. (This
is a bit different from wiping the felony off his record.) A few moments
later, Dan Rather artfully described the drug dealer whom Clinton
released from prison nine years early. "Carlos Vignali was convicted of
shipping 800 pounds of cocaine from Los Angeles to Minneapolis, but"
(and you knew the "but" was coming, didn't you?) "he was a first-time
offender and many political figures—a sheriff and a Roman Catholic
cardinal—lobbied the White House for the sentence to be commuted."

Here's what CBS didn't tell viewers: Janet Reno's Justice Department
had rejected Vignali's appeal for clemency months before it was granted
on Clinton's final day; other first-time offenders given clemency were
small dealers, but Vignali was at the top of a huge interstate drug ring;
Vignali's father was a big-time donor to the Democratic Party; and
Roger Cardinal Mahony, cited by Rather, said several days before that his
letter asking for leniency for Vignali was "a serious mistake."

The wettest tears were saved for Hillary. "This is terrible for her,
Dan," CBS analyst Gloria Borger offered. Borger stuck with her story
the next morning: "Oh, this is just terrible for her," she wailed to sympathetic *Early Show* cohost Bryant Gumbel, who added his own shot: "But,
aside from feeding the cottage industry of the usual Republican Clinton-
bashers, is anything likely to come of this?" Borger reinforced the suggestion of cynical Republican glee: "George W. Bush is sort of floating
under the radar here. He seems to be having a very good time with this."

Those damn Republican Clinton-bashers again.

By the second night, Rather was sounding like a press release service
for the Clintons. "Two separate friends of Hillary Rodham Clinton told
CBS News tonight that Hugh Rodham, quote, 'spent considerable time

in the White House during the last month of the Clinton presidency.' Senator Clinton's mother, Dorothy Rodham, was also there for a good deal of time, according to these sources. One friend said Hillary Clinton's family has, quote, 'always been very important to her and very close to her.' Continuing to quote, 'She always has tried to have her brother and mother around as much as possible.' Also continuing to quote, '[T]hese new revelations are absolutely devastating to her and she is furious about them,' unquote."

The next day, February 22, Senator Clinton decided to hold a press conference on Capitol Hill to put her spin on the story. In *The Final Days*, Barbara Olson explained that Hillary was incredibly consistent in pushing her talking points. More than twenty times she said she hadn't known anything about what was going on. More than ten times she said she was very disturbed and disappointed. Her answers defied logic. One reporter asked, "[T]he $400,000 your brother received had nothing to do with the president's decision to pardon these two men?" to which she answered, "I believe that's the case. I absolutely believe that's the case."

Even while Democrats reacted harshly—the papers were filled with tales of Democrats angrily denouncing the Clinton shenanigans behind closed doors—the upshot for Hillary was more sympathy. Even James Carville was fairly mum, refusing to defend or attack Bill, but he cast Hillary as the victim: "You can pick your friends," he said. "But you can't pick your relatives." On *The Early Show*, CBS reporter Diana Olick quoted Hillary as saying she was "heartbroken and shocked by it, and you know, immediately said this was a terrible misjudgment and the money had to be returned," and concluded by playing up the victim spin. "The Senate spotlight has not come easily to Mrs. Clinton, only the glare of scandal. For instance, take the day she presided over the Senate for the first time. Denise Rich was hogging the headlines, claiming her donations to President Clinton had nothing to do with the pardon granted her fugitive ex-husband. And then there was the day she delivered her first speech on the Senate floor, an impassioned call for health care reform. Her husband was busy leading a mob of cameras and reporters on a tour of his new neighborhood in Harlem. Guess who made the news that night? It seems no matter how hard Senator Hillary Clinton tries to build a wall between herself and her husband's policies, it inevitably comes crumbling down."

This has to be one of the most absurd endings ever to a TV news story. Since when is a freshman senator's perfunctory firsts—presiding over the Senate, giving a floor speech—national news? It wasn't national news when it was done by other new senators at the time, even women, like Senator Jean Carnahan of Missouri and Senator Debbie Stabenow of Michigan.

Hillary also had defenders at ABC. On *This Week,* cohost Cokie Roberts declared her position formally: "There's a poll today saying most New Yorkers don't believe Hillary Clinton on all this. Now, I must say I do believe that Hugh Rodham did not tell his stern big sister about this." Former Clinton aide George Stephanopoulos agreed: "I think you're exactly right." In her online column, ABC anchor Carole Simpson made it a network trifecta when she chided, "When you express shock and outrage at Bill's and Hillary's brothers' involvement in the pardon controversy, consider what your own relatives might do if you possessed the power of the presidency." It's plausible that anyone's relatives would be entranced by the possibility of lucrative lobbying with the family influence. But it wasn't just that Hugh Rodham made the pitch—Bill and Hillary bought the pitch. So it wasn't just sleazy relatives who were at fault, but the pardoning authority who egregiously added to the fault.

The press coverage waned (even over Marc Rich), and by springtime it was another scandal successfully squashed. On the April 12 *Good Morning America,* ABC's Linda Douglass aired a supportive story on Hillary's first hundred days in office, a journalistic tradition usually reserved for presidents. But apparently it needed to be expanded to future presidents. Douglass told the devastated-victim story yet *again*: "Clinton was the new kid on the block while her colleagues were howling about her husband's last-minute pardons of questionable criminals. Then she learned her own brother Hugh was paid $400,000 to win pardons for a drug dealer and a swindler. . . . Her friends tell ABC News Mrs. Clinton was devastated, angry at Hugh, yet frustrated that she could not protect him. They say she felt cut off from her family. She is rarely seen with Mr. Clinton, though sources say he often sneaks into Washington to stay with her." There's something humorous in the notion that anonymous sources confirm that a married couple sometimes sneaks into moments of togetherness.

Douglass claimed that "back home" in New York, "the tabloids have raked her over the coals," and "her critics never give up, but "she never gives in." Viewers were supposed to be inspired. "All agree: Clinton has thrown herself into work, often putting in sixteen- to eighteen-hour days, immersing herself in details of legislation, almost never missing a committee hearing. She has been a sponsor on twenty pieces of legislation, twice that of other freshmen senators—on education, job programs, consumer protection, health care, and, ironically, tighter scrutiny of presidential pardons." Here was another outbreak of Olick Syndrome: since when is chronicling the cosponsorship of bills inspiring enough for TV news, even the shameless attempt at endorsing post-Clinton pardon reform?

On the July 16 *Today*, Katie Couric sat down for another interview with Hillary biographer and New Age guru Gail Sheehy. When Sheehy said that Senator Clinton had ingratiated herself with colleagues and taken "advantage of the fact that the Senate is the best refuge for a co-scoundrel," Couric protested: "Co-scoundrel. That's pretty harsh." But Sheehy was insistent that "the way they left the White House was very, very unattractive." So Couric returned to buffing Hillary's image, talking about how "she has also won a great deal of respect by working very, very hard, and by not pulling any kind of prima donna act." Sheehy underlined the fringe benefits of the media's constantly cooing coverage: "The wonderful thing about Hillary's position is . . . her celebrity trumps her scandals."

Washington Post reporter John F. Harris echoed the media's excitement over their favorite senator with a supportive Sunday cover story in the *Washington Post Magazine* in January 2002. The subheadline said it all: "A supportive spouse, surprisingly accepting colleagues, and a mandate to legislate. For Sen. Clinton, life is almost perfect. If only they weren't still out to get her." Hillary's paranoia was easily transferable.

HILLARY'S NEW CAREER AS HAWKISH "CENTRIST"

The terrorist attacks on New York City on September 11, 2001, were a terrible and unifying event, but it soon became clear to calculating pundits that their senator from New York could gain unusual prominence in the aftermath. "It seems almost crass to say it, but if anyone has profited from this politically it is Hillary Clinton," Rutgers University political scientist Ross Baker told the Associated Press. It didn't occur to AP or anyone else in the Clinton-loving media to reexamine the Clinton administration's terrorism record. In the early days after the awful events, with a nation still in shock, and with political differences set aside, her prominence was understandable.

Senator Clinton appeared in interviews on all three networks in the first days of national shock. Beyond the evening newscasts she was featured by CBS's *Face the Nation*, NBC's *Dateline NBC,* and CNN's *Larry King Live;* was covered by all the morning talk shows; and was afforded live coverage of her press conferences as well as her attendance at firefighters' funerals. Everywhere she spoke she expressed her horror at the attack, her gratitude that her family was safe, and her support for President Bush's emerging War on Terror. On September 14, she told Katie Couric, "I'm fully confident that the president and his advisers are preparing plans that will be effective, and we have to stand behind that."

Despite the spirit of national unity, not every event was a slam-dunk for Hillary, especially when she was viewed as taking political advantage of the tragedy. When she took the stage at a memorial rock concert in Madison Square Garden in October, the audience erupted in boos. As Byron York reported for National Review Online, "All the junior senator from New York had to do was walk on stage to hear a round of boos from the crowd, thousands of whom were the specially invited police officers and firefighters. If she had any plans for long extemporaneous remarks, the stunned-looking former first lady quickly abandoned them and retreated to the wings."

Now damage control was in order. Not to worry. The media were there to handle that task for her. The booing had been shown live by the cable TV music channel VH1, but as ABC's John Stossel illustrated in a report the next July, when the Viacom-owned cable channel replayed it, sound technicians had replaced the boos with cheering and applause. And that version is the permanent record VH1 put onto its DVD of the event. As Andrew Stuttaford quipped on National Review Online, "This is something to remember the next time you hear about the 'suppression of dissent' post-9/11."

As the nation settled into a post-9/11 reality, Hillary's Senate life quieted down, though national media figures still occasionally offered their dollops of adoration. On ABC's daytime show *The View*, TV legend Barbara Walters oozed, "I went to a luncheon yesterday and Hillary Clinton was there. And I don't get to see Hillary Clinton very much and she was talking about the problems of New York and the problems of safety. She was simply terrific. She was so well informed, she speaks without any written material, you know. We do a lot of kidding around, but boy, I was impressed."

But why the continued fascination? It certainly wasn't with her Senate leadership. In their book *Condi vs. Hillary*, former Clinton adviser Dick Morris and his wife, Eileen McGann, note that "Hillary has had a total of twenty bills passed since she entered the Senate. Of those, fifteen have been purely symbolic in nature." True, it would be tough for any Democrat to claim major legislative accomplishments at a time when the House, the Senate, and the White House were all controlled by Republicans. So what about her Senate voting record? Had the admiring press been interested in something more than cheerleading, they would have found that Hillary was emerging as one of the most left-wing members of the Senate. During her first year in the Senate, the liberal Americans for Democratic Action (ADA) awarded Clinton's votes a near-perfect 95 percent approval rating, a record that put her on a par with Senators Barbara Boxer, Chris Dodd, Barbara Mikulski, and Chuck Schumer. The American Conservative Union (ACU), by contrast, gave her a paltry 12 on its conservative scale.

How about her ratings from taxpayer groups? The National Taxpayers Union reported that she supported their position 3 percent of the time in 2001, which, said the group, "earned the dubious distinction of being the lowest-scoring member of the Senate" that year. "This is the worst score for a Senate freshman in their first year in office that NTU has ever recorded," it added. She earned an "F" rating from NTU in each of her first four years, during which time she voted against Bush's tax cuts in 2001 and again in 2003. The National Tax Limitation Committee gave her a zero for 2001–2002. Citizens Against Government Waste has given her a paltry 8 percent lifetime rating.

What about gun rights? She had an "F-minus" from the Gun Owners of America. "As First Lady, Hillary Clinton was a principal in the Clinton administration's effort to harass the NRA," National Rifle Association executive vice president Wayne LaPierre said. "As a senator, she's supported every draconian gun control effort that has come down the pike. As president, I have little doubt that she'll continue her vendetta against gun owners and hunters, and raise it to unprecedented levels." On the other hand, Hillary earned a 100 percent ranking from the Brady Campaign to Prevent Gun Violence in her first Congress.

The American Federation of State, County and Municipal Employees, which works feverishly to protect the gold-plated pensions and early-retirement privileges of public workers, gave Mrs. Clinton and Ted Kennedy identical 100 percent ratings for 2001, 2002, and 2003. Meanwhile, her lifetime rating from the AFL-CIO is 93 percent—again, precisely the same as Kennedy's.

Nor has Hillary Clinton shown any hesitation in supporting the favorite causes of the libertine left. In her first two years, Senator Clinton earned a perfect 100 percent voting score from the gay "liberation" lobby. During this time she voted against the Jesse Helms amendment to deny federal funds to public schools that would ban the Boy Scouts from their meeting rooms, and for the Barbara Boxer amendment to allow such punitive action against the Scouts with no threat to their money from Washington. Having accused her GOP opponent in the 2000 campaign of being "out of the mainstream" on gay rights, Hillary served as the keynote speaker for the Human Rights Campaign's big annual fundraising dinner in October 2001, where she pledged that she would keep lobbying for "hate crimes" legislation and "domestic partner" benefits, and declared that gays who lost lovers on 9/11 should get the same federal assistance as "other families." (She was also a leader in advocating benefits for illegal-alien relatives of the lost.) "We have to make clear that what we're fighting for is our values," she said.

That was nothing compared with Senator Clinton's fierce solidarity with the abortion lobby, which she cultivated closely in her Senate campaign. She even touted a line in the Clinton budget proposal providing a $4.5 million package to subsidize abortion clinics to purchase security cameras, motion detectors, and bullet-resistant windows. Her voting record followed suit: routine 100 ratings from NARAL Pro-Choice America, routine zeroes from the National Right to Life Committee.

The record speaks for itself, but in politics, where perception is reality, records don't mean much if you can get away with it—which means receiving a healthy assist from the press. Bill Clinton had succeeded masterfully in 1992, packaging his ticket as centrist, complete with a running mate who had twice edged Ted Kennedy out in the National Taxpayers Union's measure of Biggest Spender in the Senate. Al Gore attempted to continue the charade in 2000, but a relentless assault by conservatives and the alternative media on his liberal record neutralized the effort. When Howard Dean, arguably the most radical major political player on the national scene today, emerged as the early Democratic front-runner in 2003, the press again was anointing him—somehow—as a moderate; an inept campaign and a primordial scream put an end to his aspirations. Even John Kerry tried to run from his far-left record with a compliant media aggressively promoting the hawkish war-hero image needed to offset a lifetime devoted to leftist causes. But for the Swift Boat Veterans for Truth, it would have worked, too.

Even before capturing the New York Senate seat, Hillary Clinton was already viewed by most political observers as serious presidential timber, a testimony to the extraordinary hold she commands over the American left. But a darling of the left cannot win the presidency on that record. What to do? The answer was simple. Shamelessly sell ultraliberal Hillary as a moderate. On the January 12, 2002, *Chris Matthews Show*, NBC reporter Andrea Mitchell raved about her appeal to Democrats, with a twist: "They all gravitate to her. It's not only that she's passed out so much money, it's that she's got ideas. She's centrist. She knows how to play to a liberal constituency and she knows how to play to middle America."

In a May 31 online column, *Newsweek*'s Eleanor Clift reported how the "neutral" people understood that Hillary "blended" into the center: "Neutral observers give her high marks for the way she has blended into the Senate's clubby culture, even joining conservative Republicans in a weekly prayer group. The junior senator for New York has never been the wild-eyed liberal her critics imagine. . . . The former First Lady's makeover as a political centrist dates back to the shellacking she took as the architect of the health-care plan that almost sank the Clinton presidency."

Even the wire services ran with the spin. On July 29, Associated Press ran a story headlined "Hillary Clinton Emerges as Moderate." Washington bureau reporter Shannon McCaffrey wrote that despite conservative direct-mail language comparing her to liberals like Ted Kennedy, Senator Clinton had "belied" predictions that she would be "a liberal's liberal." McCaffrey's evidence? Clinton was scheduled to deliver "the keynote address at a Democratic Leadership Council meeting in New York" and the organization was a "centrist group." How moderate is this group? At that time, it was headed up by Senator Tom Carper of Delaware, with a lifetime ACU rating of 18 percent. Senator John Kerry (lifetime ACU rating of 6 percent) belongs to the group and received its endorsement for president in 2004. In 2005 the organization gave Ted Turner its DLC/Clinton Center award for his philanthropy, which includes all things in favor of abortion, militant environmentalism, and radical groups protesting America's military presence wherever it lands.

For the liberal media, *centrism* was a sales word, not a claim to investigate. Hillary's weakest feints toward the American middle—whether it's touting abortion as something that should be "safe, legal, and rare," or touting the Scripture collection in her purse, or showing up in Afghanistan for a shamelessly pandering Thanksgiving dinner with the troops—result in immediate press attention, with major gravitas attached. But the concrete liberalism of her legislative record is ignored.

Not everyone has swallowed the Kool-Aid on these "centrism" claims. In *U.S. News & World Report*, "Washington Whispers" writer Paul Bedard typed out this brief item: "Sen. Hillary Rodham Clinton is fast becoming known in the Senate Democratic caucus as the keeper of the liberal flame. Insiders say she often forcefully defends left-leaning positions when others talk of compromise."

Senator Clinton did go beyond sounding hawkish when she voted for military action in Iraq in the fall of 2002. On the September 15, 2002, edition of NBC's *Meet the Press,* she protested the politicization of the war effort. "I don't know that we want to put it in a political context. I'm sure that the president doesn't mean that," she offered. "This is a national security issue, not a political issue. It should come before the Congress when it's appropriate to come before the Congress." Would Congress vote to support war in Iraq? "I can't imagine that we won't. . . . This has been the policy of the United States for four years now." Senator Clinton went so far as to remind her host that while many Democrats voted against the Gulf War in 1991, she supported that war against Saddam Hussein as well.

It wouldn't be long before Senator Clinton found that hawkishness a burden as the liberal base turned increasingly toward the antiwar fervor of MoveOn.org, and her faith in President Bush's wisdom about war was suddenly a forgotten talking point, an indecent thought never to be acknowledged again.

Chapter 13
Hillary's Mangled History

I could hardly breathe. Gulping for air, I started crying and yelling at him, "What do you mean? What are you saying? Why did you lie to me?" I was furious and getting more so by the second. . . . Up until now I thought that he'd been foolish for paying attention to the young woman and was convinced he was being railroaded. I couldn't believe he would do anything to endanger our marriage and our family. I was dumbfounded, heartbroken and outraged that I'd believed him at all.

—HILLARY CLINTON's "reaction" on August 15, 1998,
to the "news" that Clinton had strayed with Monica Lewinsky,
from her memoir *Living History*

I spoke to scores and scores of journalists in Washington during that period, hundreds probably. It was a matter of joking. They took for granted that he was cheating. They took for granted that Hillary knew. And yet they chose once again to subordinate their knowledge and their suspicion and not challenge her when obviously, objectively, they would have thought she was lying.

—TONY BLANKLEY, in an interview with the authors

With two years in the Senate now under her fashionable belt, Hillary Clinton could put away the modest-freshman routine. That was especially true after the 2002 elections were a bust for the Democrats. With Tom Daschle now demoted to Senate minority leader, she had an opportunity to emerge as a Democratic leader.

That's certainly what her media supporters saw for her. As the Senate reconvened in 2003, MSNBC's Chris Matthews declared with his usual brio, "You know what's impressive? Sitting in the Senate press gallery and looking down and realizing that Hillary Clinton is the leader of the U.S. Senate Democrats. She's the boss. Everybody was circling around her when they were having that big dispute over unemployment benefits. Hillary was calling the shots. . . . She's intellectually and ideologically the center of the Democratic Party." Never mind that she had one of the most liberal voting records in the entire Senate; to her rooters in the media, she was the ideological center.

The junior senator from New York seized the opportunity, most notably by stepping up the partisan attacks on President Bush, asserting that the Bush administration was cutting millions from local law-enforcement agencies and diverting it to counterterrorism. She told the *New York Times* that the White House was involved in a "shell game" and that "it's unthinkable to raise the national threat alert and decrease the funding for homeland security."

At the same time, Daschle began giving Hillary new power and influence befitting her celebrity, if not her seniority. She was put in charge of the Senate Democratic Steering Committee, and gained a seat on the Senate Armed Services Committee to build her commander-in-chief credentials. The nation's top newspapers barely noticed the committee switch. In fact, the national media kept her nearly invisible while she supported the war effort in Iraq.

Why? Was it because a hawkish Hillary would threaten the burgeoning antiwar movement within the Democratic Party (not to mention the press)? Was it because the vision of Hillary Rodham Clinton siding with President Bush would help his cause? Whatever the reason, her floor speech in October 2002 supporting Bush's call to wage war, certainly one of the most important public declarations, if not *the* most important, of her short Senate career, was mysteriously left out of the media's "rush-to-war" template. Look for articles in Hillary's adopted hometown newspaper the *New York Times* on the senator's war advocacy as hostilities approached and you'll find almost nothing. On the cusp of bombs dropping in

Baghdad in March of 2003, Senator Clinton again publicly declared her support for the president's war position "if coercive inspections" failed to work, with her spokesman declaring that she "fully supports the steps the president has taken to disarm Iraq." The media ignored that, too.

What Hillary's supporters really anticipated in 2003 was the arrival of her thick memoir, titled *Living History*, obviously modeled on *Washington Post* publisher Katharine Graham's *Personal History*, which won great media adulation in 1997. (Like Mrs. Clinton, Mrs. Graham rose to power and influence after her own personal pain in her marriage, as Philip Graham cheated on her and eventually committed suicide, leaving her father's *Washington Post* for her to run.) Not only the titles, but even the book covers were similar, each featuring a photo of the subject staring into the camera in black-and-white.

While the press was hyping Hillary as promising presidential material, they weren't going to scrutinize her this way. No one in the media even lifted an eyebrow at the "Author's Note" that began the book: "In 1958, I wrote my autobiography for an assignment in sixth grade. In twenty-nine pages . . ." In twenty-nine pages? Even at age twelve, Hillary's ego was running amok.

As the publicity tour to promote Hillary's memoir began in June, the first official talking point was that Mrs. Clinton's autobiography was "candid." The *Time* magazine cover featuring her excerpt promised, "The former First Lady talks candidly about Bill, her public life and her private pain." On NBC, Tom Brokaw claimed that "she's a lot more candid about her personal life and feelings than many had expected." On *Today*, Katie Couric echoed, "[S]he's very candid about a very personal matter." *Today* news anchor Sara James added, "Mrs. Clinton writes candidly about the moment her husband admitted he's been unfaithful." On CBS's *Early Show*, reporter Tracy Smith touted how Hillary "describes in candid detail her pain and anguish over her husband's affair." Denied a Hillary interview, *Early Show* cohost Harry Smith interviewed her former campaign spokesman, Howard Wolfson. What was his first impression? "I was impressed with Hillary's candor." On CNN's *American Morning*, another former Clinton publicist, Lisa Caputo, chimed in that "she's quite candid in the book, as you'll see." Caputo dropped the C-word twice more before her interview was finished. (She added that it was "very candid" in her interview on *Today*.)

After all the bated breath and wild speculation, Hillary's tale of being shocked, shocked at the truth of the intern affair was, and is, simply unbelievable. She claims that she learned the truth of the Monica Lewinsky affair *on August 15, 1998*. Remember the Lewinsky scandal timeline, and not just the fact that Hillary probably knew about Lewinsky long before she ended up on a witness list in the Paula Jones case at the end of 1997. Consider what was happening during the weeks *before* she supposedly started "gulping for air" in shock. On July 29, 1998, Clinton lawyer David Kendall announced that Clinton would testify before the grand jury on August 17. On that night, ABC's Jackie Judd reported that Monica Lewinsky had saved the infamous blue-dress sample of the president's DNA. The next day, all the other networks noted that the dress had been handed over, offering plenty of euphemisms about the president's leaving "physical evidence." The FBI came to the White House to draw the president's blood for a DNA test. As all these developments unfolded, we're supposed to believe Hillary knew nothing, and suddenly gasped for breath on August 15?

Sean Hannity laughs in disbelief at all the talk of Mrs. Clinton's candor. "I have the book on tape," he told us. "I played it on the radio. 'I could hardly breathe.' At some point you've got to laugh, and that makes you laugh. 'I was shocked!' It was a bald-faced lie, one of the biggest lies she's ever told. That's all there is to it."

In her telling, Hillary was the dictionary definition of dim bulb, a woman who claimed that she never suspected a thing about Gennifer Flowers or Paula Jones or Monica Lewinsky, making Mrs. Clinton just about the only person on earth not to suspect her womanizing husband. The very thought is preposterous, and clearly defies the historical record. Hillary Clinton was so suspicious of her husband's affairs, and had been for years, that at one point she'd hired private detective Ivan Duda in Arkansas to track him. The entire Clinton political machine was so attuned to Bill Clinton's sexual proclivities that Clinton confidante Betsey Wright joked of "bimbo eruptions" along the campaign trail. Remember also that poor naïve Hillary was anything but: As George Stephanopoulos recounts in his book, upon learning of the first potential national bimbo eruption (Connie Hamzy), Hillary said, *"We have to destroy her story."*

But now Hillary Clinton was taking the charade to a new, lower level.

She wrote that all along she had felt the womanizing stories were lies concocted by her enemies. "I had little trouble believing the accusations were groundless. By then, I had endured more than six years of baseless claims fomented by some of the same people and groups associated with the Jones case and the Starr investigation."

In other words, Flowers and Jones and every other Clinton mistress (and possible sexual assault victim) were still a figment of the conservative conspiracy's imagination. Hillary was still claiming this in 2003, despite Clinton's admission to Starr's team of an affair with Flowers, despite Clinton's settling with Paula Jones for $850,000, despite Juanita Broaddrick's weeping testimony of a rape on NBC. Even now, she was still a victim of both her husband and the lying right-wingers.

A tough questioner, a journalist who valued the truth, would openly display some small fraction of the incredulity Hillary's position demanded. If one were to believe her *Living History* recollections, at the very least one would have to ask Hillary this simple question: How could someone honored as so dazzlingly smart look this amazingly airheaded? Or try this one: Given that she blamed a right-wing conspiracy for creating a nefarious legend of her husband's adultery, and given that the charges were in fact true—indeed, "proven true," to borrow the very language she had originally used during her famous January 1998 *Today* show appearance—didn't she owe conservatives a whopping public apology?

But these questions are based on a false premise. Her stated claim of ignorance was simply unbelievable.

"This is an example of what I see the Clintons doing all the time: telling a lie when no lie is necessary and a big lie when a little white lie would be just fine," *American Spectator* editor Emmett Tyrrell told us. "There was no reason for her to lie about this. It didn't save her marriage. It didn't save her in the eyes of the knowing public. It just showed her one more time in a gratuitous lie." *National Review*'s Kate O'Beirne doesn't buy Hillary's story either: "For years she covered up for a sexual predator and was only furious that he had gotten caught." Floyd Brown, who has spent years examining Clinton scandals, is equally unconvinced: "Hillary is an expert liar, and those comments were just a scripted fabrication because she not only knew about the affairs, but she actively [worked to] protect him. She owes the American people an apology."

When we asked talk-radio host Mark Levin whether he believed Hillary's story, he said, "No, she's a liar. If she didn't know that this guy was cheating on her since before they were married, since they were dating, and throughout their marriage, she ought not be president of the United States. If she's that dumb, that blind to what's going on right under her nose, then I don't want her leading the fight against terrorism. This was all a cover-up and she's still lying about it." As for the suggestion that Hillary had to endure "baseless claims" from the right, Levin was defiant: "If conservatives are the only ones—and in many cases we were—to speak out against what was going on in this White House, which includes assaulting and harassing women, then good for us!"

Rush Limbaugh agreed that it was impossible to believe Hillary knew nothing about Lewinsky, but he told us that we won't ever get an apology from Mrs. Clinton: "If you have the expectation that the Clintons have decency and character, then you would expect an apology. But you have to understand that they're total political animals. I never expected her to apologize to me. I don't expect her to apologize about anything."

But the press bought it. Her interviewers in the "mainstream" media chose to replay the surreal soap opera of Hillary, the Wronged Little Woman, and sold these dreary reruns as "candid" droppings of "bombshells." They couldn't imagine that she was pretending. ABC's Barbara Walters stuck with the spin that she was struck dumb by love: "She's either the greatest actress in the whole world, or this is really, you know, you understand why the marriage works when you see how she talks about him." CNN reporter Jonathan Karl unequivocally accepted her tale by reporting that she went on the infamous conspiracy-spinning *Today* show "unwittingly repeating his lies." CNN anchor Aaron Brown even puzzled over why anyone would care whether Hillary was lying or not. "What is all the fuss here, in a sense? What does it matter, when she actually found out or what words were used? Why is this important?" *Time* magazine columnist Joe Klein agreed: "Well, it's not important, but it's fun. I mean, the marriage was the great mystery of the Clinton administration."

The only exception was Fox News. On his show *Special Report*, Brit Hume pointed out that Hillary's account of frosty marital bitterness over a Martha's Vineyard vacation after he admitted the Lewinsky affair in

August 1998 did not match an account of a light, bantering couple contained in Clinton aide Sidney Blumenthal's book *The Clinton Wars*. National Public Radio reporter Mara Liasson countered by simply asserting that she had "no problem believing" what Hillary wrote about her "complicated" marriage.

As always the message from the media was loud and clear: *We're behind you, Hillary!*

ANOTHER PARADE OF PANDERERS AND PATRONIZERS

The media often approach political memoirs with skepticism, expecting them to be bland attempts at self-justification. But in Hillary's case it didn't matter how ridiculous her "living history" sounded or how much history her book left out. The fawning interviews continued.

ABC's Barbara Walters secured the first interview for a prime-time Sunday night special on June 8, and ABC should have been investigated for false advertising. The promos that plugged that Hillary interview promised, again and again for two weeks, to deliver "the interview we've all been waiting for, and the book that tells all. Sunday June 8. Nothing's off limits."

Were "we all" waiting for this? ABC imagined that everyone's heart bled for Hillary. "The book that tells all"? Hillary never tells all. "Nothing's off limits"? ABC should be glad they didn't offer this interview by pay-per-view, because everyone would be entitled to a refund. Barbara Walters left almost everything of importance off limits.

Senator Clinton's 528-page book should have made some effort to address and answer the alphabet soup of scandals she and her husband left as their legacy—and instead, she ignored them again. Did she hire Craig Livingstone, the goon who collected the raw FBI files of political opponents, or not? Why, after a long absence, were the subpoenaed Rose Law Firm billing records mysteriously located in her area of the White House residence? How did she make $100,000 on a $1,000 investment in cows? What role did she play in Travelgate? What role did she play in the Marc Rich pardons? What role did her brother play in the pardon of a drug dealer? What role did she play in the theft of White House furniture sent to her new residence? And speaking of that new home, how did she explain those suspicious loans that were being arranged for her? Her failure to answer these questions speaks volumes about her. And the media's failure to focus on this outrage speaks volumes about them.

When she wasn't joining Hillary on picturesque walks through her childhood neighborhood in Illinois and her ritzy new house in Chappaqua and asking her softball questions about her life story, Walters only asked questions that would please the Clinton-loving left. How could Hillary work with icky Tom DeLay, and senators who voted to impeach her husband? "I mean, no hard feelings? No remnants? Are you a saint?" She lamented that the poor Clintons were so hounded "I can barely remember a week went by when one of you wasn't being criticized and investigated."

The financial scandals were brought up—and quickly discarded. "You made investments in the commodities market, you dealt in real estate, Whitewater, you worked for the Rose Law Firm, all of which at the time you thought were very innocent. All of these things came back to haunt you. Was there anything you could've done differently?" Hillary admitted no mistakes, and no wrongdoing: "Well, Barbara, of course all of those things were made into political issues. And after all of the years of investigation, and all of the looking under rocks and all that was done, of course there wasn't anything wrong."

Hillary had the same I'm-blameless answer when Walters touched briefly on her appearance before Kenneth Starr's grand jury over long-missing Whitewater documents. "Everything that was thrown at me, everything that was said turned out to be without basis in fact," Hillary the Victim insisted, "but that didn't help at the time, because we had this out-of-control, zealous prosecutor who was on a partisan campaign to undermine Bill and me and everyone else."

Walters flashed past the "vast-right-wing conspiracy" controversy. "If I ask you straight up: Was there and is there a right-wing conspiracy to destroy your husband's presidency, would you today say yes?" What a question! Walters knew the vast right-wing conspiracy charge was a fraudulent accusation, yet rather than confront the former First Lady on her dishonesty, she was inviting her to amend it! Hillary was more than happy to comply. "There is a very well-financed, right-wing network of people, It's not really a conspiracy because it's pretty much out in the light of day" and they "really stopped at nothing, even to the point of perverting the Constitution in order to undermine what he was trying to do for the country."

It's always interesting to see Mrs. Clinton accuse someone else's husband of "perverting" the Constitution.

The biggest nail-polishing moment in the interview came when Walters turned to religion as she explained Hillary's vacation at Martha's Vineyard after Clinton was forced to admit adultery: "I don't think people realize how strong your faith is. It goes all through the book. It must have helped you then." Naturally, Hillary agreed. "It was the primary source of help to me. I was raised with faith, and that's a great gift to give a child, and I have relied on it. I've relied on prayer." Again, no one questioned whether her covering up for her husband's behavior and her long record of attacking her husband's previous accusers were a moral or religious failing. Instead, Walters insisted in one of her endless promotional interviews on ABC, "She's a very religious woman."

The most daring question came near the end, when Walters asked, "Do you trust your husband totally today?" Hillary ducked with an unsurprising answer: "You know, we've really been tried and tested. And we are at the point now that we're looking forward. I hope that we'll grow old together. That's how I look at our future." Walters replied, "Okay. I have to ask it. What if he does something in the future that is similar?" Hillary wanted the question tucked back in her zone of privacy: "You know, that will be between us. And that will be that zone of privacy that I believe in." Walters ended the interview by instructing Hillary to read a gooey paragraph from her book in which she explained how she lovingly found that her husband was still "the most interesting, energizing and fully alive person I have ever met."

Time magazine excerpted the book, and senior editor Nancy Gibbs interviewed Senator Clinton with kid gloves. When Hillary said the Bush administration was conspiring to defund the federal government's "ability to do anything other than fund defense," Gibbs followed up: "Would you call Bush a radical?" Hillary replied, incredibly, that the Bushies "are certainly more radical than Ronald Reagan." Gibbs also asked about the VRWC—but her question presumed that the charge was true from the beginning! "Is the 'vast right-wing conspiracy' bigger than you thought when you brought the term into our vocabulary?"

On TV, NBC's Katie Couric came next, and NBC dragged out her taped interview with Senator Clinton over three days on *Today*. There was plenty of talk about her Illinois childhood, and nothing on the financial scandals. True to her record of interviews with Hillary, Couric brought up the male chauvinist pigs, this time with reference to the health care debacle: "But were you surprised at the backlash? The really vitriolic, violent backlash against you in many ways? Do you think it was good old-fashioned sexism?" That drew a surprising answer. Hillary regretted the health czar job: "In retrospect, it shouldn't have happened. It was a mistake."

But on the sex scandals, Couric could only ask naïvely why Senator Clinton felt the need to discuss them: "I'm wondering how you square that with the fact that you are a feminist. That means you're against things like sexual harassment. And given some of the things your husband allegedly engaged in as president, do you think that fell under the purview of the public's right to know?" *Allegedly*? Couric couldn't even acknowledge that any of the sexual allegations had been proven true.

Hillary granted two interviews to National Public Radio. NPR's Juan Williams interviewed Hillary for the June 19 *Morning Edition*, and tried to ask about how she's criticized by both traditionalists and feminists over her marriage. He turned to her maternal role: "When I'm reading about the Lewinsky affair and I hear about your role as a mother, I think even if you are offended, you must be doubly offended for what happened to your daughter. Were you?" Mrs. Clinton said "of course," again called her marriage "tried and tested," and then added, "And as I write about my husband, he is a force of nature. I knew that when I met him. I married him with my eyes open." So how does that match the "gulping for air" section? Williams didn't ask. He did wonder if "you told him, 'This is it, bud. You've had your last chance. If you do this again, I'm out of here'? Hillary ducked: "Well, let me just say that I am going to try, as best as possible, to keep my conversations going forward with my husband between us. But, you know, we're having a good time."

But the stronger dose of liberalism came in a June 12 interview on NPR's popular *Fresh Air*, which focuses more on entertainment and the fine arts than politics, but which, when it does turn to politics, is a strong liberal brew. Host Terry Gross couldn't stop asking Hillary to explain those scandalous conservatives. "Senator Clinton, you were a kind of symbol of evil for the right when you were the First Lady. But I think that you are being less demonized now that you're actually in office as a senator from New York. Do you agree that you were more demonized as First Lady than as senator and, if so, why do you think that that's true?" Hillary acknowledged she was "more of a flash point when you have a president who is breaking down barriers and trying to move the country in a progressive direction," and then returned to her talk about how she's a Rorschach test for people's strange anxieties about powerful women.

Gross asked about the need for Democrats to be more aggressive in opposition. "Now your opponents on the right were very skilled at attacking your husband's presidency, attacking your health care campaign, attacking your marriage and your private life. The Democrats now are having a very hard time in forcefully opposing President Bush and his policies, particularly the tax cut, this unprecedentedly large tax cut at a time of war with Iraq, facing, you know, the expenses of war, facing the expenses of the occupation. . . . What do you say to those critics who think that the Democrats just aren't doing a good enough job right now?" Gross asked if the Bush administration also showed signs of being vastly right-wing, and Hillary responded with a broadside: "I don't think that this administration in reality is either compassionate or conservative. I think it is hard-edged, radical, right-wing, with a very specific view of where they want to take America."

It was more of the same on taxpayer-funded PBS. On his late-night talk show, Charlie Rose waxed sympathetic about her personal growth, as if Hillary emerged like a beautiful butterfly from the chrysalis of the Clinton White House. "But you made a decision, because of your affection, love for him, to go to Arkansas where he wanted to pursue his dream," he cooed. "You gave up some independence because there was a higher value. . . . Now, here in a sense it's come full circle for you. . . . It seems to be the emergence to me of a new independence for you since you're on your own."

These kinds of questions only fed Hillary's ego. On HBO, interviewer Bob Costas wondered what were "your best and worst qualities as a politician?" Hillary could only muster that she had too large a bleeding heart: "Probably my worst quality is that I get very passionate about what I think is right." Compare the silence over that I-can't-think-of-any-real-flaws answer to the high dudgeon reporters managed when President Bush had trouble at press conferences and campaign debates responding to questions about his biggest mistake.

Hillary wasn't risking any tough interviews with this bizarre gulping-for-air story line. On NBC's syndicated weekend *Chris Matthews Show*, former Reagan speechwriter Peggy Noonan couldn't believe this plastic air-gulping story line, given that Hillary once put private detectives on her husband's trail in Arkansas. NBC reporter Andrea Mitchell noted the obvious: "This is a way of telling her story herself. She's not telling it in a tough interview with Chris Matthews, with Tim Russert, with anyone else. This is a way of her getting out her version, so that people, book buyers, people who read it, people who read about it will hear it more in her voice, and that is politically very advantageous." But what Mitchell didn't add, and apparently couldn't bring herself to add, was the conclusion one cannot help but reach in the face of the evidence: Hillary Clinton was lying.

HILLARY EXPLOITS HER NEW BIG-APPLE ROOTS

Despite predictions by some that *Living History* wouldn't sell well (Tucker Carlson promised to eat his shoe on CNN if it sold a million copies), the publicity was resplendent and sales took off. CBS, whose sister company Simon & Schuster had published the book, publicized its own corporate success by inviting Carlson on to *The Early Show* to grovel about his staged shoe-eating bluster. On ABC's daytime show *The View*, cohost Meredith Vieira credited her cohost Barbara Walters for the sales juggernaut: "She should thank you, Barbara, because after you did the interview, after you did that interview with ABC News with Hillary, first time she was speaking out about the book, talking about it, the next day 300,000 copies flew off the shelves of that book. So Barbara, she owes you a big thank-you."

ABC reporter John Cochran told the country on July 31: "Remember the $8 million advance Hillary Clinton's publisher gave her? Turns out it was a bargain. She has earned every penny—and then some. Her book is a bestseller in eight countries. Conservatives, who have long opposed her, trashed her book as phony and self-serving. Now some conservatives worry that attempts to demonize her have backfired."

But despite all the fawning and the fainting spells by Big Media stars, a majority of Americans were not impressed. *USA Today* published a poll showing that more than one in five respondents said the book belonged in the fiction section, and a full 56 percent said they thought Mrs. Clinton was being disingenuous in her claims that, notwithstanding seven months of revelations about it, she did not suspect the Monica Lewinsky affair was real until her husband fessed up. In other words, America believed Hillary was a liar. An ABC/*Washington Post* national poll timed for the book release found that when asked if they wanted Hillary to run for president, 53 percent said she should not. After the press bubble had passed, CBS also found in its poll that more people disliked Hillary (32 percent) than liked her (24 percent), with 44 percent undecided.

John Cochran saw something else in his July 31 report. Hillary Clinton was not just a publishing smash, she was a wild congressional success: "She has not only signed 20,000 copies of her book, she has also put her name on more legislation than any other senator in this Congress. Sponsoring or cosponsoring 396 bills, ranging from resolutions on Girl Scouts Week to funds for rebuilding Iraq." No other politician in America would be hailed as effective for cosponsoring pro–Girl Scout resolutions, but Hillary was in a league of her own.

The advantage of a New York Senate perch afforded Hillary unique media opportunities. For example, when Gotham experienced a blackout in mid-August 2003, Senator Clinton made the rounds of the networks campaigning against energy deregulation. In an interview with Ted Koppel in the middle of ABC's live prime-time coverage, she raised the specter of Enron: "I think that we have a lot of unanswered questions about where we're heading in this deregulated, privatized energy world." On MSNBC she blasted the Bush administration's "failed policy of deregulation that caused so much trouble in California a few years ago. They want to actually, you know, impose it on the entire country." She gave the same sermon on CNN.

That advantage also resurfaced on the second anniversary of the 9/11 attacks, as she made the rounds of the network morning shows. While Bush administration officials got clobbered, she was treated gently. ABC's Charles Gibson asked her solemnly, "As a New Yorker and senator and whatever, how are you feeling this day?" On the same program, Gibson pressed hard on Deputy Defense Secretary Paul Wolfowitz, suggesting that we were fighting terror in the wrong place.

On NBC, Katie Couric pushed around General Richard Myers, chairman of the Joint Chiefs of Staff, on why Osama bin Laden remained uncaptured after two years and on evidence that showed "the situation in Iraq is unraveling." But Couric gave Hillary the floor to give her political spin: "Two years after September 11, two years later, how safe and secure do you think this country is?" And "What do you think the major holes are, if you had to assess them?"

On CBS, the contrast was starkest. *Early Show* cohost Hannah Storm suggested to General Myers that many were feeling the war in Iraq was a harmful sideshow. "There are people even within the military, though, who contend that all the resources and the money and the troops that we have spent in Iraq have derailed the war on terrorism," she opined on behalf of those people. "Derailed your search for Osama bin Laden and your efforts to dismantle al Qaeda. What's your response?" For Hillary, she repeated the attack, but this time as a softball for the liberal Democrat to crush: "A lot of people"—note how we'd now grown from "people" to "a lot of people"—"feel the focus on the war in Iraq has not only derailed our own security and has hurt us economically, it's hurt our credibility on the world stage. Are we suffering a crisis of leadership in this country right now?" But Hillary demurred, suggesting that she would be glad to return on a less somber day to discuss leadership failures. So Storm helpfully set her up with another pitch: "You've fought so much for the heroes of 9/11. You have sought money for firefighters, you've taken the EPA to task for toning down their report on air quality at Ground Zero. Has enough been done for the heroes, the people who fought so bravely on that day?" This time Hillary swung: "I don't think so. I feel very strongly that, you know, the people who rushed toward danger, who I think saved thousands of lives, deserve all the help that they need."

Viewers could see the difference in treatment. On one side were the Bush team, who required a whip-cracking skepticism. On the other side was Hillary, who required a royal deference.

Run, Hillary, Run!

On the long Thanksgiving weekend, Senator Clinton and a fellow liberal Democrat, Senator Jack Reed of Rhode Island, visited troops in Afghanistan and Iraq. While she was there, on November 30, the CBS show *Sunday Morning* aired another humanizing soft-soap taped profile, this time of Mrs. Clinton and her childhood friend Betsy Johnson Ebeling. CBS reporter Erin Moriarty sat with them as they giggled over old photos and drawings. High school teachers once again marveled over how Hillary turned in 75-page term papers.

They briefly revisited the impeachment era, when the friendship was said to be the most important. Ebeling recalled being angry, but when asked for her response to the charge that the Clintons had a marriage based on mutual ambition, she had a change of heart. "To be in the presence of these two people is to be in the presence of two people who really love each other," she explained. "These are two people who think alike, who constantly stimulate each other's thinking. And I can't imagine a different, better partner for her." For her part, Hillary once again insisted she could not let the odious right-wingers see her cry. "I knew exactly what the folks on the other side expected: that at some point I would, you know, show anger or, you know, some emotional breakdown, I guess, in public, which they would then use to try to stampede people into forcing Bill to resign."

On Monday morning, Senators Clinton and Reed were invited to the *Today* show to display their newfound wisdom from their experience abroad. Katie Couric may usually seem sunny in mood, but her first question to Hillary was pure darkness. "What are your impressions of the situation in Iraq? How bad is it, in your view?" Her questions to Senator Clinton were vague, not the accusatory salvos the networks use against Bush administration spokesmen: "Senator Clinton, what is the solution, then?" Hillary wanted to wave the magic wand of the UN, with no embarrassment that the UN had made a huge, scandalous mess out of its Oil-for-Food Program in Iraq—a scandalous mess that the national media have routinely ignored. "In the short term, we have to move as quickly as possible to internationalize this with a new UN mandate," Hillary said. "We need the legitimacy of the United Nations in order to move forward." Couric had no follow-up for that.

On December 7, Hillary Rodham Clinton did something she had never done before. She appeared on all three network Sunday morning shows on the same day. Like Couric's, most of the interviewers' questions were remarkably brief and uncharacteristically bland—including those from former Clinton adviser George Stephanopoulos on ABC's *This Week*. Tim Russert did press her to answer again on the vast-right-wing conspiracy charge, and she had a new answer. She regretted conservatives organizing: "I regret that, because, you know, we've made progress as a country when we, you know, maybe went a little right, a little left, but we ended up kind of in the middle, which is where most Americans live and work and raise their families." But it's not where Senator Clinton voted.

Hillary's generic message for all three networks was that Bush wasn't "leveling with the American people" on the costs of war and that Bush was putting the withdrawal strategy from Iraq on a political timetable to benefit his campaign.

Was there a better case of the pot calling the kettle black than Hillary Clinton charging someone else with not "leveling" with the American people? Did she "level" with the American people about her secret health care task force? Or her killing in cattle futures? Or her role in collecting FBI files on Republicans? Or her accusation of a vast right-wing conspiracy? Or her ignorance of her husband's affairs? Or—the list seems endless.

If there is anything stranger, it was Hillary Clinton charging that some president other than her husband timed his military adventures on a political calendar. Didn't these network stars remember how Clinton hit positively nothing belonging to Osama bin Laden in Afghanistan and hit a pharmaceutical factory in Sudan to divert attention from his Lewinsky grand jury testimony? They couldn't recall how he bombed Iraq just as House Republicans began considering impeachment charges? Apparently not. No one asked.

Mrs. Clinton was asked to defend herself against charges that it was wrong for her to tell soldiers in war zones that while everyone at home loved them, many questioned Bush administration policies. John Roberts asked, "In hindsight, would you have criticized the president while you were on the ground in Iraq?" Mrs. Clinton protested that this "didn't happen. I know that's the latest flaming charge by the right wing. But that's not what happened." She said she wasn't "going to lie" to soldiers from New York about the domestic political hubbub over Iraq.

Tim Russert also asked about that on NBC, even mentioning that former Bob Dole aide Scott Reed called her comments "un-American." Hillary replied, "I think that's reflective of the efforts by this administration to deny and divert attention from what everybody knows. I mean, it is like the old children's story, 'The Emperor Has No Clothes.'" Unclothed-emperor analogies are a bad choice for Mrs. Clinton, but Russert didn't even stutter or blink.

But the lamest part of these Sunday sessions came when all three wasted their precious hard-question time by asking the Fabulous Former First Lady if she would throw her combat helmet into the ring for the White House in 2004. Stephanopoulos fantasized about a pollster telling her that with her on the ticket, the party wins, and without her it loses. Under those circumstances, he asked, "will you accept?" Clinton retorted, "That is not going to happen, George," prompting an excited Stephanopoulos to eagerly exclaim, "That's not a no! It could happen!" NBC's Russert presented her with another fanciful scenario, this one in which a deadlocked convention turns to her for salvation. Russert followed up ten times as he pushed, pushed, pushed. Examples: "So no matter what happens, absolutely, categorically, no?" and "But you would never accept the nomination in 2004?" and that ever hopeful "I think the door is opening a bit."

On Monday morning, Stephanopoulos reprised the Hillary-as-rock-star stanza for ABC's *Good Morning America*. Cohost Charles Gibson observed the obvious: "It seems like a lot of us can't take no for an answer." He added that it was "fairly realistic" that Hillary would be pressed into service as the vice presidential nominee, and "it'll be very tough for her to say no at that point." Stephanopoulos insisted that she did the three morning shows because "she wants to be a big player in the

Democratic Party. If you look at the polls right now, if she were in the race, she'd have 43 percent of the vote in the Democratic primaries."

But what Stephanopoulos, and Gibson, and Russert, and so many other Run Hillary Run enthusiasts were overlooking—and certainly not inserting in their gushy pieces—was that Hillary Rodham Clinton remained a very polarizing figure whose candidacy, either heading a presidential ticket or as a running mate, might well doom the Democratic Party. ABC's summer polling numbers, which Stephanopoulos had cited, contained other numbers he didn't mention. There was no substantive difference between men and women in their distaste for Hillary, and 56 percent of whites, 60 percent of older Americans, and 76 percent of Republicans told ABC "never" to a President Hillary campaign. But the media weren't trying to acknowledge the polls as much as to change them in her favor. Tomorrow was always another day full of hopes that the positive press would build Hillary's mandate.

Chapter 14

Everyone Else's Abuse of Power

*There has never been an administration, I don't believe in our his-
tory, more intent upon consolidating and abusing power to further
their own agenda than the current administration. . . . It's very
hard to stop people who have no shame about what they're doing. It
is very hard to tell people that they are making decisions that will
undermine our checks and balances and constitutional system of government who don't care. It is very hard to stop people who have
never been acquainted with the truth.*

—HILLARY CLINTON, speaking over fierce applause at a "Women for
Hillary" reelection fundraiser in Manhattan, June 6, 2005

*[Hillary] gets a pass on just about everything she does, and she's got a
series of inconsistencies that nobody ever challenges.*

—SEAN HANNITY, in an interview with the authors

The **media's narrative** for Hillary never seems to change. It's Hillary the
Magnificent, Hillary the Compassionate, Hillary the Brain, Hillary
the Leader, Hillary the Moderate. Another day, another whitewash.

During her husband's presidency the cheering from the press box
allowed Mrs. Clinton to shunt aside scandal after scandal and ignore
troublesome questions raised by special prosecutors, congressional investigations, and an alternative media that had stepped up to fill the role

abdicated by the so-called mainstream press. It also helped elect her to the U.S. Senate and then vault her into the upper ranks of the Democratic Party leadership. So there was little doubt that when the cries of "Hillary for President!" began, the media would be in her corner. The consistency of the softball interviews—the sheer repetitiveness of the easy questions—offer an excellent predictor of the kind of coverage Mrs. Clinton will get going forward in her presidential campaign.

For starters, Hillary's journalist supporters made sure to rewrite history so her opponents couldn't use her scandals or failures against her. Mrs. Clinton's feminist friend Katie Couric proved up to this task in February 2004, when she interviewed Hillary to kick off a weeklong series on First Ladies. (Barbara Bush and Lady Bird Johnson were not interviewed.) Couric recounted Hillary's life story again, and struck all the same notes of flattery. "She perhaps faced more challenges professional and personal than any other First Lady in history. Now three years after she left the White House, Hillary Rodham Clinton may wield more political power than her husband." There were no questions about those "challenges" being due to Hillary's scandalous behavior and grave political errors.

Rehashing the national health care debate, Couric offered the requisite spin that conservatives should be blamed, not congratulated, for defeating Hillary's plan. "You certainly tackled some things that, that no First Lady had before you. What made you decide to do that and, and were you trepidatious [*sic*] at all going into those, those areas? For example health care. . . . Were you prepared for that backlash?" Note the word *backlash*, with the clear implication that the reaction was not just negative but personal and prejudiced. Lost with that word is the suggestion that maybe, just maybe, this was a principled stand against Hillary's socialist tendencies. Like a broken record, Couric again asked why Hillary was a "polarizing figure," to which Hillary responded that "some of it has to do with that Rorschach test about women and women's roles." *Blah, blah, blah.* Couric wrapped up the piece with this dazzling endorsement of her heroine: "Hillary Clinton's choices in just about everything have been scrutinized and analyzed by almost everyone. She hopes as more women themselves assume positions of power, voters will be less judgmental and more forgiving."

As usual, Couric didn't sound like an objective journalist but like she was conducting a sensitivity seminar on mistreatment of women in the workplace, lecturing the country that Queen Hillary would like the little people to be "less judgmental and more forgiving"—in other words, to be a mirror of the excuse-making liberal media. Once again, she enunciated the strange feminist double standard: traditionalist women should be picked apart, but feminist pioneers must go unquestioned and unscrutinized—even as they assert their right to have all the powers and responsibilities of male power brokers.

Less than two months later, Couric was granted access to Senator Clinton yet again, heralding the paperback edition of her memoir *Living History*. This time it was a prime-time book promotion on *Dateline NBC*, with a portion of it snipped out for *Today*. *Dateline* host Stone Phillips oozed in his introduction that "From the moment Americans met her twelve years ago, it was clear she was a woman to be reckoned with. Smart, tough, ambitious, she seemed tailor-made for the world of politics. So it should come as no surprise that the title *Senator* fits Hillary Clinton like a glove." In one segment played on both shows, Couric played the usual game of touting Hillary as part of a presidential dream ticket. Would Senator Clinton accept a slot as John Kerry's running mate? Couric hoped so: "If John Kerry called you tomorrow, and said, 'Hill'—whatever he calls you—'Senator, Hillary, I'd like you to be my vice president?'"

Clinton: "I'd say, 'John, I really can't do that. And I will help you, and support you in every way possible.'"

Couric (role-playing): "But Hillary, the party really needs you!"

Clinton: "Well, you know, I don't think that will happen. I made it clear I don't want that to happen. And what my answer will be, no, if it does happen. I'm not prepared to do that."

Couric couldn't stop setting her up as a national sensation. "Whatever her aspirations, these days she seems to be the life of the party—the Democratic Party. And at times she's received like a rock star." Couric walked Clinton through the "pain" of being booed by 9/11 mourners at that VH1 concert, but said even the cops and firefighters loved her now: "By last week, some of those jeers had turned to cheers. New York Fire Department and Firefighters Union officials praised her for securing an

$81 million grant for post-9/11 health screenings for rescue workers. And this week, a poll of voters in New York State showed her job approval rating as risen to 62 percent, up from 38 percent shortly after she entered the Senate."

When Couric interviewed Bill Clinton about *his* sprawling new memoir, *My Life,* on June 23, she castigated him for conning poor, victimized Hillary into spreading the vast-conspiracy garbage on the airwaves. "I guess many people don't understand, Mr. President, how you allowed her to go on national television," she complained. "How you sort of hung her out to dry while she defended you that January morning on the *Today* show. And I know you write in the book that you were ashamed watching the interview." When Clinton protested that "what she said was true," Couric, like a stern grade-school teacher preparing to withhold recess, telegraphed her lost patience: "I know you've *said* that. On the other hand, she was defending you. C'mon." Clinton insisted, "That's right, and I explain that. But what you have to come to grips with and all the people in the media have to come to grips with is that both things are true."

In his book, Clinton had written that yes, he was adulterous, but the conservatives "abused the criminal and civil laws and severely damaged innocent people" and he couldn't compound his personal errors by "letting the reactionaries prevail." It was classic Clinton, a strategy "to disparage those who accurately describe and report on the Clintons' misbehaviors by accusing [them] of violations of ethics," as Tony Blankley said in our interview. "The Republicans didn't abuse any legal process, he was the one who committed perjury, he was the one who obstructed justice, and presumably influenced witnesses. They created the phrase 'politics of personal destruction' [and then] they would go out and destroy the credibility and reputation . . . of their opponents. It's a classic strategy and it largely worked." Emmett Tyrrell added, "We didn't write sexual harassment into the criminal code. He did. We sure as hell didn't force him to lie under oath. He broke his own laws. He did it to himself."

Professor Couric didn't challenge him on any of this. But she did challenge him about making life—and perhaps a political career—more difficult for her sainted Hillary.

Fortunately for her, Couric and her colleagues were there to make things easier for Mrs. Clinton. The practiced art of the whitewash helped them do so. On a Sunday morning in April, Hillary wowed the radical abortion-on-demand crowd who gathered in Washington for the "March for Women's Lives." According to the hard-left *Nation* magazine, "No one managed to match the impact that surprise speaker Hillary Rodham Clinton had when she spoke in the morning to the gathering throngs. As she took the stage, it was as if the Beatles arrived; even progressives, who might lament that the U.S. Senator is more of a centrist than they'd like, couldn't help but scream and applaud." Nor, for that matter, could they complain about her "centrism" on abortion; she continued to maintain a 100 percent perfect voting record with NARAL Pro-Choice America. But for those who weren't at the march, the only thing they heard from Hillary was the bland sound bite that the networks ran, in which the former First Lady said that everyone should register and vote for John Kerry.

Only the Associated Press offered an additional clip from the speech that was more in keeping with the day's high-voltage atmosphere, particularly its hatred of Team Bush: "This administration is filled with people who disparage sexual harassment laws, who claim the pay gap between women and men is phony . . . who consider *Roe v. Wade* the worst abomination of constitutional law in our history." It was odd to hear Hillary accuse some other White House of being lax on sexual harassment, considering her husband's expertise in that field, and her failure to stop those violations. No one in the press saw the irony.

Hillary as Convention "Rock Star"

As the Democrats gathered in the People's Republic of Massachusetts for their convention in late July, the early controversy centered on the Kerry campaign's initial decision to exclude Hillary Clinton from the list of prime-time speakers. Were they nervous about being overshadowed? Trying to stop a potential contender for 2008? ABC's Jake Tapper did a story on the first morning of the convention on the "thorny issue" of how to treat the Clintons, "how to honor this couple so popular with the Democratic base, while not allowing them to completely steal the spotlight from this couple, John and Teresa Heinz Kerry." Tapper explained that "there are far too many Clinton lovers in the Democratic Party to let [the decision to exclude Hillary] stand, so she will speak tonight, introducing her husband."

This was what the networks considered tough coverage, repeating the internal babble of Democratic worrywarts.

Hillary dutifully made the rounds of Monday morning shows on ABC, CBS, CNN, and NBC (somehow she had no time for the Fox News Channel). All four networks focused on her presidential ambitions and whether the Kerry camp had made a boo-boo. None asked about other potential problems for Kerry, such as whether he was too liberal, his flip-flops, his stiffness as a candidate, or whether he was soft on national security.

In her third Hillary interview in five months, Katie Couric asked mostly about the new recommendations from the 9/11 Commission, but at the end brought up the speaking goof-up. "You were not originally on the list of speakers. And many people sort of theorized that the Kerry-Edwards campaign feared that you might overshadow them, and particularly given what many political observers view as your political ambitions to run for president in 2008." Hillary dismissed the fuss, saying, "I have been the subject of so many wonderful theories ever since my husband started running for president in 1991."

On ABC, Charles Gibson's interview focused most intently on her presidential ambitions. Gibson showed a clip of Bill Clinton explicitly talking about Hillary's plans for the White House, saying that she was "where I was in 1988." The host then asked Senator Clinton, "If John Kerry wins, are you shut out for some period of time?" Hillary replied with a straight face, "I don't know and I really don't care." Gibson accepted this and proceeded to his next questions, inviting Hillary to slam the president, which she was happy to do. Gibson: "Is this an election between George Bush and not George Bush?" Hillary: "I think that this race up until now has been Bush versus Bush, and Bush is losing."

There was another story ABC and NBC could have addressed that morning but deliberately chose to ignore, even though conservative talk radio, Fox News, and countless newspapers were abuzz over it. On July 25, addressing the Pennsylvania delegates to the Democratic National Convention at the Massachusetts State House in Boston, aspiring First

Lady Teresa Heinz Kerry had railed, "We need to turn back some of the creeping, un-Pennsylvanian, and sometimes un-American traits that are coming into some of our politics." Afterward, Colin McNickle, the editorial page editor of the *Pittsburgh Tribune-Review,* mildly asked Mrs. Kerry what she meant by "un-American." She denied using that term, accusing McNickle of putting words in her mouth. CNN showed the whole sequence on video: her flighty remarks, the question by McNickle, Mrs. Kerry conferring with her aides over who this impertinent questioner was, and her tempestuous return to confront McNickle. She demanded to know, in a tone of voice better directed at a disobedient gardener, "Are you with the *Tribune-Review?*" McNickle replied, "Yes, I am." Heinz Kerry retorted, "Of course. Understandable. . . . You said something I didn't say. Now shove it!"

"If I had been a member of the mainstream liberal media," McNickle told us, "the story would have been, 'Oh boy, is she going to be a liability to the Kerry campaign.'" But that's not how the press handled Mrs. Kerry's outburst. "Because I was a member of the editorial pages of a conservative newspaper," McNickle added, "then I became the story and I had an agenda, according to the liberal media."

Unlike ABC and NBC, the CBS and CNN morning shows did bring up the Teresa Heinz Kerry meltdown story with Senator Clinton, but their spin validates McNickle's point. CBS's Hannah Storm worried, "This is a very fine line that a strong woman walks as her husband is campaigning for the highest office in the land. What sort of challenges does she face, from your perspective, and what advice would you give her?" Hillary replied that Teresa didn't need advice, and "everybody gets frustrated with the press, with all due respect." CNN morning anchor Bill Hemmer tiptoed into the Teresa remarks with Hillary: "I don't know if you have much of a comment based on what Teresa Heinz Kerry said last night. If you do, I'll give you the platform here." Hillary praised Teresa as a terrific human being, and added a rave for her anticonservative moxie: "I think a lot of Americans are going to say, good for you. You go, girl. And that certainly is how I feel about it."

That afternoon, Mrs. Clinton also granted interviews to Dan Rather and Peter Jennings for their evening broadcasts, and Jennings bowed to the press-bashing with a tone of servility. "Teresa Heinz told a reporter, editorial writer to stick it, 'shove it' I think was the exact phrase. How much pressure is there on a spouse?" Hillary repeated what she'd told CBS: "Well, I think everyone gets frustrated with the press, with all due respect," to which Jennings kowtowed in agreement, "No, I quite agree with it."

At least Dan Rather asked about the conservative case against Kerry. "And what about those who don't wish him well? They say, 'Listen, he's Senator Flip-Flop, always has been, and would be as president.'" Clinton huffed in dismissal, "Oh, I think that's, you know, Republican propaganda." Rather also asked about "those who say, 'Listen, down deep, the Clintons plural did not want John Edwards to be on the ticket because it might harm Senator Clinton's chances in the future'—you say what?" She said it's "just not true." And that was that. (Not surprisingly, both Jennings and Rather would be much tougher on Laura Bush when the Republicans gathered in New York five weeks later, pounding her with hardball questions about attacks on John Kerry as if she had personally ordered the anti-Kerry ads.)

After making the rounds at the networks, Hillary made her speech to the convention in prime time. The speech was a candy box of sugary praise for John Kerry, John Edwards, and her husband, the man who can "empower the powerless," promote reconciliation of all races and religions, inspire young citizens to service (no intern jokes, please), and "bring life-saving medicine to people living with HIV-AIDS throughout the world." There was nothing memorable about this address, but that didn't stop Hillary's cheerleaders from offering rave reviews the next morning. "It was unbelievable in here after Bill Clinton spoke and it really started when Hillary Clinton took the podium. It was as if she was a rock star coming in here!" gushed CBS morning host Hannah Storm. MSNBC host Chris Jansing enthused, "I was on the floor when Hillary Clinton took to the podium and the place absolutely went wild. . . . Like a pop star, she's known by just her first name: Hillary!"

WHERE'S HILLARY?

And then Hillary Clinton disappeared.

From the moment the convention ended until Election Day 2004,

Hillary was a nonfactor on the national scene. Perhaps, as some of her critics have charged, she really did want the Kerry-Edwards campaign to crash and burn, opening the floodgates for her presidential run in 2008. This is difficult to prove, but one truth jumps off the page: As this book documents, Hillary Rodham Clinton was, and is, able to generate national news coverage at the snap of her fingers. Reporters didn't talk about it much in the fall, but Hillary and Kerry were together even less than Hillary and Bill.

Searching through the Nexis news data-retrieval database would just leave you empty-handed. We tried the word *Hillary* within fifty words of *John Kerry,* a fairly open-ended search, from September 1 through November 2, Election Day. Every news source gave you only enough stories to count on two hands. Try the *Washington Times* and you get eight articles, but nothing of substance. Same with the *Washington Post*—five articles, about polls of whom Republicans hated most, or how Judy Collins campaigned for Kerry on one day and sang "Chelsea Morning" in the Clintons' honor on the next. *USA Today?* Count 'em on one hand—three stories, with the same weak links.

How about the Associated Press? Certainly, they would show Hillary on the stump. But there were just ten stories listed. They did find two reports that vaguely hinted at Hillary's supporting Kerry, but neither showed her out on the campaign trail with him. The closest you come is an October 3 story that talked about Hillary's appearance with Coretta Scott King to celebrate the fortieth anniversary of an NAACP chapter in Portland, Maine, in which reporter Jerry Harkavy noted that Senator Clinton attended the event "prior to an appearance at a John Kerry fund-raiser." But after that, it's the same shocking absence of any evidence of a joint Kerry-Hillary effort.

The *New York Times,* the hometown press? Just nine stories, and no real linkage.

Nexis holds a heavy portion of the twenty-four-hour news content of CNN, and there you find a little bit more evidence of support, if not joint appearances. Hillary spoke up for Kerry as smarter than Bush in a brief interview on *Larry King Live* after the second presidential debate on October 8. She was spotted (but not quoted on CNN) campaigning for Kerry in south Florida on October 23, a Saturday. In the election's last weekend, CNN reported that Democratic aides were telling them "that

Clinton and his wife, Senator Hillary Clinton, have been asked to take part in interviews with local television stations in Hawaii on Sunday and on Monday." Now there's a high-profile challenge, locking up the vote in Hawaii, a rock-solid blue state.

On Election Day, *New York Times* columnist Clyde Haberman summed up: "If [Kerry] loses, the Democrats will face a vacuum for the 2008 presidential nomination. That would leave Mrs. Clinton heartbroken. Or not."

Bringing Sunshine to a Rainy Clinton Library Opening

Hillary reemerged on the national scene after George W. Bush was reelected in November. The opportunity came with the unveiling of the Clinton Presidential Center in Little Rock, a big, long concrete building that looked like a trailer dangling over the Arkansas River, and that aimed to preserve in granite the Official Clinton Version of Events. "And while scandals that dogged the Clinton era are not forgotten, they are treated here as radical-right attacks against him," explained CBS reporter Bob McNamara, without a hint of irony—perhaps because that is precisely the way the media had been reporting the scandals for years.

On the morning of the official unveiling, November 18, Mrs. Clinton again made the early rounds, with the day's talking point that the museum was "like my husband, it is energetic and spirited and expansive and open and welcoming." On ABC, Claire Shipman pitched softballs about emotional reactions, and the obligatory President Hillary questions, one of them about her electability: "There's a lot of talk about the map, the red-blue, and a lot of people now look at the great swath of red and say, 'Somebody like Hillary Clinton would not be electable in this map.'" Hillary responded, "You know, I think it depends upon the candidate, you know, and I also think we need people running for national office to try to bring our country together."

CBS's Harry Smith grew positively wistful as he interviewed the former First Lady. "Really this has been a road down Memory Lane for all of us, especially some of us who have been covering you all for a while, and I'm thinking about you sitting in the kitchen of what was the Arkansas

Governor's Mansion with the Coke-bottle glasses on, now the senator from New York, and many people say perhaps a presidential candidate in another couple of years." That was the "question." Hillary said that she looked forward to running again for the Senate. Smith ended the interview with a joke, since she wouldn't declare her campaign for president. He put his hands around her neck and joked, "You've never seen a reporter actually choke a former First Lady on television." She just smiled.

If it was Hillary interview day, NBC was sending Katie Couric to puff her again. Before she could ask Hillary to state what her favorite exhibit was, Couric worried about the former president's critics, who should stay quiet as Clinton tried to rehabilitate his reputation. "Some of his detractors are actually planning a counter-library in Little Rock with a satellite office in Washington, D.C.," she bemoaned. "What do you make of that? And is it disappointing for both you and your husband that his detractors and critics continue to pursue him?" Hillary looked sad, and replied, "You know, I have really no idea why the obsession continues, but that's fine. . . . But the real story of this library is about the peace and prosperity of the eight years of the Clinton administration, about a president who was always thinking about putting people first."

CNN anchor Soledad O'Brien interviewed Mrs. Clinton on tape for *American Morning* and also asked about those critics. "There are some critics, though, who say that the—the museum itself, a library minimizes the role your husband had in the impeachment process and the Monica Lewinsky scandal. What do you make of that criticism?" Hillary wanted it clearly understood that "the library presents a full and accurate picture of the Clinton administration."

Neither she nor O'Brien considered it important to state that the section of the library devoted to the Lewinsky scandal is titled "The Politics of Persecution."

The Avenging Angel Against a "Culture of Corruption"?

In the lead-up to the 2006 midterm elections, in which Democrats seized control of the House and Senate, the media paid close attention to the Democrats' frequent charges about a Republican "culture of corruption." This was especially rich given that virtually no one in that same press corps really wanted to address the idea that there were still Hillary Clinton scandals to cover.

Hillary's culture of corruption emerged again on January 7, 2005, when the finance director of Hillary's 2000 Senate campaign, David Rosen, was indicted on charges of falsely underreporting—by hundreds of thousands of dollars—the cost of a Hollywood fundraiser held on August 12, 2000. That was the Saturday night before the Democratic convention in Los Angeles. The "Hollywood Gala Salute to President William Jefferson Clinton," held at the sprawling ranch estate of L.A. radio mogul Ken Roberts, included both a dinner and a concert. Invitations to both cost $25,000 per couple. Another group purchased $1,000 tickets just for the concert. The singers included Diana Ross, Cher, Michael Bolton, and Paul Anka. Other celebrities in attendance were Muhammad Ali, Brad Pitt, and Jennifer Aniston. Organizers reported raising nearly $1.1 million for Hillary Clinton's Senate campaign.

It was the most fashionable ticket in town, the "the glamour gig," as the *Los Angeles Times* described it, yet in all the preconvention hubbub of fundraisers, it was hardly a target of major media coverage. But by Tuesday, *Washington Post* gossip columnist Lloyd Grove had found something to write about—a criminal connection. "Convicted felon Peter Paul—who served three years in prison two decades ago after pleading guilty to cocaine possession and trying to swindle $8.7 million out of the Cuban government—helped organize Saturday's star-glutted $1 million fundraising gala for Clinton's Senate race." At the time, Paul told the *Post* that "he only produced the gala and hasn't given or raised money for the First Lady's New York campaign." Hillary's campaign spokesman Howard Wolfson added, "And we will not be accepting any contributions from him."

By the summer of 2001, Paul had been indicted for securities fraud, and his story had changed. Aided by lawyers at the conservative group Judicial Watch, Paul held a press conference by telephone from Brazil to assert that he had funneled nearly $2 million in cash and in-kind donations into Hillary's campaign for the Hollywood gala, which, if true, would violate federal election laws.

That's where Rosen stepped into the corruption mud. Under arcane campaign-finance rules at the time, you could only use so much of fat-wallet "soft money" like Paul's to set up a fundraiser, until the gathering's costs came to 40 percent or less of the total of the smaller "hard money" donations raised. Since Hillary's gala had raised $1 million in hard money that August, the campaign could use soft money to pay for all costs up to $400,000. Rosen conveniently reported to the campaign treasurer that his price tag was $400,000, avoiding the necessity of spending any hard money on the party.

How badly did Rosen underestimate the bill for federal records? On January 5, 2006, the Associated Press reported in a brief article that the crook Paul was right and the Clinton camp was wrong: Hillary Clinton's 2000 Senate committee agreed to pay a $35,000 fine to the Federal Election Commission for underreporting the cost of the Hollywood fundraiser—by more than $720,000.

But given Paul's criminal record, his complaints against the Clintons were ignored by the liberal media for years. *Insight* magazine, a part of the *Washington Times,* was the only national publication that seemed to care enough to dig into Paul's whole sleazy story in 2002.

In 2003, the *Los Angeles Times* did report that Rosen and another fundraising figure, Aaron Tonken, had collaborated on a charitable event known as "A Family Celebration 2001," where Bill Clinton appeared with former president Gerald Ford, the cast of the *Ally McBeal* television series, Paul Anka, Michael Bolton, John Travolta, Brad Pitt, and Jennifer Aniston—a lineup very similar to the 2000 Clinton party's. Aaron Tonken would also run afoul of the law; by the time Rosen was indicted, Tonken was serving five years in prison for unrelated charges of defrauding charities of hundreds of thousands of dollars.

Put aside for a minute David Rosen's legal troubles, and think of the potential political implications of the Clintons' fundraising. Once again, they were organizing glitzy Hollywood fundraisers—with convicts. Isn't it especially strange that after all the fundraising scandals throughout the second Clinton term in the White House, involving criminals like Jorge Cabrera and foreign nationals in Asia, the Clintons seemed to have learned nothing? Or had they learned that the media's protective blanket meant they didn't have to play by the same campaign rules as other mortal politicians? The media pattern during the Clinton White House years would continue during the Clinton Senate years: Reporters had zero interest in an objective evaluation of the sleaze factor of the Clintons' fundraising campaigns.

The Clintons knew how to handle a story like this. They treated it like an irritating piece of bubble gum on their shoe. As with so many others before, they turned on their accusers as crooks who were not to be believed, and never mind that those crooks were their cronies, working on their behalf. That was good enough for the press. The *New York Times,* the local newspaper of record for the junior senator from New York, as well as a guiding star for the rest of the media, print and broadcast, regularly stuffed every development in the David Rosen trial deep inside the paper. The stories usually appeared in the Metro section, where the rest of the national media might not notice it:

• January 8, 2005: David Rosen is indicted. Page B4.

• February 9: A big explanatory story that easily could have run on the front page. The headline? "Clinton Benefit Has a Lesson: Double-Check That Donor List." The story's text box was full of spin on the story: "A tangled tale of a slick operator, the first couple and dogged Clinton haters." There was also a prominent photo of Bill kissing Hillary. Page B1.

• March 2: Federal prosecutors battle the Clinton camp's attempts to dismiss the Rosen indictment. Page B4.

• March 8: Peter Paul will plead guilty in an unrelated stock fraud case so he can be a witness in the Rosen trial. Page B4.

• April 23: Ted Kennedy's brother-in-law Raymond Reggie is revealed as a confidential informant in the Rosen case. Reggie plans to testify as part of a plea agreement. Page B2.

• May 10: "Political Drama Abounds in Trial Involving Mrs. Clinton's Hollywood Fund-Raiser," promised the *Times* as jury selection began. This time they put the story in the A section—but only on A17.

• May 11: "Clinton Link to Fund-Raiser Adds Spice to Mundane Trial." But not that spicy for the editor at the *Times*. Page C18.

• May 13: A story on the ongoing Rosen trial. Page A21.

So what was front-page-worthy for the *New York Times*? Well, on May 13, the same day the trial of Hillary's chief fundraiser was tucked deep in the A section, the *Times* ran a big front-page story on Hillary the Moderate. Reporter Raymond Hernandez highlighted her odd new link to Newt Gingrich. The story sold the new partnership as smart politics for Senator Clinton, for it "gives her the chance to burnish her credentials among the moderates she has been courting during her time in the Senate. . . . The Clinton-Gingrich connection comes as Mrs. Clinton has increasingly staked out moderate positions in several areas." Like what? She now favored "a more gradual approach to guaranteeing health care for more Americans"—in other words, a slower road to government takeover.

The Rosen trial just fell apart. Raymond Reggie's taped conversations with Rosen were removed from evidence. Neither Paul nor Tonken was called to testify. The jury acquitted Rosen on May 27. The next day, the *Times* put the story on B1, complete with reporter Leslie Eaton's political spin: "The case involved a heady brew of Washington politics and Hollywood tinsel, and longtime critics of Senator Clinton tried to use it to tar her politically."

Although the *New York Times* buried the supposed "heady brew" of the Rosen trial inside the paper, that was nothing compared with the way the networks ignored it. ABC never touched it. CBS had fifty words on the night of the indictment. By comparison, NBC was the comparatively thorough network, with one full story on the May 10 *Today*. Reporter Campbell Brown waved red flags that "we should say right up front that Hillary Clinton is not a part of the trial," but that it was "giving a new stage to her enemies." The on-screen graphic was "Campaign Against Hillary." NBC also offered an anchor brief reporting Rosen's acquittal on a Saturday morning.

Even CNN skated past the story, reporting the indictment in January, the trial's beginning in May, and then the acquittal, avoiding all stories in between. Their most astonishing episode of avoidance came when their afternoon show *Inside Politics* featured Judy Woodruff interviewing Hillary Clinton on May 26, the day the Rosen trial went to the jury for deliberation. Woodruff interviewed her for two long segments, and never brought it up—as she pressed Hillary to react to Tom DeLay's ethical troubles!

Only after the taped segment ended did Woodruff tell her viewers, "Today, jurors did begin deliberating the case against David Rosen. He's accused of underreporting the cost of a star-studded fundraiser for Mrs. Clinton's Senate race four and a half years ago."

When Hillary's campaign committee agreed to the FEC fine in January 2006, the newspapers tried their best to yawn past it. On January 6, the *Washington Post* carried just the 325-word AP dispatch. The *New York Times* gave it little more than 100 words on page B4 in a Metro Briefs section; it was buried as the sixth item in that column.

The *Los Angeles Times* had no story—even though the offending fundraiser was held in Los Angeles. Blogger Dave Pierre at Newsbusters.org had some fun exploring the bias by omission at the *Los Angeles Times.* Instead of the Hillary story the next day, the *Times* published 2,315 words in two articles on the premiere of NBC's short-lived liberal Episcopal drama *The Book of Daniel,* 1,431 words on liberal Jon Stewart hosting the Oscars, and another 1,477 words (starting on page one) on the decline in the popularity of tennis.

Nothing emerged on ABC. Or CBS. Or NBC. Or NPR. (CNN mentioned it briefly on *American Morning,* right before its brief item on the "Bubble Gum Bandit.") *USA Today, Time, Newsweek, U.S. News?* Nothing.

The "mainstream" media outlets that were supposed to expose a "culture of corruption" in Washington without fear or favor demonstrated a huge double standard as Hillary approached easy reelection. They suggested that Tom DeLay should honor his country and resign. They breathed heavily at the slightest chance to find a photograph to connect lobbyist Jack Abramoff with President Bush. They exploded with weeks of gloating coverage at the creepy instant Internet messages of Republican congressman Mark Foley and the Reverend Ted Haggard's misadventures in prostitution as the 2006 campaign wound down. But Hillary Clinton was always spared the watchdog's bite—and even the watchdog's growl.

HILLARY RAINS FIRE LIKE RAMBO
ON THE REPUBLICANS

Liberal media bias by omission continued to be one of Hillary Clinton's greatest political assets. A scathing partisan speech before her first "Women for Hillary" fundraiser on the first weekend of June 2005 drew only mild interest.

The *New York Times* reported on the front page of the Metro section that Senator Clinton blasted Republican leaders. "There has never been an administration, I don't believe in our history, more intent upon consolidating and abusing power to further their own agenda," Mrs. Clinton told the gathering. "I know it's frustrating for many of you, it's frustrating for me. Why can't the Democrats do more to stop them?" She continued to growing applause, "I can tell you this: It's very hard to stop people who have no shame about what they're doing. It is very hard to tell people that they are making decisions that will undermine our checks and balances and constitutional system of government who don't care. It is very hard to stop people who have never been acquainted with the truth."

The chutzpah boggles the mind. "It's the most accurate portrayal of Clinton politics I've ever heard summarized," said Congressman Jack Kingston in our interview. Former Reagan White House political director Frank Donatelli likewise scoffed, "It's an excellent statement of the *Clinton* administration if you just take it word by word and substitute the Clinton administration for the Bush administration." Talk-radio host Mark Levin was angered: "I don't think there's been a president in American history who issued so many Executive Orders and who so abused the doctrine of executive privilege as Bill Clinton. In terms of honesty and truthfulness, he's the first elected president in American history to be impeached. And she stood by his side through all this, either facilitating it or encouraging it. She is in no position to point the accusatory finger at

George Bush—or anybody else for that matter." Republican strategist Mary Matalin saw nothing but brass-knuckled politics in Hillary's remarks. Hillary, she told us, "is not stupid. She is smart, methodical." Matalin pointed to the "lack of evidentiary-based arguments" so often advanced by Democrats who blithely follow the dictum "When in doubt, attack."

Mrs. Clinton, however, wasn't finished. She described Republican leaders as messianic in their beliefs, willing to manipulate facts and even "destroy" the Senate to gain political advantage, a reference to the fight over Democratic plans to filibuster Supreme Court nominees. She also took a shot at the House of Representatives, calling it "a dictatorship of the Republican leadership." Referring to the congressional leadership, she said, "Some honestly believe they are motivated by the truth, they are motivated by a higher calling, they are motivated by, I guess, a direct line to the heavens." When we asked former Republican National Committee chairman Ed Gillespie about these comments, he responded, "It demonstrates that Hillary Clinton is one who believes conservatives aren't just wrong, they're evil."

To most of the media, however, Hillary's hyperbolic screed and its echoes of her own husband's presidency weren't worth exploring. One who did cover that speech was CNN political analyst Bill Schneider. He loved it. On the June 7 *American Morning* he began, "Hillary Clinton, if she does decide to run for president, is going to have to demonstrate she's strong, she's tough." CNN then aired a sound bite from Hillary's speech in which she proclaimed, "You know, the president has two principal financial priorities: the tax cuts for the wealthiest among us and funding the war in Iraq. . . . He's the first president in history that took us to war and cut taxes at the same time." Cohost Soledad O'Brien asked Schnieder, "Okay, she sounds strong. Is she wrong or right?" Schneider replied, "Well, I think she's right."

"THE GREATEST OF HYPOCRISIES"

The double standard in covering Republicans and Democrats was obvious when Senator Clinton and Senate Majority Leader Bill Frist, who was a heart surgeon, made the medical rounds of the morning shows of ABC, CBS, and NBC on June 16. All three pounded the Republican leader on the latest developments in the Terri Schiavo right-to-pull-the-plug case, since a medical evaluation had declared that she had massive brain damage; the interviewers accused Frist of presumptively diagnosing her from the Senate floor when he wondered out loud if she was really in a vegetative state.

Fair enough. The Schiavo case was of national import, hugely controversial, with both national parties weighing in heavily on the issue. It was perfectly acceptable, even welcome, to have the media ask Senator Frist some tough questions.

But the same held true for Senator Clinton. Any number of questions were credible, and deserved to be posed to the Woman Who Would Be President: Did she believe Terri Schiavo should die? Did Schiavo's husband have the right to put her to death? If Schiavo's parents and her siblings wanted to care for her, shouldn't they be allowed to do that? How could a Democrat ever hope to win support of the pro-life community by supporting euthanasia?

The interviewers, however, asked Hillary only about the subject du jour—a bipartisan effort to stop medical errors—and bland political questions, including the perennial ones on Hillary's presidential prospects. CBS's Hannah Storm asked if the country could see more bipartisanship. NBC's Matt Lauer asked about a vote up or down on UN ambassador nominee John Bolton.

Later that day, another controversy exploded. Conservatives started protesting remarks from Senator Richard Durbin of Illinois, the Senate's number-two Democratic leader. Standing on the Senate floor two days earlier, Durbin had read an e-mail from an FBI agent about terrible conditions for Muslim detainees at Guantánamo and said, "You would most certainly believe this must have been done by Nazis, Soviets in their gulags, or some mad regime—Pol Pot or others—that had no concern for human beings. Sadly, that is not the case. This was the action of Americans in the treatment of their prisoners." The media maintained a stony silence as Republicans exploded in fury. The networks stayed almost totally quiet until Durbin apologized, six days after the furor began. (NBC aired one brief item before the apology.) Even after

Durbin apologized, CBS still avoided it. Senator Clinton had no comment, and no one in the liberal media was interested in obtaining one, either. There were more important political matters that needed to be addressed.

So what was more important than a report on Senator Durbin's apology for the slur against his country? On the day of Durbin's apology, June 22, top Bush adviser Karl Rove told a New York Conservative Party dinner, "Conservatives saw the savagery of 9/11 and the attacks and prepared for war. Liberals saw the savagery of the 9/11 attacks and wanted to prepare indictments and offer therapy and understanding to our attackers." Within hours of reading the remarks in the *New York Times*, reporters pounced. The evening news was full of rancor against Rove, and at the top of the celebrity list attacking Rove was . . . Senator Clinton.

ABC showed her insisting to Defense Secretary Donald Rumsfeld at a hearing that "I would hope, Mr. Secretary, that you and other members of the administration would immediately repudiate such an insulting comment from a high-ranking official." (Would she repudiate the worse-than-insulting comment from her high-ranking Democratic colleague?) NBC showed Hillary at a press conference complaining, "And to have someone like Karl Rove go to New York City and say what he said is just almost unimaginable." (As unimaginable as comparing the U.S. government to the Nazi regime?) MSNBC aired a sound bite of Hillary saying, "So either he said something in a hasty, ill-conceived reckless moment . . . or he said it deliberately, intentionally, as part of a continuing effort to divide Americans. So the only way we'll know for sure as to what his real intention was last night in New York City is whether or not he retracts these comments and apologizes." (Would she demand an apology from Durbin?) CBS News, trying to stay consistent in avoiding the news, avoided the Rove story as it had covered up the Durbin story.

"It's a double standard," Gillespie told us. "Anytime a Republican says anything bordering on controversial, it is going to evoke a spate of coverage in the traditional media, and that coverage will persist until said Republican offers an apology." And what of Democratic controversies? They are "met with a yawn and the referees swallow their whistles. . . . Every Republican is held accountable for anything any Republican says and Democrats aren't held accountable for any stupid thing said by any Democrat anywhere." Matalin concurred. The media's double standard in their coverage of Durbin versus Rove was, she said, "the greatest of hypocrisies, the worst of the outrages of the hypocrisies of the press."

After all the outrage over Rove, the media should have been asked to think about this question: How precisely did supposedly hawkish President Clinton fight his war on terror, if he waged one? Preparing an indictment in absentia of Osama bin Laden in Manhattan offered no resolution to Americans whose relatives died at the hands of al Qaeda terrorists in our embassies in Kenya and Tanzania, or aboard the USS *Cole*. He lobbed a few cruise missiles, timed precisely to distract attention from his testimony in the Monica Lewinsky case, and then stopped as quickly as he started. This means that Mrs. Clinton should have been pushed harder to think twice about the boldness or effectiveness of her husband's antiterrorist responses before taking offense at indictment quips.

Chapter 15
Hillary's Cakewalk

From the time Hillary was a child, she was imbued with the notion that in order for her life to have meaning she had to do something more than succeed in personal ways. She had to give something back.

—BILL CLINTON in a video testimonial aired at the New York State Democratic Party convention, May 31, 2006

We're beyond evidence now. If any conservative comes up with any information about Hillary Clinton, whether it's been heard before or not, it no longer matters.

—CAL THOMAS, in an interview with the authors

After national journalists spent more than a decade building Hillary Rodham Clinton into a legendary, even historic figure, especially during her first Senate campaign, the second Senate campaign turned out to be the incredible shrinking story. The Clinton machine wanted to project the idea that they took her reelection seriously, not as an annoying little speed bump on the way back to the White House. But her media supporters never took the race seriously.

True enough, any pundit could see early on that Republican opponents would have an uphill climb. Polling in the summer of 2005, more than a year before the election, put Hillary 25 or 35 points ahead of the somewhat minor figures who were rumored to be running, like Edward

Cox, a son-in-law of Richard Nixon, and Jeanine Pirro, the district attorney of Hillary's adopted Westchester County. No one of any stature in New York GOP circles—not Governor George Pataki, not Rudy Giuliani, not even former congressman Rick Lazio—was interested in the risk of being trounced, and fiercely denounced. Who would want to step into the junior senator's "personal space" after watching the 2000 experience, with the media pounding on the man they called "Little Ricky"?

Still, while Hillary's reelection seemed a foregone conclusion, anyone who bothered to examine the situation in New York would notice that even in a projected blowout, Hillary was registering numbers below other statewide Democrats. In November 2004, for instance, the senior senator from New York, Charles Schumer, had won reelection 71 to 24 percent. By the time November 2006 rolled around, Democrat Eliot Spitzer would win the governorship by a whopping 69 to 29 percent over Republican opponent John Faso. Hillary would actually end up with slightly worse numbers in her own rout, winning 67 to 31 percent.

But the media seemed interested mainly in portraying Hillary as the juggernaut, with the Senate reelection campaign merely a pesky chore to be completed before she could grab control of the Oval Office.

A few networks showed a fleeting enthusiasm for the New York Senate campaign when Pirro entered the fray. "This is one we'll sure all be watching," professed CBS anchor Bob Schieffer when Pirro announced. CNN talked it up as a plausible race before Pirro announced, and Wolf Blitzer guessed on air that political people would hear the name Jeanine Pirro a lot in the months ahead. But they didn't. Neither CNN nor CBS aired another story on Pirro for Senate.

In truth, Pirro was a disaster as a candidate. When she announced her candidacy at a press conference on August 10, 2005, she lost her place in her remarks and had to ask an aide, "Do you have page 10?" She froze up for half a minute, an eternity in television time. The networks ignored the announcement, but on a *Meet the Press* discussion that Sunday, *Washington Post* columnist E. J. Dionne mocked the gaffe: "I think that Ms. Pirro's challenge is not to have her entire campaign defined by the sentence, 'Do you have page 10?' It was really a remarkable moment." *Time* magazine highlighted the sentence in its "Verbatim" notable-quotes feature in the front of the magazine.

What was odd was that the outlets that did pay attention to the New York Senate race decided to do some aggressive investigation . . . of Pirro, not Hillary, of course. A *New York Times* reader would barely have to glance beyond the headlines to see the agenda behind the coverage of Pirro. In the first days after she entered the race, stories included "Company Accused of Mob Ties Contributed to Pirro Campaign" and, believe it or not, "Lobbying Panel Investigating Tea Ticket Received by Pirro." (It was a free ticket to a tea honoring the governor's wife, thrown by a pharmaceutical company.) Perhaps the oddest one was the Gennifer Flowers–phobic, trooper-distrusting, Paula Jones–dismissing *Times* digging into a story about Pirro's husband fathering a child out of wedlock: "Pirro Is Forced to Address Chapter of Husband's Past." Left unsaid was that it was the *Times* that "forced" the candidate to address the story.

Albert Pirro had also been convicted of tax fraud, making him and his wife prime targets for the *New York Times*. Never mind that *both* candidates had a wandering-husband-with-scandals problem. The *Times* saw one husband as a heel, and the other as a hero. An August 13 story on Pirro carried a text box that emphasized in large type, "A husband convicted of tax fraud gets no mention from his wife," and the piece opened with a sentence that said the candidate had "finally appeared in public with what may be her biggest liability: her husband, Albert J. Pirro." On September 3, a *Times* headline suggested that the Clintons looked much better: "In Contrast to a Republican Rival for the Senate, Clinton Has Her Man Stand by Her." Reporter Raymond Hernandez began that story, "Senator Hillary Rodham Clinton brought her husband along to the New York State Fair on Friday, drawing a sharp contrast with her likeliest Republican rival in next year's Senate race, who has mostly kept her scandal-plagued husband out of public view since announcing her candidacy."

Talk about a scrutiny imbalance. Hernandez didn't find Bill Clinton comparably "scandal-plagued." While the article detailed Albert Pirro's past offenses, nowhere did it mention Bill Clinton's lying in the Paula Jones case, or impeachment, or business partners convicted of multiple felonies in the Whitewater scandal.

The *New York Times* article seemed to enjoy picking up Pirro gaffes or scandals from the Hillary war room. The Clintons had so often decried the "politics of personal destruction," but Hillary couldn't stop employing them even when she led by 30 points. On October 23, 2005, Hernandez authored an article headlined "No Gaffe by Pirro Passes Unnoticed, the Clinton Campaign Ensures." He reported, "Mrs. Clinton's political operation and its Democratic surrogates have gone on the offensive, offering a harsh running critique—mostly through a barrage of e-mail messages and press releases—of the mishaps plaguing the Pirro campaign. Their apparent aim is to make Ms. Pirro appear inept and overwhelmed" and add the perception that her advisers are "out of their league."

Pirro withdrew from the race on December 6, which oddly led National Public Radio's evening newscast *All Things Considered* to do its first story on her. (You can almost hear the NPR staffers saying to one another, "It's safe now. She pulled out.")

Left behind as the Republican nominee-in-waiting was John Spencer, a conservative whose highest political office was mayor of Yonkers, the largest city in Hillary's Westchester County. Like Al Pirro, John Spencer was also introduced to the public as a philanderer. On the March 22, 2006, edition of NPR's *Day to Day* (coproduced with the liberal website Slate.com), NPR political editor Ken Rudin joked that "the Republicans are looking in the phone book" to find a Hillary challenger and noted in passing that Spencer "has a history of marital infidelity." What is it about the Clinton-loving media that they seem so enthusiastic to point out the adultery of Clinton opponents as an in-your-face rebuke to conservatives?

On the whole, though, the national media were barely interested in breathing Spencer's name. One light moment on MSNBC's *Hardball* suggested the media mood. Chris Matthews asked, "What is he, mayor of Schenectady or something? Mayor of something up there. I guess he's mayor— oh, you're laughing, Howard." *Newsweek* political reporter Howard Fineman responded, "Because I don't know."

Time mentioned Spencer once in passing in March, but neither *Newsweek* nor *U.S. News & World Report* ever noticed him. CBS and NBC never mentioned the Republican challenger once, not once in the entire 2006 cycle—even when Hillary lowered herself to two televised debates in late October. ABC's Jake Tapper featured Spencer in one

World News story in July, noting that he had an Internet ad showing Hillary "alongside Osama bin Laden." Their pictures were side by side, but Spencer wasn't saying they were allies or look-alikes. The ad suggested that Hillary would leave American vulnerable by repealing the Patriot Act and NSA terrorist-surveillance programs that "helped stop another 9/11." Spencer told Tapper, "We are in a real war and I don't believe Hillary Clinton and her friends understand that." Hillary quickly appeared on screen to denounce the Spencer ad as "beyond outrageous" when we should be "trying to work together." Apparently, Hillary was never, ever a partisan warrior.

When the election was over, CBS star Bob Schieffer giggled at Spencer and said, "Hillary spent 29 and a half million dollars, I believe it was, and I've already forgotten who it was she was running against. . . . She could have spent $100 and won that race in New York." That's especially true considering that CBS never uttered John Spencer's name. The "free media" weren't going to give the conservative candidate any "free media."

At Hillary's postelection celebration, the national cameras homed in on the Clintons and the confetti as the victory song offered a clear message of greed for the presidency: "You Ain't Seen Nothin' Yet," a 1974 rock-and-roll hit from Bachman-Turner Overdrive. Apparently no one noticed that the song begins with the lyrics "I met a devil woman / She took my heart away / She said I've had it comin' to me / But I wanted it that way."

HILLARY PLAYS THE "PLANTATION" CARD

While the media were happy to report every Hillary Clinton campaign attack suggesting Jeanine Pirro was the gaffe-a-minute candidate, they weren't so interested when the junior senator made her own verbal mistakes. On the Martin Luther King Jr. holiday on January 16, 2006, Mrs. Clinton marched into a Baptist church in Harlem with Al Sharpton and gave a fiery speech. First, ignoring her own scandal-plagued White House years, Hillary charged that President Bush's team was historically filled with corrupt cronies, that his presidency "will go down in history as one of the worst." Then, with Sharpton proudly looking on, she threw the race card on the table with a big, noisy thwack. "When you look at the way the House of Representatives has been run, it has been run like a plantation, and you know what I'm talking about," she sneered. Not only was Bush corrupt, Speaker Dennis Hastert was a slave master.

Imagine what would have been the media's response had these racially inflammatory words been uttered by a Republican, say Senator Trent Lott.

But the media displayed their usual knee-jerk instincts to downplay and protect Hillary from her own mouth. The Associated Press reported the story first on Monday night, and the local TV news channel NY-1 offered footage for television, but the story was of little interest to the national networks. On Tuesday morning, ABC and CBS offered little anchor briefs, and NBC reporter David Gregory brushed past it briefly in an anti-Bush speech roundup on *Today*.

Talk radio and conservative blogs were blazing, but the "objective" national media didn't want to be dragged along. On Wednesday morning, NBC's Andrea Mitchell touched on it again, but mostly to note Hillary was standing firm. On ABC's *Good Morning America*, liberal senator Barack Obama was asked very vaguely about the remarks, and he underlined how Hillary was right that the GOP House displays a "further and further concentration of power around a very narrow agenda that advantages the most powerful."

If the networks seemed asleep at the switch, consider how the print media covered this brazen appeal to racial tensions. Quite simply, they just didn't want to mention the "plantation" or "worst president in history" remarks. *USA Today* skipped it. The *Los Angeles Times* skipped it for three days before allowing one article. (At the same time, this titanic liberal newspaper of the West emphasized, in stories on three different days, Pat Robertson's remarks on Ariel Sharon's stroke being caused by God for "dividing God's land.") The *Washington Post* mentioned the remarks on page A6, in a story headlined "White House Disputes Gore on NSA Spying."

The *New York Times* skipped a day and then boiled the controversy down to one little word *(plantation)* in one sentence in the fourth paragraph of a story about how Hillary was delicately building a political network for 2008 while sharpening her tone against Republicans. It was as if the story was dictated by Hillary herself. Raymond Hernandez reported that her remarks were "causing a stir," but that she was a fundraising dynamo: "By and large, Mrs. Clinton's visits around the country have drawn the kind of reaction one would expect with a person of her immense celebrity and political stature." *Time* and *Newsweek* just printed the "plantation" quote without comment or analysis.

Cable television chewed the story over for a good day or two. The Democrats quickly caught up with a balancing spin: evidence that Newt Gingrich and other Republicans used the "plantation" metaphor against Democrats in the 1990s, often in reference to their firm grip on 90 percent or more of the black vote. While it can be argued that it was rhetorically excessive for Gingrich to compare himself and other congressional Republicans to leading a plantation slave rebellion against Democratic rule, the distinct difference between Newt's and Hillary's remarks is that Gingrich was not accusing Democrats of racism.

TEATIME WITH HILLARY

Hillary maintained her policy of doling out few interviews and making few political splashes on her way to victory in 2006. One of the rare instances of her granting the media access came at the end of August, when she allowed a crew from ABC's *Nightline* to follow her on the campaign trail in upstate New York for a day. Voters saw plenty of Hillary shaking hands and posing for pictures with voters, but little tough questioning.

The broadcast began with Hillary and ABC anchor Cynthia McFadden sipping morning tea and exchanging pleasantries. After asking Hillary about whether campaigning was fun, McFadden asked what adjective she hoped people used to describe herself. *Real,* said Mrs. Clinton, insisting that there was "kind of a cottage industry [giggle] in trying to turn me into a caricature of what I am." McFadden didn't ask what the caricature was, but she had hinted at it in her introduction, when she said that Senator Clinton had been "accused of being calculating, opportunistic, even of lacking any principles in regard to the war in Iraq and her marriage."

The only tough questions in the half hour came from the liberal perspective—three inquiries about why she wouldn't retract or apologize for
her vote for the Iraq War. As for the Clinton marriage, despite McFadden's opening promotional language that it would be put "under a micro-
scope" and that "nothing's off limits," in reality McFadden insisted that
anyone who didn't insist on limits was incredibly rude.

She asked, "Is your marriage fair game? The *New York Times* clearly
thinks so. Front-page article about how many days you spend with your
husband, fourteen is their answer, a month. [Another giggle from
Hillary.] How angry did that article make you?" Hillary claimed, "Not
at all. You know, I just don't pay attention to it. I really don't. My attitude
is I have *no* control over what somebody wants to talk about or write
about." (Emphasis hers.) McFadden looked shocked: "Really?" Hillary
replied, "Really." McFadden seemed to want outrage. "It didn't hurt?
It doesn't make you mad? I mean, I'm—it would sure make me mad, I
think."

The article in question was three months old, appearing in the *Times*
on May 23, 2006. Reporter Patrick Healy wrote that the *Times* had come
up with the fourteen-days-a-month average after talking to fifty Democratic Party insiders and Clinton aides and cobbling together the calen-
dars of Hillary and Bill. To be precise, the Clintons were apparently
together for *fractions* of fourteen days a month: "Sometimes it is a full day
of relaxing at home in Chappaqua; sometimes it is meeting up late at
night."

But here's where Hillary's desire to be seen as "real" gets very strained.
Does anyone believe that the *New York Times* would work with top
Democrats and Clinton aides for weeks to address what they said was
"Topic A" among Democratic decision-makers, and Hillary could plausi-
bly say of it, "I just don't pay attention to it"? With her long and persistent record of stressing the withholding of information and wanting
complete control over a supposedly unruly Clinton-bashing media, isn't
it more likely that she reviewed the calculations before letting the *Times*
have it? Would she sit idly by and suggest that she had "*no* control" over
what her aides and supporters talked about to the newspaper?

Rather, the marriage story appears more likely to have been a calculated leak. Discussing the story on the NBC-syndicated *Chris Matthews*

Show back on June 3, *Time* Washington bureau chief Michael Duffy said that if the *Times* hadn't done it, someone else would have, since top "Democratic worriers for the past couple of months had been asking reporters to sort of look into this, because I think they don't want to get down the road in a year or two with a front-runner who's no longer viable." NPR anchor Michele Norris insisted, "If you talk to people who are close to the Clintons and their reading of this, it sounds like they don't welcome this discussion, but they realize it's a discussion that has to be had. . . . They recognize that this, it's almost better that this gets out there now, that people deal with it."

The Clinton war room liked dealing with a story through friendly media, and then they liked to follow up by saying anyone else who was still asking questions was dealing in "old news." If the Clintons curbed curiosity about the marriage in the middle of 2006, then it would be "old news" by 2008. The *Times* wasn't rifling through underwear drawers and searching for sex partners. They were conducting a very friendly investigation of personal recollections about where Bill and Hillary were, and yet a very supportive Cynthia McFadden could only strike a pose of disgust that anyone was asking.

The next cautionary moment for anyone who thought Hillary was tremendously "real" came when McFadden asked whether Hillary was thinking about running for president. "I am not thinking about it at all. . . . The truth is, I don't think about it." Then came the "surprise" moment when Bill Clinton arrived at an event for a "Hey, girl . . . Hi, honey" moment. (That's what Bill and Hillary said to each other on camera.) Bill said she *was* thinking about the White House: "We talk about it, and I, you know, I've urged her to think as little about it as possible," since rule number one is never to look past the next election. In other words, in saying she didn't think about the presidency "at all," Hillary ended up looking like that "calculating and opportunistic" caricature, and not "real."

McFadden wrapped up her day of staging events with Hillary in a dreamy tone: "It was an almost pitch-perfect day of campaigning. A Hollywood director could not have done better. Even the sunset obliged." If that wasn't syrupy enough, McFadden added a final thought that ABC "by chance" ended up in the same restaurant as the Clintons after sundown and spied the lovebirds "down in the restaurant's garden, alone in the candlelight, a man who had been president and a woman who says she's hasn't yet decided if she wants to be, eating dinner and laughing."

"Love Her" or "Hate Her"?
We Know the Media's Answer

The biggest splash of the summer occurred not long before *Nightline* ran its gooey profile of Mrs. Clinton. The August 28 cover of *Time* magazine featured a flattering black-and-white photo of Hillary's profile, and over it the headline was a poll question with two little boxes to check: "LOVE HER" or "HATE HER."

Wait, someone didn't love her? In fact, *Time* discovered that its readers were very mixed. They were surprised to receive more than 4,500 covers in the mail with the boxes checked. "That's a lot of snail mail in this digital age," they wrote. "Love her" drew 2,286 votes, while "Hate her" was very close behind, at 2,122. (Neither was checked on 131 covers.) Their admittedly unscientific online poll was also very tight, with 40,821 "love" votes, 39,289 "hate" votes, and 29,928 "neither" votes.

This newest cover story stood out, since it was not the normal *Time* magazine Hillary cover, which could be mistaken for the cover of *Ladies' Home Journal.* This was the tenth cover story for Hillary Clinton since she had appeared on the national scene hitched to Bill Clinton's wagon in 1992. That must be a record of sorts, at least for someone who is not yet president. The royal covers about her came with titles such as "Ascent of a Woman," "Turning Fifty," "Hillary in Her Own Words," and the late-Lewinsky-scandal classic, "'It's Nobody's Business but Ours.'" (There was one exception. A cover in 1996 carried the caption "The Truth About Whitewater" and featured a harshly spotlighted Hillary. That, however, wasn't advertising a *Time* article inside, but an excerpt from James Stewart's Whitewater book *Blood Sport.*)

This cover was evenhanded, but the story inside was, unsurprisingly, not nearly as neutral. Reporter Karen Tumulty's piece carried the usual courtier's curtsies, starting with talk of the "outsize status of both

Clintons" and how Hillary's husband was, hands down, "the best Democratic political strategist on the planet." They were "the most fascinating tango act in politics," even if now "the choreography is reversed." Bill Clinton was "still the superstar," and yet Hillary pleased her neighbors by having "storytime for tots the day she picked up her public-library card." In a sidebar, their Chappaqua fans confessed that they're not usually "royal-watchers."

The story read like a Democratic club newsletter. In more than 4,000 words, there was not a single conservative or Republican detractor quoted—not one. *Time* explained that since the question of Hillary's forthcoming presidential campaign was so sensitive, the Clintons had declined to speak on the record and had discouraged all their insiders from speaking on the record. So the whole article was filled with the Clinton inner circle, often speaking anonymously.

That's not to say the Clinton insiders didn't ponder how Bill and Hillary's marriage might be a political problem, or how he might outshine her on the stump, or how she might be seen as liberal. But imagine *Time* devoting an entire cover story to anonymous insider chatter from Reagan or Bush insiders, without a single sound bite from a liberal critic. Then see a doctor for shortness of breath if you can't handle the incessant laughter.

Conservatives were referenced in the story, but only (surprise!) as vicious attackers. Hillary's campaign for the White House could face every attack Bill faced, and more, Tumulty wrote, since "he never had to contend with the blogosphere or the newer kind of independent operation that turned *swift boat* into a verb in the 2004 presidential election." John Spencer's name didn't surface.

Tumulty's most ridiculous sentence was this one: "Hillary has already figured as Lady Macbeth in enough volumes to fill a bookmobile, and in the next year the publishing industry will be adding to the collection with such titles as *Liberal Fascism: The Totalitarian Temptation from Mussolini to Hillary Clinton* and *Whitewash: How the News Media Are Paving Hillary Clinton's Path to the Presidency.*"

Despite the early plug for this book (using an old working subtitle), the sentence was just servile exaggeration. There isn't a bookmobile of anti-Hillary books—maybe a bookshelf—just as there isn't a bookmobile of George W. Bush–bashing books. But in her unanimously liberal story, she was only making the conservative argument stick: the first way the media pave Hillary's path to power is by publishing cover stories in which only the Clinton political family is allowed to speak.

That's why the love her/hate her boxes were inadequate. What many conservatives hate is not Hillary but the glaringly obvious way in which the national news media circle around the Clintons like royal scribes and Secret Service protectors, incapable of telling a story straight, all the while insisting that their final product is "objective news reporting."

The conservative opinion leaders we interviewed were unanimous on this point. Cal Thomas was discussing the power of the Hillary Boosters when he made the comment quoted at the top of this chapter, that "if any conservative comes up with any information about Hillary Clinton, whether it's been heard before or not, it no longer matters." Thomas added that "it's not all ideological, some of it's commercial"—a woman president would be fresh and compelling and therefore draw more viewers and readers—but the results, he said, are the same regardless. "And those results are that Hillary Clinton so far has not come under the kind of scrutiny that any conservative woman or any conservative man or Republican would come under if the circumstances were the same."

Rush Limbaugh said, "The drive-by media, as I call them, is a giant cover-up machine for the Clintons. To this day it's participating in helping write a legacy for Bill Clinton because his administration did not produce one that is suitable and positive, so the quest goes on to write the positive. . . . Hillary is part of it."

Sean Hannity told us, "I mean this sincerely, the single biggest contributor to the [Hillary] Clinton '08 campaign is going to be the mainstream media . . . as they were to Bill's campaign and Bill's presidency." According to Hannity, the media "are not going to do their job."

They haven't for fifteen years. Why would they start now?

Conclusion
"Is Hillary Clinton Unbeatable?"

When you are attacked, you have to deck your opponents, and that is what I believe you do.

—HILLARY CLINTON, January 2007

[Hillary's] presidential candidacy is due to one thing—that is, she is owed it. . . . It's her turn and she's entitled. That's it. That's the sum total, and in that theory you have every explanation for why the liberals love her. Why the liberals do not challenge. Why the liberals back her up. She's one of them.

—RUSH LIMBAUGH, in an interview with the authors

Ever since *Time* magazine introduced her to the country in 1992 as an "amalgam of Betty Crocker, Mother Teresa, and Oliver Wendell Holmes," Hillary Rodham Clinton has benefited from a form of favoritism unique in modern American politics. From the start, America's hardiest news consumers have witnessed a parade of fawning interviews more fit for a monarch than the wife of a democratically elected president, never mind a scandal-ridden politician. It's a sad stack of so-called journalism, a parade of panderers and patronizers, flatterers and flunkies, a stuffed thesaurus entry under *S* for *servility*.

The vast majority of Hillary interviews over the years have been tightly controlled, taped and edited to perfection. Journalists will insist that there are no ground rules in a Hillary interview, yet the topics covered usually range from *A* to *Abacus*. It seems essential to stress that she has a beautiful mind and is a victim of intolerant conservatives because of it. No one ever dares to ask a question that would crease a royal wrinkle.

The carefully staged interviews are, of course, just the beginning. As has been documented here, there's also the consistent pattern of omission: the refusal, time and again, to report important, newsworthy information that might harm Hillary's standing. In this regard the networks are the worst offenders. They have provided that great boost to Hillary, since they remain the biggest source of news for Americans, even in this era of cable television, the Internet, and talk radio.

It is no accident, then, that she emerged as the 2008 presidential front-runner before she was even elected to the Senate. To be sure, she had never held elective office to that point, and her one previous foray into national politics—her effort to ram socialized health care through Congress—was an unmitigated disaster. But she had the liberal news media—her media—in her corner. Her record, such as it was, was irrelevant.

Had it not been for the "alternative media," which began to emerge in force while her husband was in the Oval Office, finally threatening the liberal media's long-held monopoly, America never would have learned of virtually any of the scandals swirling around this woman. Because these new outlets dared to assume the responsibility abdicated by the traditional news media, and because of the threat they pose as a result, Hillary and her press supporters have peddled the line that she's been persecuted by a "vast right-wing conspiracy" of "Clinton-haters."

After her cakewalk reelection to the Senate, however, Hillary Clinton found herself in an unexpected fight for the 2008 Democratic presidential nomination. Her competition got a big boost from the unlikeliest of sources: the same national media that heretofore had served her so loyally. Enter Barack Obama, the first-term liberal senator from Hillary's home state of Illinois. The liberal media collectively swooned.

As our colleague Rich Noyes has so thoroughly documented, in late 2006 and the early months of 2007 the media couldn't stop gushing about Obama. NBC *Today* cohost Meredith Vieira surely did predecessor Katie Couric proud when she told Obama in October, "You are the equivalent of a rock star in politics." ABC's Terry Moran was wowed, telling *Nightline* viewers a few weeks later, "You can see it in the crowds. The thrill, the hope. How they surge toward him. You're looking at an American political phenomenon." Moran's ABC colleague Claire Shipman, in January, enthused, "Barack Obama, with his fairy-tale family, has personal charisma to spare." Those over-the-top reactions were fairly typical of the way the media caught Obama fever.

The young senator benefited from something else that has marked Hillary Clinton's time in the spotlight: a lack of scrutiny from the networks. For example, on Sunday, March 25, 2007, the *Chicago Tribune* ran a long investigative story headlined "The Not-So-Simple Story of Barack Obama's Youth," showing that the account of his life that Obama presented in his memoir was sometimes at odds with the facts. "Several of his oft-recited stories may not have happened in the way he has recounted them," the *Tribune*'s Kirsten Scharnberg and Kim Barker reported. "Some seem to make Obama look better in the retelling, others appear to exaggerate his outward struggles over issues of race, or simply skim over some of the most painful, private moments of his life." While it's a virtual certainty that this sort of detailed reporting on a major Republican presidential candidate would be picked up all over the national media, the networks ignored the *Tribune* story. The only mention of Obama on the networks' Sunday morning talk shows came from NBC's Tim Russert, who asked former senator Bill Bradley this penetrating question: "Do you think Barack Obama is someone who has tapped in to idealism in our country?"

Had Hillary Clinton's long stretch of luck finally run out? Had her boosters abandoned her at last?

Not at all.

In the age of twenty-four-hour news coverage, news cycles have become remarkably short, and as a result our memories tend to be short as well. In politics, whatever is happening at the moment is treated as the most important and the most astounding development ever to come down the pike. What happened only a matter of days ago, even if it was the subject of breathless, around-the-clock coverage at the time, now seems to be ancient history—gone, forgotten, unimportant.

That is why it is so important to take the long view with Hillary Rodham Clinton. The only way to understand her is to revisit the whole arc of her career in national politics. By doing so, we see that Obama's press coverage—fawning, no doubt—has been but a brief honeymoon compared with the sustained fifteen-plus years of whitewashing that Hillary Clinton has received from the national media.

In fact, by the summer of 2007, the pro-Hillary forces in the media were fighting back with a vengeance.

"HILLARY CLINTON IS INEVITABLE"

A sure sign that Obama Mania couldn't overwhelm the Hillary-loving media came in June on the *Today* show. Meredith Vieira, who just months earlier was touting Obama as a "rock star," was already rethinking that position. "What happened to the Obama buzz?" she asked. "Why are people moving away from Barack Obama?"

These questions came during a conversation with two former Clinton aides, Lisa Caputo and Dick Morris. It is interesting that *Today* didn't have Morris on in 2004 to discuss *Rewriting History,* his bestselling book debunking many of the claims Hillary made in her memoir, but did welcome him now, when the segment's headline was "Decision 2008, Is Hillary Clinton Unbeatable?" The well-known Clinton critic answered that question with a resounding yes ("I'm against her, but she'll win").

Vieira used her whither-Obama questions to tee it up for Caputo, Hillary's former press secretary, to make an impassioned speech on behalf of her candidate. Caputo said, "The more that [the American people] see of Hillary Clinton and they stack her up against the other candidates in the Democratic field, I mean, the choice becomes clear. Whether it's her performance in the debates or if they are watching her through her town halls throughout the country, I think people are becoming very comfortable in the direction she'll take the country." Some viewers probably expected Hillary to appear at the end of this performance and declare, "I'm Hillary Clinton, and I approved this message."

In case *Today* viewers hadn't gotten the point, Vieira drove home that Hillary was unbeatable by saying to Morris and Caputo, "But the point is you both think it's a done deal."

The very next day, *Washington Post* media reporter Howard Kurtz began his article with this sentence: "Hillary Clinton is inevitable." He added that this was "the consensus view of media wizards, strategists, pollsters, and other kibitzers, that HRC is a virtual lock for the nomination. An official with a rival campaign told me that Hillary has an 80 percent chance of being the party's candidate, and most neutral observers would probably go with a higher number."

Why all the talk of Hillary's inevitability nearly a year and a half before the 2008 election? Could it be that the very media making this declaration had something to do with it?

They had everything to do with it. Meredith Vieira touched on this idea in her interview with Caputo and Morris. "Could [Hillary] possibly be the Teflon Candidate?" Vieira asked. "I'm thinking of these two books that just came out. Highly critical of her and her husband and they don't seem to have made any dent in her popularity."

Ah yes, the two books, which Vieira didn't even name. They were *Her Way*, by Pulitzer Prize–winning reporters Jeff Gerth and Don Van Natta, and *A Woman in Charge*, by Carl Bernstein, one-half of the famous Watergate wrecking crew that put Richard Nixon in the scrap yard. The two books, released the same week in June, would have stopped the Clinton candidacy dead in its tracks had they been afforded the coverage they deserved. Instead, the media allowed Hillary's camp and her press supporters to trot out their well-rehearsed lines about "old news." And when they bothered to cover the books, they dutifully parroted Clinton talking points.

For instance, on *Good Morning America*, ABC's Chris Cuomo (son of liberal icon Mario Cuomo) interviewed Gerth and Van Natta, and was dismissive from the beginning. He introduced the interview by playing up Mrs. Clinton's inevitability and casting the authors as pesky attackers of the kind that had always harassed Hillary: "Just as [Hillary Clinton] seems to be cementing her position as front-runner, here comes *Her Way* . . . billed as the book Hillary Clinton does not want you to read." For one question, Cuomo might as well have read a Clinton press release: "The campaign said it is an Ambien substitute. They say the book is just a rehash. How do you respond to that, that your book is a sleeper? It's all been done before. You only needed a library card to report this out. Your response?"

This was not only an incredibly shallow rerun of a Clinton attack line. It suggested that Cuomo acted more like a Cuomo and less like an objective journalist. He felt no need to read a single page of the book before dismissing it as a rehash. In fact, the Gerth and Van Natta book was stuffed with new and original reporting on Hillary, including a thorough look at her Senate career. Once again, this was not a "Clinton-hater" book, or a conservative book. They wanted to talk about Hillary's vote for the Iraq war as an embarrassment. A news anchor might suggest that the new scoops were not earth-shattering. But this news anchor relied on snotty verbiage from party hacks for his "library card" taunt and suggested something that simply was not true.

As for Bernstein, that venerated icon of investigative reporting, NBC's *Today* gave him a respectable six minutes of coverage—which is about six minutes more than conservative authors of Clinton books typically receive. (Add Andrea Mitchell's dismissive "pundits say it won't hurt Hillary" news story on the book, and it's eight minutes of airtime.) But *Today* did nothing to hype the interview at the beginning of its broadcast, and other NBC news figures didn't pick up on the story thereafter.

Contrast that with the coverage NBC had given to the most recent book by Bernstein's former reporting partner, Bob Woodward. Woodward's book, *State of Denial*, was a scathing attack on the Republican administration, released just four weeks shy of the midterm elections, and it was all over NBC (and the rest of the media). *Today* gave Woodward's book a full fifteen minutes of coverage, and Tim Russert welcomed the reporter on *Meet the Press* the next Sunday. Also, Russert discussed the Woodward book as a serious factor against the Republicans six times over the course of six days. That's a publicity avalanche, and far more than what Bernstein will ever hope to recover.

Like the rest of the elite media, *Newsweek*, in its "Conventional Wisdom Watch," yawned at the two Hillary books—just as Hillary's campaign would want: "Her marriage has been troubled! Some good details, but we've heard it all before."

Aside from yawns, the other media response was to revisit the Poor Hillary story line. Many journalists somehow lumped in Bernstein, most famous for bringing down a Republican president, and Gerth and Van

Natta, both from the *New York Times*, with the "Clinton-haters." Under the headline "The New War on Hillary," *Newsweek* ran a story blasting Clinton "haters," who in their "fury" had turned the former First Lady "into a comic-book villain." According to *Newsweek*, the "narrative of depravity" about Mrs. Clinton was simply a "tissue of inventions by conservatives."

This comment ignored the obvious fact that many elements of this "narrative" did not come from conservatives. For instance, the *Newsweek* piece mentioned allegations that Hillary "threw lamps at her husband" and "communed psychically with Eleanor Roosevelt." But it was *Newsweek* itself that launched the lamp-throwing rumors nationwide in 1993, in a pro-Hillary story by Eleanor Clift. (Clift downplayed the charge, writing that "Washington dinner parties were buzzing with stories of Hillary throwing—take your pick—a lamp, a briefing book, or a Bible at Bill.") As for the séance allegation, the reporter who revealed that one was Bob Woodward back in 1996. Of course, *Newsweek* wasn't happy with the story back then, either. Evan Thomas defensively noted that "unlike Nancy Reagan, Hillary never tried to use psychic powers to influence her husband." This was the same piece in which Thomas described Mrs. Clinton as "a Joan of Arc figure, persecuted for her righteous crusade."

And Carl Bernstein, a "Clinton-hater"? Asked by Alan Colmes on Fox News whether he would vote for Hillary after writing his book, he offered a qualified and liberal yes: "If the circumstances were right—and against most of the people running against her in the other party—so far, yes."

HILLARY'S "RIGHTEOUS CRUSADE"

The "righteous crusade" remains a familiar element of what we might call the national media's "narrative of saintliness." Thus even her biggest failures can somehow be spun in Hillary's favor. During a 2007 town hall meeting with Hillary principally devoted to the subject of health care, *Good Morning America* coanchor Robin Roberts could come up with nothing more penetrating about Hillary's failed 1993 scheme to nationalize one-seventh of the economy than to state as fact that "many people felt" the plan was "ahead of its time."

Ahead of its time? This was all a serious journalist could think to say about Hillary's health care plan, which crashed and burned? Even ardent supporters of Hillary would concede that the First Lady badly mismanaged the process—and that's to say nothing of the socialist nature of the plan itself. Roberts's comment shows that Sean Hannity was exactly right when he told us Hillary "gets a pass on just about everything she does."

But that lack of scrutiny, that cheerleading, that rewriting of the historical record are precisely why Hillary Rodham Clinton is such a formidable presidential candidate. Though she certainly would have preferred the easy path to the Democratic nomination that her media boosters— and probably she herself—envisioned, she has shown she can weather storms that would sink almost any other candidacy. She is smart enough, and ruthless enough, to exploit the extraordinary advantages the national media have handed her.

In our interview, Rush Limbaugh aptly described the advantage the "drive-by media" give Hillary: "She doesn't have to answer questions. She won't go anywhere where she has to answer hard questions. . . . *I want to have a chat with the American people. I want to know what's on their minds.* It's a trick. It's the same trick she used when she ran for Senate. The media love it. It wows them to say . . . she only wants what's best for the people." Hillary sits back and lets the media spread useful myths about her.

But Hillary has what should be a fatal flaw. America is simply not prepared to embrace her socialist agenda. Cue the media's greatest mythology, the argument, presented as fact, that Hillary Clinton is a political centrist.

In politics, perception trumps reality every time. So the reality of Hillary's hard-left voting record—remember, she retains a near-perfect voting record with the liberal Americans for Democratic Action and a 100 perfect record with NARAL Pro-Choice America—is immaterial. It takes only one line in one speech—abortion "represents a sad, even tragic choice to many"—to earn her instant headlines around the country as a moderate on that volatile issue. It takes only one vote supporting President Bush's decision to go to war in Iraq for her to be positioned as a military hawk, even though she has embraced one leftist international cause after another in her adult life and has recently been tripping over herself to try to win back the vocal antiwar elements on the far left of her party ever since Iraq went sour. It takes only her claiming that "I am, you know, adamantly against illegal immigrants" to have the press fawning over her bold moves toward the middle, even though she led the fight for illegal aliens who lost relatives in the 9/11 attacks to get federal compensation.

Thus we hear CNN host Anderson Cooper claim on his prime-time show, "Most Americans, of course, stand stubbornly in the middle, as has [Hillary] Clinton, at least for the four years she's been in the Senate. She's lost the vast-right-wing-conspiracy rap, changing into a queen of compromise, eager to reach across the aisle, a successful strategy so far." Or we read a *New York Times* "news" story that proclaims, "In fact, Mrs. Clinton has defied simple ideological labeling since joining the Senate, ending up in the political center on issues like health care, welfare, abortion, morality and values, and national defense, to name just a few." These are but two of countless examples of the media's up-is-down reporting on Hillary.

The 2008 presidential race is going to be fascinating. The so-called mainstream media are thoroughly giddy over the prospect of victory, and will stop at nothing to see its realization. They have ignored Hillary Clinton's radical past and far-left Senate voting record and will continue to do so until the very end. Mark our words: Throughout the presidential campaign you will never hear, or read in the national press, labels like *pro-abortion*, *pro-tax*, or *pro-gay* used by reporters to describe her positions. You will never find them using adjectives like *far-left*, *hard left*, or even just *leftist* to describe her philosophical bearings. You won't find anyone in the national media describing her as *intolerant*, *ruthless*, *calculating*, *zealous*, or *manipulative*—all labels used by journalists to describe conservatives. And yet every single one of these adjectives applies to her.

The alternative media will have their plate full in the 2008 campaign. Talk radio, the Fox News Channel, the websites, the bloggers, the columnists—it will be up to them, collectively, to expose and neutralize the liberal media's activist agenda to elect a president. We are fortunate that the liberal media's monopoly has begun to crumble at last, even if they still retain extraordinary influence. Just a couple of decades ago their fictional narrative about Hillary Clinton would have passed unchallenged. Now tens of millions of Americans watch, read, and listen to what the conservative media say. They can call attention to the serious issues that, if examined in anything more than cursory fashion, expose why Hillary Rodham Clinton should not be elected president.

But the task will not be easy, not with the ceaseless assault that is sure to be waged by CBS, ABC, NBC, MSNBC, CNN, the *New York Times*, the *Washington Post, USA Today*, the *Los Angeles Times*, the AP, and on and on. Nor will it be easy for any conservative candidate who has to face Hillary in the general election. What CBS attempted to do to George W. Bush through the dishonest Memogate story in 2004 is sure to be but an appetizer for what will follow.

Despite what Hillary's legions of supporters would have Americans believe, conservatives who criticize Hillary Rodham Clinton are not irrational "Clinton-haters" with a personal vendetta against the former First Lady or her husband. The matter is simple but essential: many feel she is unfit to be president.

Sean Hannity captured this perfectly when he said that the most disturbing facet of Hillary Clinton is not her failure to apologize for the smears she has made against conservatives, but her camp's refusal to be forthright on the issues. "I'm not looking for an apology," Hannity told us. "I want America to have a healthy, vigorous debate on issues on the economy, on terrorism, the War on Terror, on border security, on social and cultural issues, and how this country is going to look when we hand it off to our children and grandchildren."

If it were up to Hillary's cheerleaders in the national media, the nation wouldn't have this debate. It's up to others to reveal the truth the media won't tell Americans.

Acknowledgments

Bringing fifteen years of uncomfortable facts to the table on just how dramatically the media favor Hillary Clinton would be impossible but for the daily work by editors and content analysts at the Media Research Center (MRC), who have been capturing and cataloging the evidence since 1991. Brent Baker has headed up the news analysis team for twenty years now. Rich Noyes not only helped direct our research effort, but the original idea for this volume was his as well. They were indispensable to this effort.

The MRC research team today includes media analysts Geoff Dickens, Brad Wilmouth, Scott Whitlock, Justin McCarthy, and Matthew Balan. Clay Waters runs the MRC's TimesWatch project and helped us flesh out Hillary's "hometown" coverage during her Senate career. Others who helped compile the research over the years have included Jessica Barnes, Brian Boyd, Brant Clifton, Nick Damask, Eric Darbe, Mark Drake, Gene Eliasen, Jim Forbes, Andrew Gabron, Patrick Gregory, Mark Honig, Kristin Johnson, Steve Kaminski, Marian Kelley, Tim Lamer, Megan McCormack, Mark Rogers, Michael Rule, Ken Shepherd, and Paul Smith. Interns Kyle Drennen and Patrick Skeehan helped with some heavy early research requests for this project.

We also required extensive use of the MRC video archive for this book, and we thank Michelle Humphrey and her dedicated staff for their helpful research assistance. And then there is Brent Bozell's assistant, the effervescent Danette Williams, without whose help the entire project would be incoherent mush.

Once the research was compiled, it was necessary to turn to experts in the conservative community for their analysis: Tony Blankley, Floyd Brown, the Honorable Dan Burton, Ann Coulter, Don Devine, Frank Donatelli, Joe Duggan, Tony Fabrizio, the Honorable Ed Gillespie, the Honorable Newt Gingrich, John Goodman, Sean Hannity, Laura Ingraham, the Honorable Jack Kingston, Wayne LaPierre, Mark Levin, Rush Limbaugh, the Honorable Bob Livingston, Mary Matalin, John McLaughlin, Colin McNickle, Greg Mueller, Kate O'Beirne, Phyllis Schlafly, Jerry Seper, Craig Shirley, General Jack Singlaub, Cal Thomas, and Bob Tyrrell—all provided illuminating perspective. We are indebted to them.

As we are to the wonderful folks at Crown Forum, beginning with editor Jed Donahue, whose talents are equaled only by his patience. We are also grateful to Patty Bozza, Jie Yang, David Tran, Lauren Dong, Mary Choteborsky, Tina Constable, Kristin Kiser, Amy Boorstein, Christine Aronson, Donna Passannante, and the others at Crown Forum who made this book a reality. Craig Shirley and Diana Banister and their colleagues at Shirley & Banister Public Affairs handled the promotional aspects with their signature efficiency and we thank them all.

Tim Graham thanks his wife, Laura, and his children, Ben and Abby, for their patience and support and great hugs, and always thanks God for his parents, Jim and Ann Graham.

Brent Bozell echoes those sentiments with his wife, Norma; his children, David and Laura, Brent IV and Dawn, Joey, Caitlin, and Reid; his parents near and afar; and his new granddaughter, Molly, who proved it is possible for an author to edit and burp a baby simultaneously.

Index